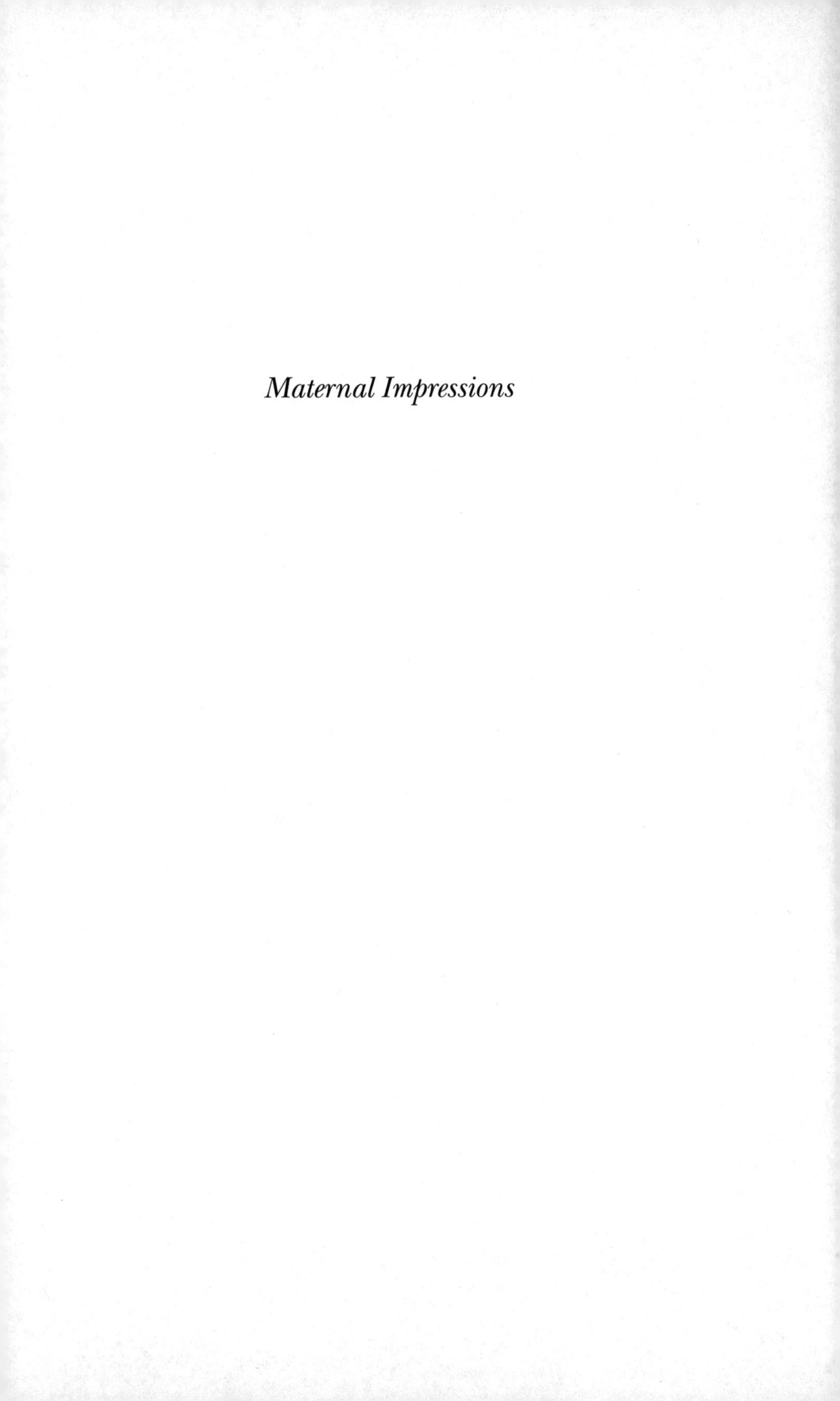

Maternal Impressions

MATERNAL IMPRESSIONS

Pregnancy and Childbirth in Literature and Theory

CRISTINA MAZZONI

Cornell University Press

ITHACA AND LONDON

First published 2002 by Cornell University Press

Printed in the United States of America

Library of Congress Cataloging-in-Publication Data

Mazzoni, Cristina, 1965-
Maternal impressions : pregnancy and childbirth in literature and theory / Cristina Mazzoni.
p. cm.
Includes bibliographical references and index.
ISBN 0-8014-4035-1 (cloth : alk. paper)
1. Pregnancy. 2. Maternal-fetal exchange. 3. Pregnancy in literature. 4. Pregnancy—Psychological aspects. 5. Pregnancy—Social aspects. 6. Pregnancy—Folklore. 7. Childbirth—Folklore. I. Title.
RG551 .M396 2002
618.2'4—dc21

2002005101

Cornell University Press strives to use environmentally responsible suppliers and materials to the fullest extent possible in the publishing of its books. Such materials include vegetable-based, low-VOC inks and acid-free papers that are recycled, totally chlorine-free, or partly composed of nonwood fibers. For further information, visit our website at www.cornellpress.cornell.edu.

Cloth printing 10 9 8 7 6 5 4 3 2 1

For my mother,

Stefania Mazzoni

Contents

Preface

The phrase "maternal impressions" describes the belief that the fetus can be affected by its mother's desires, fears, experiences. In the first chapter of this book I discuss some of the theories underlying this belief and its ramifications in folklore, science, and literature. Used as a title for my book, however, the phrase "maternal impressions" will, I hope, be read more generally as the impressions of a mother: the impressions others have of mothers, the impressions mothers have of others—and of themselves. This is my subject throughout the book. How does a mother impress an other, the fetus (the belief in maternal impressions, Chapter 1)? How does an other, the fetus, impress a mother (the epistemology of quickening, Chapter 2)? What impression does maternity make on the mother's body (the perception of maternal deformity, Chapter 3)? And how impressive is it to become a mother, anyway (the experience of childbirth and paradox, Chapter 4)? *Impressions* is what I chose to emphasize in the title of this book, as in the titles of its chapters, because impressions, as the above questions attest, can be used to describe the readings I undertake throughout, and because the spatial and temporal indeterminacy of impressions well reflects the uncertainties of maternity and of its discursive elaborations.

Impression is a dual word. An impression can mean a strong effect on one's mind or body, but it can also be a vague awareness. (An impression can also be an imitation: Since my experiences of pregnancy and birth are past, perhaps I am making an impression, an impersonation of the pregnant and birthing woman.) Impressions are dual in terms of space (Are they deep or superficial?), but also in terms of time: They can be first impressions, they can be lasting impressions. And with their ambiguous meaning of both surface and depth, brevity and length, impressions evoke the fluidity necessary to any prolific discussion of maternity: maternity with the outside of its big belly and the depth of its placenta and uterus, maternity as a swollen exterior and a growing interiority, but also maternity as birth, that never-ending moment of passage between the inside and the outside to the point that the two concepts, ultimately, make little sense. Hence the movement, within my discussion as well, between the first impressions maternity gives and the lasting impressions it makes, between the impressiveness of the maternal self and also its continued impressionability.

The first impressions this book will give are in turn also multiple I predict. Maternalist readers may find *Maternal Impressions* insufficiently celebratory of motherhood, inadequately impressed by its power, while other feminists may protest its focus on a historically dangerous aspect of women's lives—reproduction as a source of women's oppression rather than a sign of our impressiveness. Some readers may also be negatively impressed by the subtitle's apparent deceptiveness: *Pregnancy and Childbirth in Literature and Theory*. There is not enough perhaps of what is traditionally referred to as literature in the following pages, and where do texts such as "Rapunzel," Luke's account of the Visitation, or Freud's case of the psychotic Schreber belong in this literature–theory dichotomy—not to speak of Paolo Mantegazza's and Cesare Lombroso's treatises on the nature of woman? Neither literature nor theory can easily claim any of these texts, I admit. But my hope is that, after reading *Maternal Impressions*, these skeptical readers will be impressed instead by the continuities among the different discourses I invoke, as well as by the discontinuities present within the texts themselves. If literature, folklore, religion, psychoanalysis, and science, for example, are impressed in analogous ways by the workings of maternity, still pregnancy and childbirth expressly prevent these disciplines from oppressively reducing maternity into a linear, noncontradictory, teleologically sound experience. Consequently, I have tried to remain impressionable to the demands of maternity in my own thinking and writing, so that readers may find their reconstruction of maternity, in the following pages, to be not a labyrinth with a single prescribed itinerary, but rather one of those colorful jungle gyms mothers are well familiar with, where many paths are possible and encouraged, and where the object of the game is a productive practice leading to improved understanding of and skill in the diverse activities involved. And I hope, through this practice of leaping and sliding, climbing and wandering, holding and letting go, in the maternal impressions of my title the reader may recognize and acknowledge the first impressions through which we, of woman born, come into being, as well as the lasting impressions that we, as human beings, make on others and on our world.

I owe impressive debts to many for contributing to the conception and delivery of this book. The initial and final stages of research for *Maternal Impressions* were aided by two Summer Stipends from the University Committee on Research and Scholarship here at the University of Vermont. Early drafts of sections two and three of each chapter were previously published in *Annali d'Italianistica, Rivista di Studi Italiani,* and *Italian Culture;* I thank their kind editors, Dino Cervigni, Anthony Verna, and Mario Mignone. Most practically, I am immensely grateful to the staff at the Interlibrary Loan Office here at the University of Vermont, Bailey-Howe Library, without whose efficient and courteous labor the birth of this book would have been impossible. Finally, I must thank Bernhard Kendler at Cornell University Press for his encouragement of this project since before it was even born and for his suggestions of titles for both *Maternal Impressions* and, a few years back, *Saint Hysteria;* the Cornell anonymous readers were of great assistance to me with their careful and well-conceived critiques. The editors, especially Cathi Reinfelder, did wonders with my non-native blunders.

Whenever an acceptable translation of foreign-language materials was easily available, I have used it, but unless otherwise noted, all translations are mine. All references to Cesare Lombroso's *La donna delinquente, la prostituta e la donna normale* are to the 1893 edition; exceptions are noted. For reasons of both space and style, there are no notes in this book. References are given parenthetically, and other intellectual debts are acknowledged in the extensive bibliography.

Less easily worded acknowledgments are due to the many people in my life who continue to sustain my multiple maternal practices. Some of the health professionals who have helped me give birth to and learn to take care of my children, especially Marti Churchill and Joe Hagan, un-self-consciously yet persistently dismantle the generalizations about the imperialism of medicine that emerge throughout the pages of this book. At the University of Vermont, Joyce Boyer, Sue Breeyear, Catherine Connor, Kathy Doyle, Patrizia Jamieson, Donna Kuizenga, Kate Marvin, Gayle Roof-Nunley, and Janet Whatley have provided professional support that has repeatedly and joyfully spilled over into a sustaining maternal practice. The friends who bore and delivered children during the years I worked on this book generously shared with me thoughts, feelings, insights, hand-me-downs, books, and child care: Carol Begley, Carolyn Ciampa, Rita Coté, Maria Kenney, Cetti Mangano-Perry, Maria Rosaria Palumbo, Hyun Ja

Shin, Sandy Soucy, Marci Szurley, Helen Williams, and my sister Silvia Mazzoni. Other dear friends nurtured me and my family in maternal ways: Patrizia Jamieson, Miriam Sheehey, Ed Stone, Silvana Tropea, Tiziana Zampini, my brothers Pietro and Stefano Mazzoni, and my sisters Sabrina and Paola Mazzoni. My grandmother, Nonna Ida, has bestowed on me the gifts of female genealogies and many witticisms about mothering. My father's brave shift from doctor to patient painfully and lovingly illustrates for me, every day, the bond between courage and humility. My mother Stefania was there at every stage of my life, though only when I became a mother myself did I begin to grasp and acknowledge my debt to her commitment, and to learn that someone could have fallen in love with me as instantly and as profoundly as I fell in love with each of the little persons who had just come out of me. Because she continues to give birth to me, and helps me give birth to my own children, it is to her that I dedicate this book. My children, Paul, Gemma, and Sophia, teach me every day moving lessons of joy in attention and responsibility, as well as the transforming virtues of faith, hope, and charity; my prayer is that I may learn those lessons as well as they are teaching them. And, *dulcis in fundo* . . . I cannot adequately describe John Cirignano's role in my maternal practice and thinking. He fills my life with love and laughter, challenges me into honesty and simplicity, and generously gives me the space, time, and strength to read and write. He was there for every day of my pregnancies and every moment of my births, and although he has not yet touched this book with his hands, it is as much his as it is mine.

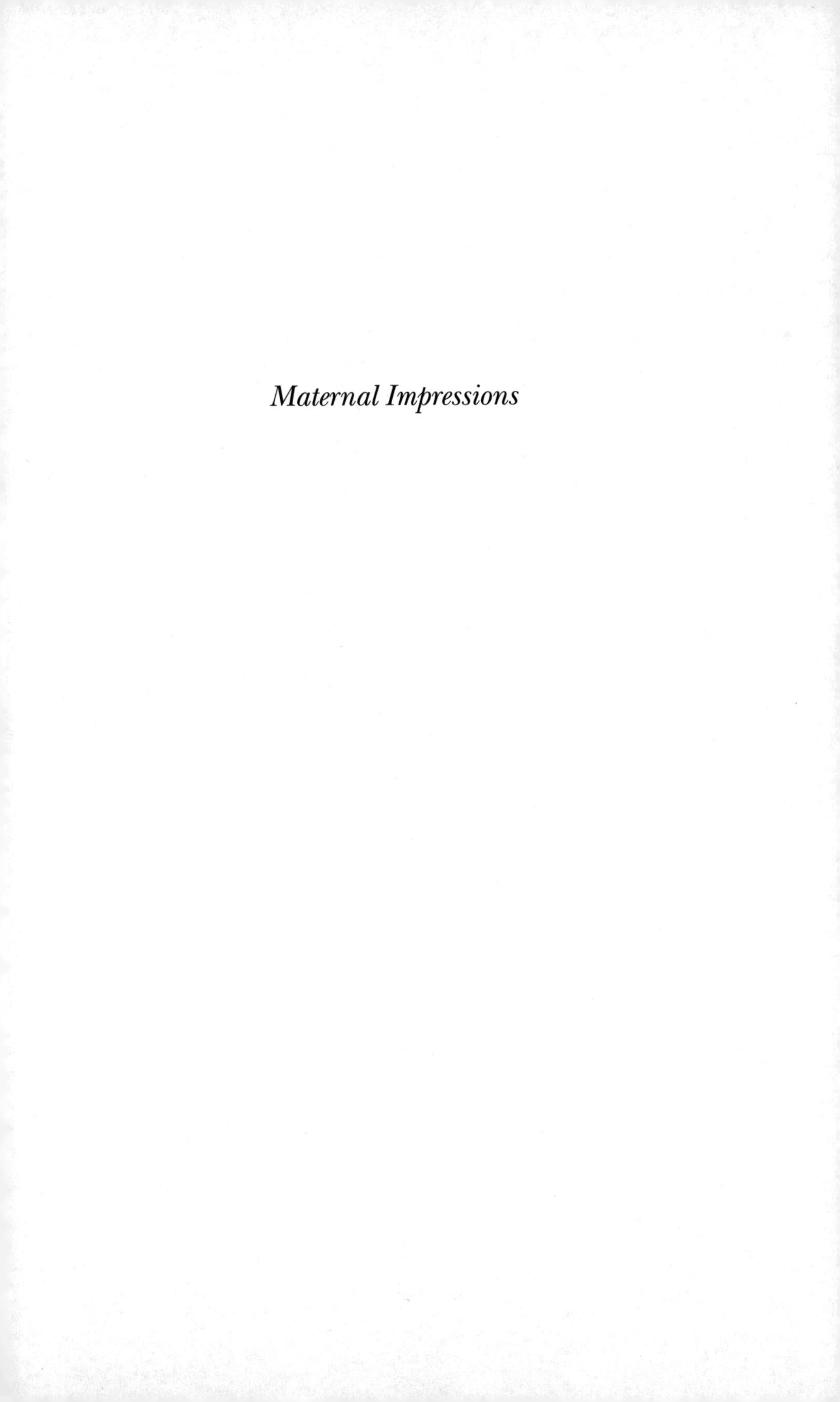

Maternal Impressions

Introduction

Personal Impressions

"Recovering mothers' voices in the rites of passage of pregnancy and childbirth is a formidable task at best, and at worst, a hazardous, volatile venture" (Miller-McLemore, 138). With these words, an academic, theologian, and mother describes her scholarly undertaking, and in these words, I—an academic and a mother—recognize my own task. After becoming an academic, and before becoming a mother myself, my encounters with mothers had been rare. Most of the women I associated with were not mothers. The few who were rarely spoke to me of their motherhood, perhaps for reasons that I now begin to understand: reserve and modesty, fear and embarrassment, paradoxically bound up with pride and pleasure, joy and pain. Thus, even recovering the maternal voices of my own peers would have been a formidable, probably a hazardous, and maybe a volatile labor. How much more must this be the case in this book, given my choice to start with mothers' voices from a century ago and to continue with maternal texts that are difficult and removed in geographical, temporal, and cultural ways from my own limited position? My hope is that in what follows the insights will outweigh the mistakes, as the joys have, for me, far outweighed the hazards in this at once scholarly and personal venture.

That the personal is political, that the body recapitulates culture, that individual language and subjectivity are embedded in society: These are by now truisms in the discourse of cultural studies. It nevertheless bears noting, however, that I began work on this book because of my experiences of bearing, giving birth, breastfeeding, and mothering my three children. Becoming a mother shocked me with its impact, delighted me with its passions, stunned me with its intensity. It changed me, transformed me even, well beyond the permanent extra pounds. Why was it all so new? Why did it seem that nobody told me, warned me how it would be? What made it so inexplicably shocking, delightful, intense—as well as, at times, frightening, irritating, angering? Being an academic, I started searching in books: I wanted to know how mothers who were writers had made sense, and literature, of their experience. In discovering what shaped, influenced, molded their understanding of maternity, I hoped, among other things, to shed light on how my own experiences came to be. In the process of this research I found that I was not alone in my questions, wonders, obsessions.

Many feminist thinkers have in recent years discussed the topic of motherhood—though early motherhood, or what I call, following Italian usage, *maternity* (pregnancy, birth, postpartum, breastfeeding), boasts a more limited bibliography. Some of these works have acquired the status of classics and, for all the controversies they have inspired, have one way or another changed the way we think about motherhood: Adrienne Rich's *Of Woman Born*, Nancy Chodorow's *The Reproduction of Mothering*, Mary O'Brien's *The Politics of Reproduction*, Ann Oakley's *The Captured Womb*, Emily Martin's *The Woman in the Body*, Sara Ruddick's *Maternal Thinking*, the works of the so-called French feminists—Luce Irigaray, Hélène Cixous, Julia Kristeva—as well as the works of lesser-known Italian feminists, such as Adriana Cavarero and Luisa Muraro. Other important critical texts examine motherhood in more specific disciplinary contexts. Examples include Alice Adams's *Reproducing the Womb*, Clarissa Atkinson's *The Oldest Vocation*, Sarah Blaffer Hrdy's *Mother Nature*, and Robbie Kahn's *Bearing Meaning*. Still others provide critical overviews of this abundant literature on motherhood: Patrice DiQuinzio's thorough and provoking *The Impossibility of Motherhood*, for instance, and Michelle Boulous Walker's *Philosophy and the Maternal Body*. These are just a few examples, limited to works I have found particularly stirring; more on these and other texts will be said throughout *Maternal Impressions*. Nor should this apparently well-endowed list obscure the fact that, as Italian psychoanalyst Silvia Vegetti Finzi puts it, "Only in the past few years has attention focused on the need to rethink motherhood. The poverty of both theory and experience in this domain is painfully obvious" ("Female Identity," 139).

Nestled in this rich maternal context, drawing from it support and motivation, *Maternal Impressions* is the record of my search, a professional and personal search carried out over the past several years in the fragmented way mothers know well. With the birth of my first child in 1994, mothering had become so central to my life that research in any other topic made little sense to me. Being a feminist critic gave me the opportunity to explore my obsession and—how nice!—make it count as part of my job. This was not an insignificant factor in those pre-tenure years (I finally and thankfully received tenure in 1999, when my third child was one year old). Maternal thinking has productively blended, for me, with thinking about the maternal. In this I was privileged and blessed, since my husband and I could arrange to take turns being with the children with minimal outside help. His sacrifice of a traditional career and my many lost moments with the children are part of the price we paid for this privilege. The other part? The inability to hang out with colleagues in the hallways and at lunch or to attend a weekend conference because the children needed tending, a baby needed nursing, or classes had to be prepared meant a painful lack of friends and allies among those with whom I share so much else that is important to me. I never could have known, before 1994, to what extent mothering would alienate me, in practical as well as intellectual ways, from the active professional and social life that I always believed I could claim. (And yet, at the same time, having children has also made me aware as I had never been before about the political and social issues we encounter in daily life.) Pregnancy, childbirth, and breastfeeding are still, in many communities—including the academic ones I have belonged to—unspoken, perhaps unspeakable.

Yet without that sense of maternal community, it is difficult for many mothers not to remain silent, almost closeted about maternity. Mothers are often alone in pondering difficult questions such as, Is it okay to honor female generativity, to acknowledge our body in relation, to share the pleasure and the pain that our children bring to us? Is it worth risking a dangerous essentialist identification with biology by publicly recognizing the joy of experiences such as pregnancy and childbirth that hopelessly entangle us in our bodies? (In feminist theory, *essentialism* is the belief in a transhistorical, transcultural, unchanging essence that defines woman and without which a being is not a woman; it is a controversial topic that recurs throughout this book.) Can maternity make theory, and especially can it make good theory? Could pregnancy possibly function in ways analogous to, say, Luce Irigaray's shockingly corporeal image of the two lips (drawn, like pregnancy, from female morphology and sexuality, and suggesting closeness while avoiding closure), or even to Donna Haraway's radical figuration of the cyborg (a figure of relationality evoking, like pregnancy, patterns of interconnectedness and affinity—though a figure, I must add, suspicious of procreativity)? But has maternity not been used to reiterate essentialist notions of womanhood as motherhood? Have women's biological association with and ideological encapsulation in maternity not in fact silenced us? And is procreativity not the rock upon which liberal feminism, egalitarian feminism, repeatedly and unavoidably stumbles? Can equality survive the differences through which, as which pregnant bodies announce themselves?

In this process I have been striving to imagine and use the potential of maternity to question conventional representations of subjectivity—and by maternity, again, I mean the period of early motherhood, a period most imbricated with the body: pregnancy, childbirth, postpartum, breastfeeding. These maternal practices resist individualism; they intrinsically acknowledge difference and the resistance that difference poses to our quest for control and manipulation. They demand to be reinscribed as body and as language. Pregnancy can quicken our reflection on notions of difference, of radical and irreducible difference, as it is both visibly inscribed on the body (thus, for a change, establishing a female body—an odd and swollen female body, to boot—as paradigmatic) and conducive to mutual understanding through a process of epistemological and bodily growth and change. At the same time, the subjectivity to which the pregnant, birthing woman accedes is always specific. She is always *a* particular subject and not *the* subject; subject and object of a division in process. She is clearly not *Woman.* This necessary recognition can best be realized through a "different" subject—such as, indeed, "a" pregnant, "a" birthing woman. Women's bodies, then, must be treated in terms relevant to female specificity—not just as "other" or, even worse perhaps, as "same," as utterly heterogeneous and abject or as mercilessly homogenized. Maternal difference can be conceived of, for example, in the ways that the Italian feminist thought known as *pensiero della differenza sessuale* (thinking of sexual difference) or *pensiero della differenza* (thinking of difference) has taught us: a primary, original sexual difference demanding to be explored in autonomous ways; a difference both natural and biological as well as ontological and essential, social and cultural-historical. A difference that, according to Irigaray, "is one of the major philosophical issues, if not the issue, of our age" (*An Ethics of Sexual Difference*, 5). Although resistant to a reductive definition, sexual difference must be elaborated particularly with respect to those areas in which women have traditionally been domesticated: maternity and the female body, then, as well as language and subjectivity.

Autobiography, my own embodied genealogy, what Italian feminists call "il partire da sé" (starting from one's self), is unavoidable and perhaps desirable in this context. First of all, it helps me to deconstruct the opposition between subject and object of knowledge by implicating myself, my story, my body, into the web of stories and bodies I spin in this book. The subjectivity of knowledge as it is grounded in the body is highlighted by my self-inscription and description. My own theoretical and personal elaboration of this need was crystallized in reading Elizabeth Grosz's eloquent statement that "where feminism remains committed to the project of knowing women, of making women objects of knowledge, without in turn *submitting the position of knower or subject of knowledge to a reorganization*, it remains as problematic as the knowledge it attempts to supplement or replace" (*Space, Time, and Perversion*, 40). In the autobiographical references of my book, then, the reader can participate in the never-complete project of reorganizing one's position (mine, yours) of knowing, and its effects on the objects known (both self, then—me, you—and other texts). Furthermore, autobiography stages the happy fact that pregnancy cannot possibly claim to be among those fetishized "universal human experiences" so dear to humanism, and so it is also a subject that tends to resist formal academic language. I do not have delusions of avant-garde grandeur in my own writing, for what follows, let the reader be warned, or reassured, is no *écriture féminine* (though I talk about *écriture féminine* in Chapter 2). But I also do struggle, in these pages, to strike a satisfactory balance between the relatively abstract critical language in which I have been trained and the visceral response that the texts I analyze have elicited in me because of their most intimate connections with that vital aspect of my life that is the experience of maternity.

I mentioned above some of the influential critical works on maternity of the past few decades. But I must admit that I found a most touching continuity between my experience of maternity and that of others within literary texts penned by Italian women during the late nineteenth and early twentieth centuries. These are writers who were popular in their own lifetimes and who for the most part have been forgotten, for a complicated web of reasons. When I started reading more in depth the work of Neera, Grazia Deledda, Carolina Invernizio, Annie Vivanti, Sibilla Aleramo, Maria Messina, and Ada Negri, my scholarly life and its bond with my daily occupations changed dramatically. Why were these writers returning time and again to the subjects surrounding maternity? What was the meaning of these textual tensions between womanhood and pregnancy, and why were there even tensions if, as bourgeois ideology made it so clear, women's role was to become and to remain mothers? How could the fulfillment of a social, cultural, even religious ideal entail so much fear, pain, self-destruction even? What were the connections, because I immediately knew that there were, that there must be valid connections, between these writers' paradoxical constructions and the unanswered questions I kept encountering in my own experience as an academic mother? And how do these connections fit within the discourse of sexuality and reproduction that modernity privileges as the site of production of truth about the subject?

I hope that my modest contribution can be included within that feminist project that Sara Ruddick has effectively described as "the construction of an image of maternal power which is benign, accurate, sturdy, and sane" ("Maternal Thinking," 345). Still I have written with the poignant awareness that there is no single accepted, acceptable theory of maternity, that feminist theory must forever struggle with paradox, that motherhood involves insoluble dilemmas, contradictory solutions, implacable objections to every theoretical elaboration. As Patrice DiQuinzio aptly put it, "motherhood is impossible: it is impossible for feminist theory to avoid the issue of mothering and it is impossible for feminist theory to resolve it" (xx). I propose that, rather than lament this impossibility, we revel in it, deriving from it multiple meanings and messages, for, as Renee Heberle has so concisely written, "Feminism itself must recognize the significance of the resistance of its own objects of analysis to encapsulation in thought" (125). Many possible ways of interpreting this resistance and this impossibility arise in the pages of *Maternal Impressions*, but let me leave you with a striking one right now: "Could it be that maternity evokes for a woman levels of reality that she has never practiced before, and that it changes her way of being—with stunning force, at times—because maternity is the situation in which she is socially authorized and culturally empowered to activate her body, its drives, and can exercise an active part in social relationships?" (Muraro, *Maglia o uncinetto*, 80).

The many questions that kept arising in the course of my research converged around four general patterns, which in turn move the meditations I tell in the four chapters of this book. What role does the pregnant woman have on the physical and psychological development of the child in her womb, and how is female desire constructed in this process (Chapter 1)? What relationship, what knowledge develops when the child starts to perceptibly move within the mother's womb, and how does this knowledge figure a critique of epistemology (Chapter 2)? How does the child-in-womb and the pregnancy itself affect, change, shape a woman's body and psyche, her subjectivity, and how does the grotesque body convey meaning (Chapter 3)? And finally, what is the significance of the act of giving birth to another human being—for a woman's life, for a woman's self—and why does it entail so much paradox (Chapter 4)? These questions, repeatedly asked by women writers of a century or so ago, are comparable to those animating the proliferating genre of advice manuals on pregnancy and childbirth today, and they find analogues in other discourses that I examine in the four chapters.

Consequently, each of the four chapters is in turn divided into four sections. The first section of each chapter deals with pregnancy and childbirth advice manuals and other culturally relevant and well-known texts: the tale of Rapunzel in Chapter 1, the account of the Visitation in Luke's Gospel in Chapter 2, Freud's case study of Schreber in Chapter 3, and Chris Bohjalian's best-selling novel *Midwives* in Chapter 4. The second section starts with symptomatic readings of turn-of-the-century Italian scientific texts, primarily by Cesare Lombroso and Paolo Mantegazza, in order to develop discussions of the construction of "woman" in science. The need to open up scientific discourse to the analytic practices of cultural studies is especially evident in the texts I read in this section of each chapter, for they were aimed at the general public as well as the scientific community. And, to quote Jill Matus, "Biological accounts of reproduction and sexuality are not the origin from which ideas about men and women and sexual difference then radiate and circulate; rather the relationship between scientific knowledge and cultural imperatives is one of interplay and exchange" (7). The third section of each chapter is devoted to Italian literary texts from the late nineteenth and early twentieth century: Grazia Deledda's *Cosima* in Chapter 1, Neera's *L'indomani* (The next day) in Chapter 2, Deledda's *Elias Portolu* in Chapter 3, and Sibilla Aleramo's *Una donna* (A Woman) in Chapter 4. Do these texts consolidate or undermine the scientific fields to which they point? How do they construct or shape what we read as cultural and social experiences—pregnancy, childbirth, reproduction? Finally, the fourth and last section of each chapter is devoted to contemporary feminist writers and theorists, primarily Adriana Cavarero, Hélène Cixous, Luce Irigaray, Julia Kristeva, and Luisa Muraro. The connections among scientific, literary, popular, and theoretical discourses, underlined by the questions informing each chapter, will point, I hope, to a continuity between the two turn of the centuries (the last one, our own) both in terms of pregnant and birthing women's concerns and in terms of the concerns of society: What *should* a pregnant woman, a birthing woman, a mother, be concerned about, impressed by? What are the important maternity matters?

"It is difficult to see how our current scientific ideas are infused by cultural assumptions; it is easier to see how scientific ideas from the past, ideas that now seem wrong or too simple, might have been affected by cultural ideas of an earlier time," Emily Martin has written in *The Woman in the Body* (27). The details, the assumptions, the prejudices between the turn of the last century and our turn of the millennium might be different, even wildly divergent at times, but overall the questions are surprisingly analogous. If nineteenth-century doctors had no hesitation about asserting women's biological inferiority and weakness, contemporary obstetricians subject healthy women to a systematic clinical gaze even as they reject a vocabulary of outright domination. Significantly, the questions I have chosen to emphasize dwell on relationship and interdependence, mediated by language and subjectivity. They display the inseparability between the personal and the political, the complex connections and interactions between bodies and power, the reliance of power on knowledge and/of the body, and the omnipresence of power as understood in Michel Foucault's sense: Can we distinguish between women's concerns and those that society imposes on us, between our corporeal bodies and the culturally inscribed bodies of social representation? Indeed, can we even have access to a purely biological body, or is the body not always-already inhabited by society, by culture? Is the body an effect, an impression of language? The self-monitoring of the pregnant woman, discussed especially in Chapter 2 in the context of quickening and fetal movement, is an obvious example of the imbrication between the individual and the establishment, of the way in which the latter's control of the pregnant woman is inextricably linked to her own self-monitoring.

On the other hand, the focus on the late nineteenth and early twentieth century in the two center sections of each chapter is theoretically grounded in the need to avoid ahistorical generalizations—often a problem in feminism of difference and in the exaltation of maternity as empowering for women. By drawing attention to specific cultural-historical contexts of mothering, I hope to acknowledge the dilemma of difference and to negotiate the dangers of essential motherhood, even as I recognize the impossibility, implicit in the very texts I read, of a totalizing account of mothering. The period I have selected, about a century ago, is especially crucial because it is the time that began to see a transition in childbirth from home to hospital and an increased trust in the specialist obstetrician as the individual best qualified to survey motherhood. Doctors in eighteenth-century Italy were already campaigning against lay midwives, and schools began a medical training of midwives that replaced informal, oral and practical training. It was not until the second half of the nineteenth century that the move from home to hospital, or at least from midwife to doctor, began in the cultural imagination as well as in practice. This shift was caused by multiple factors, which I refer to throughout this book. Most prominent among these are improved health outcomes (the scientific explanation) and the imperialism of the medical profession (the feminist explanation). This shift is culturally significant because it has entailed not only a dramatic, though controversial, improvement of maternal and infant health but also a transformation of some of life's most fundamental experiences as well as a decreased attention to mothers and a diminished trust in maternal knowledge. As Ann Oakley eloquently puts it,

> This is probably the most critical aspect of motherhood's fate in the twentieth century—that women's own knowledge of it has become, in the professionalized image, inauthentic. Stripped of its internal authenticity, motherhood becomes an exercise in professional consultation, an axis of self-doubt, and a black hole into which 'liberated' women disappear only to be besieged by visions of all they gave up (or never had) in order to fulfill this one great intimate destiny. ("Feminism, Motherhood and Medicine," 134)

So while many feminists in the early 1900s turned to medicine to make motherhood safer, nowadays it is feminists who most vociferously criticize the medical profession for its objectification of women and its erosion of female knowledge.

Knowledge is a recurring theme when maternity is explored. Knowledge has been the link between my personal experience of maternity and my professional quest to understand it. Knowledge has been and in altered ways continues to be the battleground between midwives and doctors, between caregivers and mothers themselves: for the one who knows more is the one with the decision-making power. But, more positively, knowledge is what prolifically explodes with the experience of maternity; it is an embodied knowledge hardly available to the dispassionate scientific gaze. Maternity brings epistemological possibilities productively theorized from various perspectives—linguistic, philosophical, theological, psychoanalytic, for example. One of these perspectives, of which I like to be reminded and which fits well within my emphasis on cultural-historical specificity, is articulated by Susan J. Pitt:

> As a historian of childbirth, I am reluctant to discuss how childbirth should be organized in the present. This is not because I do not believe that my work could have a political impact in the present—but because I believe that truly radical thinking can come only by laying aside assumptions about beneficial outcomes as though they were pan-historic constants. It is too easy when dealing with contemporary history to slip from discussions of what is

> useful for feminists today into assuming those same needs for women in the past. (192)

Yes, slipping is easy, though difficult lessons can be learned if we keep reading and thinking about what women in the past have written of their needs and wants in the experience of maternity.

In the course of this book, I hope to blend maternal theories with the maternal wisdom, the maternal knowledge that has matrilineally survived until today, even if in fragments, details, clues. It is knowledge grounded in the process of sustaining another—in gestation, in birth, in lactation, and beyond, throughout maternal practice. If its epistemological insights are reserved for mothers who alone are rooted in the bodily experiences I discuss, I do not intend with my emphasis to dismiss the labor of women and men who mother in other ways: adoptive parents, foster parents, maternal fathers, as well as those who engage in lovingly sustaining others in the myriad ways available; on the contrary. (Nor do I assume that all mothers are models of ethical behavior, but that is the subject of another, more painful book; I am also leaving out of my discussion the subject of new reproductive technologies, on which many excellent texts are available.) For in the affirmation of others, our own humanity is confirmed and valued. I am dwelling on maternity because it is comprised of fundamental experiences that have been all too often, all too deeply, left unspoken. And in the needed exploration and discovery of maternal matters, all who are involved in sustaining others might find existential, perhaps bodily analogues that meaningfully, impressively even, speak of the process of tending life, of nourishing and supporting otherness—with bodily, intellectual, emotional, political practices. I hope the following pages can become part of that conception, of that gestation, of that birth of ideas, words, texts about mothers and maternity.

ONE

Rapunzel's Mother, or the Craving Body

Impressions of Pregnant Desire

Maternal Impressions in Advice Manuals and "Rapunzel"

Salmon patches, strawberry marks, café-au-lait spots: these are not items on a fusion-cuisine menu, but rather some of the names given to the newborn's birthmarks in the popular pregnancy and childbirth advice manual *What to Expect When You're Expecting* (Eisenberg, Murkoff, and Hathaway, 303). These evocative, appetizing names point to the theory of maternal impressions—that is, the description of the ability of the pregnant woman to influence in a bodily or psychological manner the child she carries. Very often, this belief was related to foods. If a pregnant woman's craving is not satisfied, the belief goes, then a sign of the desired food will appear on the skin of the child she carries. Two vivid memories spring to mind when I think of this theory. The first is the joyful picture of the *salumiera* behind her deli counter in my Italian hometown, offering my pregnant mother samples of anything she wanted. The *salumiera* did not want to be responsible for possible birthmarks or other abnormalities on the body of my future brother. For if my mother saw something she craved on that well-stocked counter—some plump buffalo-milk mozzarella, perhaps, or slices of pistachio-speckled mortadella, or a bowl of Gaeta olives—and could not eat it, there might be corresponding birthmarks (white, pink, brown) on my brother's skin. And so my mother, obligingly, sampled.

Recent polls as well as the dissemination of this belief in contemporary television commercials in Italy suggest that the theory of maternal impressions, especially with respect to food cravings, is still deeply rooted among many Italians. If the only socially acceptable desire for a woman is to have a child, then the desiring pregnant body is granted attention and understanding through its food cravings. Hence the familiar image of the concerned husband running all over town to find strawberries in January or, in this country, pickles and ice cream. My mother recalls sending my father on a three-hour expedition in nearby Rome to find the watermelon she craved while pregnant with me in the dead of winter. Nobody wanted me to be born with reddish half-moons on my skin. Americans today do not share the belief in birthmarks as results of a pregnant woman's cravings, and no such connection is implied in the pages of *What to Expect When You're Expecting.* Yet in this manual, too, the bond between pregnant mother and in utero child is repeatedly mediated by food. During my first pregnancy I remember reading this manual and obsessing over every single bite I took, for it was implied that whatever I was eating I was also feeding my child; this, naturally, and guiltily, did not keep me from consuming unnecessary calories, sodium, sugar, and caffeine. Indeed, there runs through the pages of *What to Expect When You're Expecting* an opposition between baby and expectant mother that "surfaces most acutely in the discourse around food," positioning "the baby's health against the mother's 'appetites' " (Michie and Cahn, 26). This connection does prevail, and it has a fascinating history.

The other memory arising from thoughts of mother-induced birthmarks feels more ominous and stars my flamboyant paternal grandmother. Her story is linked not to food cravings but to the more general ability on the part of the pregnant woman to influence the child she carries through the force of her imagination. Nonna Peppina spent the last few years of her long, full life confined to a bed in our home. She would get vociferously angry if anyone with any deformity or plain ugliness came in the house during my mother's pregnancies. She insisted that all of her ten children were so attractive because in the course of her pregnancies she never set eyes on anyone who was less than beautiful. In fact she also made it a practice, as she untiringly told me, to look at herself in the mirror as frequently as possible so that all her children might be as beautiful as she! Thus also the protagonist of Ada Negri's short story "Il suo diritto" (Her right), explains the beauty of her son and daughter as a consequence of her intentional actions: "During my two pregnancies, I had covered the apartment walls, especially in the bedroom, with photographs of angels by Verrocchio, Perugino, Raphael; and I spent very long hours contemplating them, in the hope of thus influencing the bodily beauty of my children" (*Prose,* 304–5).

Though my stories may be humorous, the control and self-control that their ideological premises exact of women have a dark side as well. Both anecdotes point to the power that a pregnant woman has over the child she carries. The first type of power is a negative, marring power, while the second indicates a more constructive ability on the part of the pregnant woman. Although maternal impressions, which recur time and again in the works of late-nineteenth- and early-twentieth-century scientists and women writers, are quickly dismissed as superstitions on the rare occasions in which they are mentioned in today's pregnancy advice manuals, they have very real counterparts, poignant translations into the language of contemporary popular and medical culture. The subject of fetal harm, through drug and alcohol addiction for example, raises issues of sexual difference and reproductive responsibility; for some, it is imperative to involve men, public institutions, and social structures into the woman's individual responsibility in such matters (Daniels, 83–98). Even more pervasive are the injunctions to healthy foods and healthy habits that permeate the pages of all pregnancy advice manuals. In this perspective, the very genre of the advice manual could be seen as dangerously manipulative; as Helena Michie and Naomi Cahn note, "the mother's every move, whether it be taking a bite of dessert or choosing underpants, is carefully inspected, calibrated, and quantified with respect to the baby inside her" (25).

Yet I find it helpful to be reminded of the cultural relativity of such injunctions. For example, in Neera's novel *Il romanzo della fortuna* (The novel of fortune, 1906), we read of a scientifically up-to-date female character who "maternally" encourages a hesitant pregnant neighbor to help herself to some Marsala, a Sicilian fortified wine, because of its healthfulness in pregnancy (266–7). More recently, in Dacia Maraini's *Il treno per Helsinki* (The train for Helsinki, 1984), the pregnant protagonist's friends bring her red wine when she is hospitalized following heavy bleeding, and encourage her to drink it because it is good for her blood and for her health (63). What was deemed cheerfully healthful even just a generation ago (Marsala, red wine) is now demonized as fatefully harmful. What constituted a different kind of order (the powerful cravings of pregnancy) is perceived by medicine as a cultural disorder (wine to a pregnant woman?); we ridicule what we cannot understand. And since the medical gaze cannot envision cultural relativity, examples such as my memories as well as Maraini's and Neera's stories are quickly dismissed as old wives' tales, at best meaningless, at worst damaging.

In Alan Guttmacher's *Pregnancy, Birth, and Family Planning* (1973), for example, we read in a section entitled "Maternal Impressions"—one of the few manuals that even speak of this matter—that "there is no shred of scientific evidence that any component of a baby's make-up is influenced *in utero* by factors other than heredity, maternal diet, intrauterine conditions, and maternal health" (80). That we may not be sure what particular diet is best for the future child, and that perhaps maternal and fetal health cannot be gauged by blood tests and medical examinations alone, is a different, unexamined story. Furthermore, although some of the terms have changed, the connection between pregnant mother and in utero child still arouses fears, suspicions, questions, doubts. Many studies are devoted to the issues related to the pregnant woman's rights to privacy and self-determination as they impact the health claims of the (future) child. An exemplary title is Deborah Mathieu's *Preventing Prenatal Harm: Should the State Intervene?,* which explores situations that have come to be known as "maternal-fetal conflicts" or "preventable prenatal harm." Examples of these conflicts include consumption of alcohol and/or recreational drugs by the mother. In a society where abortion is every pregnant woman's legal right, it is indeed not so easy to justify the enforcement of the protection of the fetus—hence the lengthy debates of bioethicists on this subject.

More insidious perhaps are contentions couched in the terms of a believable psychology. George Feldman's *The Complete Handbook of Pregnancy* (1984) progressively reduces the certainty of its scientific claims. While it starts by claiming that "There is *no factual evidence* to prove that a mother's emotions affect the fetus so directly" (contradicting the claims of "mothers and aunts" that an "unhappy and anxious" pregnant woman will give birth to an "unhappy and anxious" infant), it slightly modifies its statement in the next section: "It is *doubtful* that a fetus can sense and respond directly to his mother's emotions" (73, my emphasis). The book then implies that a woman who "feels positive" will have an easier labor and a better "attitude" in early mothering, further stating that "Whether [children] can pick up these emotions while still in the uterus *remains a mystery,*" and concluding that "*Certainly,* if stress, anger and anxiety are chronic and unrelieved a pregnant woman should try to resolve the problems causing it *for her own sake as well as for her unborn child's*" (73, my emphasis). So we are still left with the question: Does an unhappy, anxious woman give birth to an unhappy, anxious infant? Twenty pages later a physiological rather than a psychological perspective appears: "Anxiety, fear or other emotional upsets, for example, alter the mother's hormonal balance and heart rate and respiration and blood pressure increase. The same hormones that cause these changes in the mother cross the placenta and enter the fetal bloodstream, resulting in an increase in the activity level of the baby" (92). Were mothers and aunts right, then, perhaps?

It is important to place some of these contemporary issues in their historical context, which is little-known and frequently oral. It is important because cultural forgetfulness has its consequences. Even many of today's feminist critics who discuss the disempowerment of pregnant women in contemporary society often fail to place their considerations in any historical framework, falling into generalizations that may be rhetorically powerful yet historically unfounded. The constraints imposed on the pregnant body by a society seen to increasingly valorize the fetus as subject at the expense and objectification of the expectant woman are now a topos in feminist considerations of pregnancy. Sociologist Barbara Katz Rothman, for example, writes: "Previously the uterus was thought of as a protected nest, but now the nest seemed unsafe, inadequately protected . . . Before this fall from grace . . . the mother's body was believed to do the work of protection," whereas "now . . . the uterus is no longer seen as a fortress" (*Recreating Motherhood,* 92, 159). Rothman is clearly placing her claims in a historical continuum defined by a sharp break between "then" and "now." "Where gestation was itself once the most natural of processes," claims cultural critic Valerie Hartouni with a singularly romantic view of nature, "it has now become treacherous" (41). Again, Hartouni implies that things were different in the past, things used to be better for pregnant women. In her essay "Look Who's Talking, Indeed: Fetal Images in Recent North American Visual Culture," E. Ann Kaplan accuses contemporary culture of reading the woman's body as being "in the service of the fetus," and in need therefore of external constraints and regulations: "Culture now imposes constraints on this body, dictating what the mother will, or will not, use her body for. . . . No longer is the womb the safe, idyllic sanctuary it has long been mythically celebrated for" (132). "Now," "no longer" (Kaplan); "once," "now" (Hartouni); "previously," "now," "before" (Rothman). Can this *laudatio temporis acti,* this rhetorical praise of the good old days, hold?

The constraints on the pregnant body are not new. I would argue on the contrary that this "mythical celebration," to use Kaplan's expression, is itself a mythical construction without historical bases. It is furthermore an unabashedly ideological construction, one aimed at buttressing the unwittingly essentialist argument that, in matters of pregnancy and abortion, "mother knows best." It seems that the pregnant woman instinctively, "naturally" knows what is good for her and for the fetus she carries, and needs and wants no help in deciding the latter's, and thus her own, fate. Furthermore, this argument identifies the construction of the fetus as subject and of the womb as a dangerous place as the work of contemporary prolife ideology. In order to construct the myth of the womb as "protected nest" and "fortress," however, the entire history of pregnancy, barely available as it is, needs to be erased. For as the theory of maternal impressions attests, the womb has not been perceived as a "safe, idyllic sanctuary" for a very long time.

The theory of maternal impressions has a long history, though not as long as one might think, given its pervasive status as folklore. The peculiarities of its trajectory make it a point of contact between popular and high cultures. In the eighteenth century the theory of maternal impressions was at the center of a lively intellectual debate. It was used to signify the close relationship between body and soul, and was discussed at length, for instance, in that manifesto of French Enlightenment, the *Encyclopédie.* Interestingly enough, even though today this theory is considered a remnant of folkloric belief, it first arose as an intellectual theory sometime around the fifteenth century, in humanistic texts from Florence, and was most richly articulated by hermetic and Neoplatonic thinkers of the Renaissance. In these writings the unity between mother and fetus was emblematic of the unity of the world and of the magic relations that governed the universe. This in turn confirmed the connection between human beings and the cosmos, between microcosm and macrocosm, between body and soul. Belief in the theory of maternal impressions also highlighted the creative power of women in the mysterious process of generation. The deference of early modern medicine toward antiquity probably motivated the appropriation of a different, ancient theory. This theory stated that what *the couple* (or, starting with Galen in the second century C.E., the woman) *saw* (or, again starting with Galen, imagined) *during the act of coitus* influenced the appearance of the offspring. This appropriation in turn gave rise to the impression among both the medical community and the people in general that the belief in the theory of maternal impressions always existed and was shared by all.

As the theory developed after the Renaissance and throughout the seventeenth century, it acquired more ominous features in terms of its representation of women. For if at first the theory gave women an impressive reproductive power, this "impressiveness" soon came to be seen as a sign of their disordered and capricious nature, making woman profoundly, perhaps essentially different from men. The birthmark was a sign of woman's unruliness and ambiguity, of woman's failings toward her children, and, ultimately, of her need for medical control. So in the eighteenth century the debate on the strength of the maternal imagination involved not only doctors but also philosophers and scientists. Those who opposed the theory usually supported scientific enlightenment and rational medicine. In the process of denying the power of the mother's imagination they also claimed that there was no relation between body and soul, and no communication between mother and fetus. But this relation, this communication, was probably the reason for its capillary diffusion among people of all levels of education. Those who supported the theory of maternal impressions, on the other hand, accepted the mystery of the mother–fetus link, though from a conservative and no longer viable view of the body. Both sides of the debate shared a fundamental ideological assumption, namely that the bodies of women needed to be defined and disciplined by medical and, more generally, intellectual discourse.

In the nineteenth century, the theory of maternal impressions began to be banished from the discourse of the intellectual elite; it was certainly no longer accepted, Claudia Pancino argues in *Voglie materne* (Maternal cravings, the book on which I based the above summary and to which I refer the reader for a detailed account) from 1870 on. Significantly, however, it remained alive and well not only in the popular imagination but also in literary texts and even in scientific treatises such as Cesare Lombroso's *La donna delinquente, la prostituta e la donna normale* (The woman criminal, the prostitute and the normal woman, 1893), to which I return in the next section of this chapter and throughout the book. In excluding the theory of maternal impressions from its official repertoire, the medical discourse forgot the intellectual origins of this theory, attributing its invention instead to the prejudices of the common people and, especially, to women's unbridled imagination. What nevertheless remained active throughout nineteenth-century medicine and to this very day is the belief in the connection between mother and fetus (previously rejected by those who opposed the belief in maternal impressions), and thus that the mother's well-being is fundamental to the well-being of the fetus she carries. This belief in turn supported the doctor's relatively new role as specialist and guide not only of woman's health but also of her psychological and physical balance, of her feelings and thoughts.

One of the most lasting remnants of the theory of maternal impressions is found in the fairy tale "Rapunzel." It is perhaps only through Rapunzel's story that contemporary generations in this country have heard of this previously pervasive theory. (Though in the popular imagination Rapunzel is not about cravings but about hair.) Being enamored of beautiful princesses with long, long hair, my daughter Gemma's own favorite is Paul O. Zelinsky's lavishly illustrated *Rapunzel*, published in 1997 and winner of the prestigious Caldecott Medal, awarded to the best picture books produced each year. Zelinsky's version is particularly rich because it reaches beyond the standard Grimm brothers' version, first published in 1812–1815, to two other important texts: the late seventeenth-century

French literary tale of which the Grimms' version is a rewrite, "Parslinette" (1697), by Marie Rose Caumont de la Force (1650–1724), and the Italian "Petrosinella," by the Neapolitan Giambattista Basile (1575 ca.-1632). Basile included "Petrosinella" in his lively, racy collection written in Neapolitan dialect, *The Pentamerone* (1634–1636). The intertextual (re)placement performed by Zelinsky is significant because the Grimm brothers erased in the later editions of their version of the story, whether out of prudishness or the more practical eagerness to find a wider audience, all references to the protagonist's and her mother's pregnancies. Indeed "Rapunzel" had been singled out by critics of the Grimm brothers' time as "a tale particularly inappropriate to include in a collection of tales that children could get their hands on. 'What proper mother or nanny could tell the fairy tale about Rapunzel to an innocent daughter without blushing?' " (Tatar, 18).

The story of Rapunzel, although well-known and available in many variants, is worth retelling. After years of infertility, a married couple is finally expecting a child. But the pregnant woman develops an insatiable craving for a certain plant: in the Grimms' Northern European version it is rapunzel, or rampion, while in the Mediterranean versions, such as Basile's and de la Force's, it is parsley. This plant grows in the garden of a neighboring enchantress. Afraid that the pregnant woman may die of such a craving, the father-to-be (or, in some variants, the woman herself) repeatedly steals the plant; although the pregnant woman devours it, she is never quite satisfied and insatiably desires more and more. When the enchantress discovers the theft, she demands the child—who turns out to be a daughter, named Rapunzel after the object of craving—in exchange for the plant. The enchantress raises the child as her own and when Rapunzel reaches puberty the enchantress places her in a secret tower to which she alone has access, by climbing up the girl's braided hair. When a prince discovers the girl's existence and the means to reach her, the two fall in love. As soon as the enchantress discovers the tryst—and, in some versions, the girl's pregnancy—she cuts off the girl's long hair and banishes her to a wasteland. In the Grimms' variant, the enchantress also blinds the prince, though his eyesight is restored when he and Rapunzel (and their twins) are reunited. This is where the Grimms' first edition ends, though in their final 1857 text and in Zelinsky's version the two lovers and their children find their way back to the prince's kingdom and live happily ever after.

A bodily detail links the story of Rapunzel in Zelinsky's version to the turn-of-the-century pregnancy texts I discuss later in this book. The enchantress, who is an older woman as well as a mother figure of sorts, discovers Rapunzel's pregnancy before Rapunzel herself, when she realizes that the dress has become tight around the girl's waist: " 'If you please, Stepmother, help me with my dress. It is growing so tight around my waist, it doesn't want to fit me anymore.' Instantly the sorceress understood what Rapunzel did not. 'Oh, you wicked child!' she shrieked. 'What do I hear you say? I thought I had kept you safe, away from the whole world, but you have betrayed me!' " (Zelinsky, 21). This sign of pregnancy, as it separates Rapunzel from her sterile stepmother, also links her to her biological mother, for in Zelinsky's book the mother discovers Rapunzel's existence in her womb in the same way: "one spring, the wife felt her dress growing tight around her waist. Joyfully she said to her husband, 'We are going to have a child at last' " (1). This epistemological link, like all references to pregnancy, is absent from the Grimm brothers' later editions. Already in 1819, seven years after the first edition, as well as in the final 1857 text, Rapunzel betrays herself by asking the enchantress why she is so much heavier to pull up the tower than the prince is. As folktale specialist Jack Zipes notes, while editing the texts of their tales the Grimms "eliminated erotic and sexual elements that might be offensive to middle-class morality, added numerous Christian expressions and references, emphasized specific models for male and female protagonists according to the dominant patriarchal code of that time" (74).

Unlike his predecessors, however, Zelinsky completely avoids the theory of maternal impressions: the husband's fear is that his wife may die from her craving, as she herself states unequivocally ("If I cannot eat some of the rapunzel from the garden behind our house, I am going to die," 3), and not that the unsatisfied craving may have any ill effect on the child she carries. Indeed there is no sign in this book that it could; this is perhaps because such an effect would be incomprehensible to the majority of those young American readers to whom the book is aimed. The irresistible urges and cravings of pregnancy, on the other hand, are still a part of the way in which our culture understands this period in a woman's life, as many pregnancy manuals attest: pickles and ice cream is a notoriously favored craving, appealing only to a pregnant woman's perverted appetite. Indeed, food cravings are given a preferred epistemological status by being listed as possible early signs of pregnancy (Eisenberg, Murkoff, and Hathaway, 124, 3, Curtis, 39). But although science allows us to believe in the reality of such cravings, they are frivolous, capricious, lacking physical consequences for mother or child. This is quite unlike the Grimms' husband's fears that, in the first edition, he communicates to the merciless enchantress: "he apologized as best he could, explaining that his wife was pregnant and how dangerous it might be to deny her anything in her condition" (Grimm, "Rapunzel," *About Wise Men and Simpletons*, 40). No specific mention of possible impressions is made in this passage, yet the danger is clearly understood as life-threatening—and not as the exaggeration of a whim.

An aside: Many versions of Rapunzel available to young readers today are completely bowdlerized, following the spirit of the second edition of the Grimms, thus losing much of their cultural impact. Marianna Mayer's adaptation for the Little Golden Books series is a prime example of this. Rapunzel's mother has no problem getting pregnant nor giving up her child; her craving was caused by the enchantress's evil spell and not by her own exceptional-because-pregnant body. Rapunzel herself does not of course get pregnant out of wedlock, and she is banished simply because of her illicit encounter with the prince—which, unable to lie like a good girl, she does not keep from the enchantress. There is however one interesting point of contact between the girl's impressionable body and her mother's impressive pregnant craving: "her eyes were blue as the blue-flowering plant she was named after" (Mayer, 237).

It is in "Petrosinella," Basile's Neapolitan "Rapunzel," that the theory of maternal impressions is the very motor of the narrative. This story was clearly written for a different audience than the later Grimms' versions and joyfully presents pleasure-seeking and pleasure-filled bodies. Petrosinella is named after parsley, *prezzemolo* in Italian and *petrosino* or *petrosello* in dialect, for that is the plant her Mediterranean mother most craved during her pregnancy. After all, while not many people in Italy would know of, much less long for rampion, parsley is the very synonym of ubiquity, given the favor it finds among Italian cooks. If you are "*come il prezzemolo*" (like parsley), the expression goes, you are just about everywhere. Furthermore, parsley is associated with erotic and talismanic powers. Upon seeing an ogress's bed of parsley, Pascadozia, Petrosinella's mother, "was seized with so great a desire to have some that she nearly fainted" (Basile, 135). Pascadozia is described as "unable to resist the desire," and excuses herself to the ogress "because she was pregnant and feared there might be a crop of parsley on the face of her child when it was born" (136). Pascadozia's delicious parsley soups avert any disfiguring birthmarks on her beautiful daughter's face, but the longed-for parsley makes its mark on more than just the girl's unusual name: "when the time came, Pascadozia gave birth to the most beautiful baby girl, a joy to behold, and she gave her the name of Petrosinella, for on her breast was a mark like a fine sprig of parsley" (136).

So the mother's craving does reappear as the child's birthmark, both termed *voglia* in Italian, yet the effect is never described as disfiguring—quite the contrary. For after Petrosinella, like Rapunzel, is locked up by the ogress in a hidden, unreachable tower, she does meet her prince whom she lets in using her long hair as ropes. And when the prince finally enters the tower after a period of courting, their lovemaking is described in the appetizing terms connected to the culinary origin of the girl's first name: "he sprang into the room and there feasted with that sprig of parsley at the banquet of love" (137). The metaphor is delightfully complex: the parsley is most specifically found in the birthmark, not coincidentally placed on Petrosinella's breast—an erogenous, erotic zone. And the parsley is by double metonymy the girl herself: the parsley stands for the breast, and the breast stands, synecdochically, for the whole body; and the name stands for the girl: Petrosinella is the pretty parsley girl.

Pascadozia's desire for food transforms itself, through the intermediary of Petrosinella's nubile body, into the prince's sexual desire. What the mother reproduces, in the course of her pregnancy, is therefore not only another person—another woman, her daughter—but also desire itself. While this double reproduction assumes more ominous undertones in later literature—particularly, as we will see in the rest of this study, in the scientific and literary writings of the late nineteenth and early twentieth century—in Basile's tale it retains a jocular and life-affirming tone. Indeed, an important difference between Rapunzel and Petrosinella is that the latter outwits her captor and thus actively regains her freedom through her own intelligent use of magic helpers; the more physically and intellectually passive Rapunzel, on the other hand, after wandering the wilderness with her twins, accidentally stumbles upon her blinded lover. The ambivalence of the mother figure is in turn dramatized by her dualistic, Kleinian split into a "good" mother (Pascadozia as birth mother) and a "bad" mother (the ogress as stepmother). Through her botanical and bodily connection with her biological mother, Petrosinella can negotiate the tension between matrophobia and matrophilia, unlikeness and likeness, separation and unity. Thus, if we can read beyond its surface as trite and heterosexist romantic narrative, what we find in the Rapunzel/Petrosinella tale is a complex imbrication of female identities set in motion by the power of maternal desire and the daughter's subjectivity, and an instance of that mother–daughter plot whose rarity is so poignantly and rightly lamented by poet and critic Adrienne Rich in her seminal book *Of Woman Born*. The embodiment of desire flows from mother's to daughter's body, subverting the self-identity of the subject of hysterical conversion and exposing a womanly genealogy that expresses itself through bodily connection but also through language and the power to name: Rapunzel, Petrosinella.

Maternal Impressions in Turn-of-the-Century Science

The simple statement "Ho una voglia di caffé" could be translated from the Italian into English as both "I am craving some coffee" and "I have a coffee-colored birthmark," alternately signifying desire or body, one's own appetite or one's mother's. In romance languages such as Italian, French, and Spanish, the homonymy of craving and birthmark (*voglia* in Italian, *envie* in French, *antojo* in Spanish) points to a popular etymological link in turn based on the conviction that if a pregnant woman's craving goes unsatisfied it will translate itself into an indelible colored spot on the unborn child's skin. The spot is both metonymy of woman's desire, because it is causally contiguous with it, and metaphor of its object, because it is morphologically similar to it. What is reproduced in the course of pregnancy, then, is not only the species, or a socially desirable reproduction, but also, more dangerously, woman's own desire. A belief in the strength of the latter underlies this homonymy and grounds it in cultural as well as physical anthropology: Female desire is so powerful as to be deforming to the next generation; as a consequence, it needs to be observed, disciplined, even cured. Fairly innocuous birthmarks were not the only outcome of unsatisfied urges, for the intimate connection between pregnant mother and unborn child could lead to multifarious abnormalities: the mother's craving for milk could lead to a white stripe of hair, a mother's fear of pigs could lead to a cleft palate, her stepping on the hair thrown out the window by a barber could lead to an abnormally hairy child, and so on (Zolli, 16–18). The list of dangers to which the pregnant woman could expose her child is endless, and although its details vary depending on history and geography, the belief in maternal–fetal connections touched and to some extent continues to influence the Italian peninsula.

As Jacques Gélis notes in his survey *History of Childbirth*, "It was generally believed that during the pregnancy the child saw what the mother saw, heard what she heard and felt what she felt. Any unpleasant sight or unsatisfied desire was echoed, with greater or lesser intensity, in the body of the fetus. Thus the mother's body had a dual function. Part screen, part filter, it protected the child from excessive heat or cold; but it was also a conductor which transmitted to the child various influences, some of which were far from beneficial. The mother's dreams and fantasies could make a harmful 'impression' on the fetus" (53). Historically, then, we are far from a conception of the womb as "protected nest," "fortress," "safe, idyllic sanctuary" as critics such as Rothman, Hartouni, and Kaplan would have us believe. Let us take an eloquent example from an early-twentieth-century Italian writer. In Maria Messina's *A House in the Shadows* (1921), Alessio, who grows up to be a sickly boy and dies young, is influenced in utero by the death of his mother's father and its nefarious effects on his pregnant mother. At his birth, Alessio is "a tiny, sickly baby, who seemed kneaded by the suffering of those months of mourning and by the melancholy that emanated from the house" (28). The fetus, like dough, is "kneaded" with pain and melancholy.

Not unlike Messina's view is the injunction of the title "Calm down, or it's going to be a girl," of a report in the Italian newsmagazine *L'Espresso* (September 16, 1999). According to this report, based on a Danish study published in the *British Medical Journal*, if a pregnant woman is afflicted with grave family worries in the months preceding or following conception, the newborn will "probably" be a girl. I am not so much interested in the scientific study itself, but rather in the way it is presented to the magazine's audience. From this perspective, two points need mentioning. First: Giving birth to a girl is assumed in the title to be an undesirable outcome to one's pregnancy, in a country where the standard wish for a newlywed couple often still is "Best wishes and may you have male children" ("Auguri e figli maschi"). Second: According to the report highlighted in *L'Espresso*, the likelihood of giving birth to a male under stressful circumstances is 49 percent, as opposed to 51.2 percent in nonstressed pregnant women. Statistically significant, perhaps, but is this a significant statistic? Can one truthfully say, as *L'Espresso* does, that this study reveals that if you are stressed during your pregnancy you will give birth to a baby girl? Yet the article insists on the mother's impressiveness and on the fetus's impressionability.

From a different perspective, sociologist Ann Oakley describes the theory of maternal impressions as a "key theory about pregnancy commonly held prior to the modern obstetric era," which "stated that the condition and viability of the fetus was profoundly influenced by the mother's mental and emotional state—a view that, of course, fitted well with the prevailing model of successful pregnancy as guaranteed only by a life-style properly balanced in accordance with natural dictate." And most fundamentally, according to Oakley, "Until well into the nineteenth century [in our case, as we will see, at least as late as 1893 in Italy], the question for most medical men who contended this matter was not *whether* maternal impressions could cause deformed fetuses, but *how* they did so" (*The Captured Womb*, 23–24). This once-prevalent theory of maternal impressions and of the fetus's susceptibility to its mother's sensory and emotional experiences (primarily, unsatisfied desires and terrifying sights) constitutes an overlooked chapter in the history of the body as a product of symbolic and cultural, as well as biological and psychological discourses. It is a theory that has provided one powerful way of accounting for the intricate relationship between the psychic and the somatic and for the passage from the former to the latter.

This is the very relationship that, during the same years I consider in much of this study, was occupying Sigmund Freud: *Studies on Hysteria*, Freud's first book-length study, co-authored with Josef Breuer, was published in 1895. The theory of hysterical conversion, based on the fluidity of the distinction between body and mind, displays several analogies with that of maternal impressions. In both cases, the line between body and mind is blurred; in both cases, we are faced with undisciplined female bodies. Thus it is perhaps significant that, in the case study of Anna O., the analyst realizes the existence of transference only when Anna performs the pantomime of a hysterical pregnancy and birth. In the etiology of hysteria, psychic traumas are converted into bodily symptoms: pregnancy and childbirth, but also blindness, paralysis, convulsions, and so on. In the etiology of birthmarks, the mother's trauma or desire is converted into a bodily sign on the fetus: a colored spot or a veritable deformity.

In developing its grip on the pregnant body, turn-of-the-century medical science incorporated the popular belief in cravings, so attractive, and convenient, into an ideology that insistently reduced woman to her body, female nature to univocal physiology. It did so by borrowing from an anthropological model that late-nineteenth- and early-twentieth-century women writers, I argue, both integrate and challenge. The pervasiveness of this theory of folklore-turned-science may be read in those turn-of-the-century texts, literary as well as scientific, that deal with the various stages and aspects of maternity, especially pregnancy. It constitutes an important intersection where we can read the dialogue, carried out over the female body, between literature, and especially literature written by women, and science as the positivistic, anthropological and/or gynecological interpretation of woman. The workings of maternal impressions form one aspect of the relationship between maternal and fetal body that is confronted—in a more or less subtle, subversive, or submissive way—in much female-authored literature of the late nineteenth and early twentieth century. This literature in many ways rewrites the impact of anthropological findings on the female body. Kroha notes indeed that "The years after 1880 saw an explosion of women writers unlike anything that had ever taken place in Italy before, all the more significant because it took place at a time of considerable social and political turbulence" (1).

The turbulence was cultural and scientific as well, and two of its most active agitators were Cesare Lombroso (1835–1909) and Paolo Mantegazza (1831–1910). The name of the latter should be familiar to readers of Freud's case study of Dora, the hysterical teenager who derived much of her knowledge of sex (such as, most notably for her symptoms, of the practice of fellatio) from stolen readings of Mantegazza's work—his *Physiology of Love,* according to most critics, but more likely one of Mantegazza's more sexually explicit texts, such as *The Sexual Relations of Mankind.*

Older than Lombroso, Mantegazza was best known during his lifetime for his successful popularization of many concepts of medicine and hygiene. A physician by training, Mantegazza worked in Florence, where he managed to combine his medical practice with his passion for anthropology. As a professor of anthropology at the University of Florence for forty years, he promoted and for a long time directed the National Museum of Anthropology and Ethnology, which he also first opened in 1869. He was popular among the general public and admired within the scientific profession, and his renown continued long after his death. A positivist, Mantegazza divided the human psyche and physiology into four aspects: love, hatred, pleasure, and pain. This simplification doubtless contributed to his success among the lay public. His popular writings reflect Mantegazza's attitude as a scientist and man of letters (he also wrote some novels), whose almanacs and those publications he called "elements of hygiene" presented scientific facts with the didactic tone of an old sage. Regardless of our evaluation of his works, it is believed that his contemporaries generally considered these "of great prestige and scientific accuracy, even when some of the results appeared controversial or debatable" (Minuz, 115). Mantegazza and Lombroso started out as friends before becoming intellectual antagonists and personal enemies.

Lombroso, from 1876 a professor of legal medicine at the University of Turin, is considered the founder of criminal anthropology, a discipline based on the technique of anthropometry: measuring bodies, comparing sizes and weights, calculating averages—all performed to impose order on an otherwise rather messy humanity. As one of Lombroso's disciples succinctly put it, the idea that dominated Lombroso's mind "is, on the one hand, that a man's mode of feeling, and therewith the actual conduct of his life, are determined by his physical constitution; and, on the other hand, that this constitution must find expression in his bodily structure" (Kurella, 18). It is this belief that guides Lombroso's research on woman as well as his studies of criminals, geniuses, madmen, religious leaders, and, at the end of his career, spiritualism (and his fascination with and belief in parapsychological phenomena tarnished, in his later years, his reputation as a scientist). Lombroso is noted for two controversial theories: that genius is closely related to insanity, and that criminals can be identified by physical signs, by the stigmata of degeneracy: low foreheads and small, pointed ears, for example. Like Mantegazza, Lombroso also founded a museum, the Museum of Psychiatry and Criminal Anthropology, in Turin in 1898.

During much of their careers, Lombroso and Mantegazza elaborated an ever-more-comprehensive and more or less intentionally popular discourse on the female body that was largely based on the findings of both physical and cultural anthropology. Lombroso carried out this project primarily in the voluminous treatise *La donna delinquente, la prostituta e la donna normale.* Partially translated into English as *The Female Offender,* this book was written in collaboration with his son-in-law Guglielmo Ferrero. It has been described by Harrowitz as "probably his most problematic work" (17) and by Landucci as "an authentic compendium of European culture regarding normal women, women criminals, and prostitutes" ("I positivisti," 483). According to De Giorgio, the book constituted for many years the ultimate authority on female psychology, despite some suspicions of superficiality and prurience ("Italiane fin de siècle," 214).

Mantegazza's contribution to the study of women is most obvious in his two-volume *Fisiologia della donna* (The physiology of woman), which, in its various chapters, discusses woman in terms of anatomy and biology, history and geography, clothing and artificial deformity, psychology, sensibility, emotions, and feelings, beauty, love, religion and morality, motherhood, vice and crime, intelligence, fundamental missions, place in social hierarchies, education, and future. It is an eloquent coincidence that both Lombroso's and Mantegazza's treatises on woman were first published in 1893.

In one respect the date was no coincidence, for in the last decade of the nineteenth century "a national female typology" began to be constructed (De Giorgio, "Italiane fin de siècle," 212). Thus by 1899 Lodovico Frati could rightly refer in his compendium *La donna italiana secondo i più recenti studi* (The Italian woman according to the most recent studies) to "the extraordinary quantity of works and pamphlets which have come to light in Italy, especially in these last years, concerning any question related to woman" (vii). Giacanelli underlines the cultural relevance of these treatises when he notes that "Positivist scientists become public personae, authentic and official protagonists of national life, inasmuch as they tend to concretely modify its reality through the affirmation of their ideas" (14). This interaction moves in both directions since Lombroso regularly makes use of those "unscientific, experiential categories of common opinion," and his ideas, as Giacanelli accurately notes, display a "power of penetration" and an "exceptional popular resonance" that "go beyond their 'absolute' scientific value, which is certainly mediocre" (18–19, 9). For example, Lombroso continually cites proverbs, sayings, and literary references as a direct, unquestioned source of knowledge. Conversely, Lombroso's theories constituted a fertile source for many writers who were his contemporaries and fascinated with the findings of his idiosyncratic science—such as, for example, Gabriele D'Annunzio and Luigi Capuana.

The scientific writings of the late nineteenth century do not contemplate for women the possibility of deviating from a rigid standard: The norm of motherhood should provide the fulfillment of women's biological, psychological, and cultural functions, beginning with physiology. It is evident, according to positivistic science, that woman's body has her maternal destiny written all over it, down to her very skeleton, and Mantegazza adopts Lombroso's method of physical anthropology when he inscribes woman's bones with her maternal mission: Her ribcage, for example, is more flexible to allow her to breathe better throughout her pregnancy (*Fisiologia,* 1:60). Pregnancy determines and molds woman's skeletal shape. In addition to anatomy, anthropological evidence also allows Mantegazza to scientifically posit motherhood as woman's first and only destiny: "Woman, I will never tire to repeat it one hundred times, is worth as much more as she is more of a mother" (1:123). As her body confirms, it is in fertility and the potential for motherhood that woman finds the fulfillment of her gender and of her very being: "Woman is truly woman during those thirty or thirty five years of fertility which she is given" (1:128); "*Woman is mother,* and around this kernel or biological skeleton all her energies are clustered" (1:263); "Maternity is woman's first and essential mission" (2:7–8); "The human female's mission is to make men" (2:213).

Through his repeated use of the word *mission,* Mantegazza underlines maternity as a fundamental and quasi-religious social function, aimed at reproducing and thus at creating and educating new citizens. This was at that time a more pervasive view than Lombroso's, for whom maternity was primarily tied to the reproductive instinct necessary to the propagation of the species. As a consequence Lombroso, unlike Mantegazza, viewed maternity as relatively exempt from any moral value. Nonetheless, for both Mantegazza and Lombroso, if motherhood is what makes woman "valuable," it is also, paradoxically, what constitutes her intellectual, and therefore social and political inferiority. Woman, for Mantegazza, "will always find in maternity too great an obstacle to be able to compete with us" (2:317). Both viewed maternity as incompatible with intellectual and artistic activity:

> Making men is a great and powerful thing and it requires so many and such great efforts as to make aesthetic and intellectual creation impossible (aside from a few exceptional cases). Illustrious women who were also fortunate and affectionate mothers are always the exception and almost all of them, at least until today, pay for their privilege with strange and painful neuroses; with infinite neurasthenias or, what is worse, with fatal deficiencies in their heart. (2:190)

The incompatibility between the maternal and the intellectual functions underlines the way in which woman, precisely because she mothers, is always on the verge of physiological or psychological debility. Lombroso reaches the same conclusion, drawing his "anthropological" evidence from the entire animal kingdom:

> intelligence in the entire animal kingdom varies in inverse proportion to fertility; there is an antagonism between reproductive and intellectual functions. . . . Now, since the work of reproduction is for the most part assigned to woman, for this biological reason she has remained behind in terms of intellectual development. (*La donna*, 179)

Again, as Lombroso's disciple Hans Kurella put it, sexual differentiation for Lombroso is based on "the fact that the whole organization of woman is predestined to motherhood, and [on] the fact that any other professional activity of whatever kind is hardly possible for her, or, if possible, only on account of an abnormal and degenerative predisposition" (57). A similar argument is made, at around the same time, by positivist sociologist Scipio Sighele, who notes in *La donna e l'amore* (Woman and love) that "Between intellectuality and maternity there has always been an antithesis. . . . It is therefore logical to conclude that the excessive development of woman's cerebral activity, and in general of her social and political functions, will proportionally diminish her ability to completely carry out her function as mother" (255). Cultural historian Bram Dijkstra notes similar lines of reasoning in turn-of-the-century writers and thinkers of other European countries (August Strindberg, George Romanes, Carl Vogt, Paul Möbius), whose ideas he succinctly summarizes as follows: "If the normal maintenance of the 'seat of reproduction' already consumed all the vital energy which might otherwise have fed the brain, the extent to which pregnancy and childbirth ravaged women's mental capacity was truly immense" (170).

An eminent through relatively isolated dissenter in turn-of-the-century Italian science was physiologist Angelo Mosso, who bravely stated that there was no evidence confirming the incompatibility between maternal and intellectual functions (126–32). But for the vast majority of scientists at that time, reproduction is incompatible with thinking, fertility with intelligence, and perhaps womanhood with health itself. It is especially disturbing, then, to recognize that "It is enough to open haphazardly any of Lombroso's writings to find a surprising homogeneity with contemporary culture" (Giacanelli, 19), and to entertain "the doubt that a large part of the research of positivist scientists tended to give a 'scientific' foundation to pervasive feelings and customs" (Landucci, "I positivisti," 488). It seems reasonable to deduce, then, that the reference to "the normal woman" in Lombroso's title is painfully ironic. The ostensible paragon that the normal woman constitutes, aimed at making women criminals and prostitutes more clearly recognizable, turns out to be an impossibility, a figment of the scientific imagination. For all women, "normal" ones included, fall within the scope of the criminal anthropologist. Indeed normal women are particularly unstable because indistinguishable from occasional criminals and prostitutes.

The physical connection between maternal and fetal bodies extends well beyond the theory of maternal impressions for Lombroso—though this theory can provide a crucial entry point for his discussion of the woman as mother. According to Lombroso, first of all, "maternity is an eminently physiological phenomenon" (499); as such, it is perfectly suited to the physical anthropologist's examination. It is characteristic of Lombroso's method to ignore psychological and especially sociocultural causations, making the body its privileged, even its exclusive object of study and source of data. In a sense, maternity is itself one of those mysterious cravings of the female body that keep it forever on the brink of infirmity: "maternity is even almost a physiological need which, if it should remain unsatisfied, would become the source of physical and psychical disease" (532). Later in his treatise, Lombroso downright conflates the normal with the pathological in the case of pregnancy, as well as menstruation and menopause, making the distinction between health and sickness a question of mere degree: "One of the special features of the mad criminal woman, which is only an exaggeration of her normal state, is that she gets worse during the menstrual period, pregnancy, and menopause" (593). Mantegazza concurs, also pathologizing the postpartum period and breastfeeding: "pregnancy, the post-partum period, and breastfeeding influence woman by disturbing her nervous system" (2:174–5). Woman's "mission," to return to Mantegazza's ideal vocabulary of maternity, is sickness. This vision of woman's inherent pathology has legal effects as well. In 1881, for the legal physician G. Ziino, the "abnormal states" brought about by menstruation, childbirth, and the postpartum period underscore the inadequacy of a legal system where men and women are treated as equals (Babini, 29–34).

This view is supported by the official stance of Italian gynecologists at the turn of the century. Prominent doctors such as Luigi Maria Bossi and Muzio Pazzi concur that, maternity being the physiological aim of the female organism, the maternal function is alone responsible for woman's health, both physical and psychological, and that maternity is the main cause of women's mental disturbances. The latter were called, with an ample nosographic category, "post-partum madness," a diagnosis used as a blanket term extending from the beginning of pregnancy through the entire breastfeeding period. Even more generally, other scientists have claimed that "woman's mental inferiority was the product of a *physiological dysfunction*," and that "if illness, then, is an abnormal state in man, it is a *normal physiological* state in woman" (Minuz, 127).

It is because of this cultural convergence, which assumes every healthy body to be unchanging (like the paradigmatic healthy body of an adult and not-yet-old male) and which Mantegazza and Lombroso, among others, turn into a scientific fact, that feminist critic Elisabetta Rasy justly notes that "Menstruation, pregnancy, childbirth are in some ways an illness with respect to the progressive temporality of society, they reintroduce with respect to the reality principle the pleasure principle, although in reverse . . . they bring in an irreparably and incoercibly autonomous temporality" (*La lingua della nutrice*, 119). A fair representation of the body, particularly of the female body, demands an adjustment of cultural perceptions of time, progress, reality, even. If patriarchal health shows no place for the rhythms of maternity, then the maternal body can only find a place, in this fixed universe, as a sick body. Philosopher Iris Young nonetheless observes that "Regular, noticeable, sometimes extreme change in bodily condition . . . is an aspect of the normal bodily functioning of adult women. Change is also a central aspect of the bodily existence of healthy children and healthy old people, as well as some of the so-called disabled. Yet medical conceptualization implicitly uses this unchanging adult male body as the standard of all health" (56). Although the "sickness" of the other-body—that is, not adult, male, and "healthy"—could be initially valorized as an epistemological advantage, as the clearer view from the edge, it also risks a marginalization entailing silence and ultimately erasure.

In support of his pathologizing theory, Lombroso goes on to cite a fascinating and telling list of mad pregnant women in the throes of desire. They are a rather curious lot: one woman had the urge to kill her husband, whom she usually loved, every time she was pregnant; another could not resist such an urge and after killing her husband salted his body and ate it (a rather extreme food craving, clearly!); yet another poisoned one of her children and threw herself in a well with the other three; a downright comic case involves a pregnant woman who could not resist the urge to steal a chicken on display at a butcher's shop. This odd list is an example of Lombroso's "shocking capacity . . . to collect facts, data, information from the most diverse provenances, his untiring curiosity for every piece of news that could in some way give rise to a problem or serve as anthropological scientific document or demonstrative support of his theories" (Giacanelli, 16). The pregnant woman's cravings are by definition insatiable, her behavior utterly unpredictable: "In conclusion, in this state . . . woman is capable of anything" (593), Lombroso predictably concludes, ending his discussion of the madness of pregnancy by linking it to woman's atavism. *Atavism,* or the tendency to reproduce ancestral traits, brings woman closer than man to the lower species: "During pregnancy . . . a kind of animal instinct dominates woman, and it can drag her to any excess" (594). Anthropological and medical evidence collude to transform childbearing into a potentially dangerous object of scientific gaze and legal control. And in fact the pathologization of pregnancy, as it has been pointed out from a sociological perspective, was ideologically necessary because, as Oakley justly notes, "The ideological transformation of the 'natural' (having babies) to the cultural (becoming an obstetric patient) is difficult, since obstetricians must deal with the fact that 97 percent of women are able to deliver babies safely and without problems" ("A Case of Maternity," 609–10).

In the medical gaze, the pregnant woman is clearly not herself, though the alterity within her—which one could interpret, from a feminist perspective, as an epistemological prerogative— can be diagnosed as a form of hysteria, a disorder of the uterus-as-animal (as in the view of Plato and numerous others before and after him) that leads women outside the realm of reason into the unknowable, the dark continent of femininity evoked by Freud: being "capable of anything" (Lombroso, 593), she can be "dragged to any excess" (594) and is therefore in dire need of control. In fact, as Minuz underlines, "there is a radical equivocation in the numerous writings that anthropologists and physicians dedicated to woman between the 1800s and the 1900s. Although they are presented as the rigorous answer of science to the 'eternal mystery' of woman, these writings were answering instead another question: which place should woman occupy in modern society?" (114). Having replaced religion and morals as the arbiter of the culturally acceptable, science becomes the discourse designated to put woman in her place.

Pregnancy is a productive "case study" when analyzing the reduction of women to mothers. In a sense pregnancy may be said to recapitulate motherhood. In the nine months of pregnancy the mother's body prepares the fetus's to leave it, just as the mother more slowly, in the course of the years, prepares her child for independence from her. The literary and cultural construction of pregnancy, then, can perhaps provide a concentrate, a preview, a symptom of the mother–child relation that is to grow out of it. With this observation, we can return to the theory of maternal impressions. In the chapter of his *Fisiologia della donna* dedicated to motherhood, Mantegazza vividly describes the corporeal interdependence between pregnant woman and fetus: "the new organism which develops in the uterus acts continuously on the one that envelops it, and the latter reacts on the smaller one, like two body parts irrigated by the same blood" (2:54). The connection between the two bodies, maternal and fetal, is reinforced by an agricultural metaphor of irrigation and a rhetoric of leakiness. Their physical permeability to one another's fluids embodies the psychical and grammatical permeability between their subjectivities and their personal pronouns, as well as embodying the "splitting" (of flesh and language) which takes place within the maternal body and its amniotic fluid.

For scientists as for writers, neither mother nor fetus is ever a totally autonomous self, both of their bodies being open (to each other's fluids, in Mantegazza's metaphor), heterogeneous: "grotesque," to use a definition by Mikhail Bakhtin. Bakhtin distinguishes between two antithetical representations of the body: the "classical body" is harmonious, monumental, homogeneous and, most important in this context, closed, impenetrable; while the "grotesque" body could be linked to femininity and is defined by Bakhtin as material, corrupt, threatening, and, above all, "open." According to Bakhtin, the grotesque body "is a body in the act of becoming. It is never finished, never completed; it is continually built, created, and builds and creates another body" (317). This is an apposite definition of the pregnant body, which is the open, penetrable body *par excellence.* The pregnant body lacks precise boundaries and permanently confuses the distinction between the self and the other in its creation of an-other body. The physical splitting thus accomplished entails a dissolution and/or a transformation of the self, of the signifier. And geographically, the grotesque body is the lower body, as opposed to the classical, upper body of the head and rationality, of the heart and feelings. The grotesque body is the site of orifices and discharges, and also the site of impregnation and childbirth. As Bakhtin observes, "all these convexities and orifices have a common characteristic; it is within them that the confines between bodies and between the body and the world are overcome: there is an interchange and an interorientation" (317). From a philosophical perspective, Young likewise notes that "In pregnancy I literally do not have a firm sense of where my body ends and the world begins" (49). And Nancy Hartsock extends this deconstruction of boundaries to female physiology in general: "There are a series of boundary challenges inherent in the female physiology—challenges which make it impossible to maintain rigid separation from the object world. Menstruation, coitus, pregnancy, childbirth, lactation—all represent challenges to bodily boundaries" (156).

The chapter "The woman as mother," in Mantegazza's *Fisiologia della donna,* significantly begins with the section "Cravings." Optimistically, or self-deludedly, Mantegazza writes that the belief in cravings, which he defines in this passage as a prejudice, has disappeared thanks to the progress of science. But then he contradicts himself by admitting that this theory contains "a kernel of truth," since "everything that acts on the mother, exerts an influence on the child as well." Moreover Mantegazza has to admit that such a belief is "still widespread among many people of high social status" (2:54). Through a subtly misogynous explanation, intensified by his medical and scientific self-distancing from popular gullibility and prejudice, Mantegazza attributes a corollary of this erroneous yet convenient credence—namely the theory that looking at beautiful people and things can make the fetus beautiful—to woman's need to conceal her adulterous misconduct. According to this author, the belief that it is dangerous for pregnant women to look at "monstruous or disguised people" and that it is instead useful for them to look at beautiful women, pictures, and statues, "has been very useful to unfaithful women to explain some strange resemblances between the child and family friends. By seeing them and looking at them again and again, the child looked a lot like, looked too much like the friend and too little like the husband" (2:55). It was in fact argued in the nineteenth century that it was women themselves who invented the theory of maternal impressions as a deception against their husbands (Pancino, *Voglie materne,* 172–73).

At the same time as he debunks woman's power to exert a positive influence on her children, however, Mantegazza has no trouble in attributing children's epilepsy and idiocy to their mother's encounters with war, revolution, and epidemics, nor in stating that it is from their children that pregnant women "inherit" food cravings and aversions (2:56). By attributing to the mother a purely negative power over her child (her desire can stain but it cannot paint, it can deform but it cannot mold, my *salumiera* had a point, my grandmother did not), Mantegazza's discussion of birthmarks and cravings points back to the picture he had painted at the opening of his chapter on motherhood, a scene in which the pregnant mother and unborn child dyad is touched, indeed must be touched by the husband's healing hand (I return to this scene in the next chapter).

Lombroso clothes his discussion of cravings and birthmarks with a more self-consciously scientific and more overtly misogynous language: Unlike his colleague and former friend, whose pedagogical aims are obvious throughout his works, Lombroso's popularity had a different, more somber tone. (It is precisely on the grounds of Lombroso's overzealous, even fanatical allegiance to the anthropological method that Mantegazza rejects him and his theories, *Fisiologia,* 2:43). Lombroso unambiguously pathologizes pregnancy by claiming that pregnant women are congenital neurasthenics whose willpower cannot resist because it is weakened by the sickness implicit in pregnancy. In pregnant women, according to Lombroso,

> psychic exchange is slower, the will is weaker, actions are less deliberate. The intensity of desires is the cause of those so-called moles or birthmarks, on which I cannot dwell at this point. It is certain though that some of these pregnant women have a most lively desire for certain things, and they form such a vivid image of what they see or otherwise feel that they succeed, through a mechanism which I cannot deal with right now, in determining the vasomotor mechanisms of the fetus, something which I do not deny: by now literature has collected a not insignificant quantity of cases of maternal moles, which are always, according to all the accurate observations that have been made, related to a lively yet unsatisfied desire and with the greater emotional impressionability of the pregnant woman. (*La donna,* 1915 edition, 325)

While Mantegazza, with a reasonable argument, claims that birthmarks cannot be caused by the mother's desire because, unlike the latter, their spectrum of shapes and colors is extremely limited (2:54–55), Lombroso posits a photographic relationship between pregnant woman and her desire that is in turn reproduced in the relationship between pregnant woman and fetus. Conveniently, however, Lombroso twice procrastinates the explanation of its causes: "on which I cannot dwell at this point," "which I cannot deal with right now."

Because of the physical and psychological alterations she undergoes during gestation, the pregnant woman is "impressed" by her desire, visually or through any of the other senses. As a result, her desire "impresses" itself on the fetus's forming body. What is reproduced is not only the child but also, quite literally, the mother's desire. These pathogenic cravings which lead to birthmarks, then, the result of woman's uncontrollable and unsatisfiable desire, are for Lombroso due to pregnancy as a "neurasthenic state," characterized by a decrease of high intellectual functions and an increase of instinctual life, "against which manifestations the pregnant woman cannot oppose the same resistance of feelings, ideas, modesty, as when she is in normal conditions" (*La donna,* 1915 edition, 325). Among the effects of woman's cyclical, and therefore, according to this masculine model, unhealthy physiology, pregnancy needs to be controlled, for it is an abnormal, even a neurasthenic condition in the course of which the pregnant woman jeopardizes the good health of her child and thus the very future of the human species.

In his 1912 speech against feminism, published in 1913 as *Femminismo e maternità* (Feminism and maternity), Doctor Cesare Serono is comparably wary of the pregnant woman's influence on the child she carries and afraid of the lack of influence the man (i.e., the father) has in this situation. Particularly, Serono fears the recurrence of ancestral psychological traits (akin, in his discussion, to diseases such as hemophilia) carried over from a woman's genealogy. Physical and psychological heredity are in his speech one and are likened in turn to the theory of maternal impressions: Both are dangerous because irretrievably lost to the father's control. During pregnancy, Serono warns, "woman has all the time she needs to mold her offspring according to her own being" (21). Luckily, woman is also eminently impressionable, much like the fetus she carries: just as her intelligence and culture develop quite unconsciously by making an impression on her psyche, "so also she models on her husband the external physical characteristics of her offspring; she absorbs his most salient psychological features, which she transmits to her children; but these features are much weaker than hereditary ones" (27). Like a fetus, a mother is impressionable; like a pregnant woman, a father is impressive. And through this reversal, although imperfectly (since hereditary connections are still stronger), the paternal discourse of turn-of-the-century science can claim as its own a mysterious mechanism it at once despised and feared.

Maternal Impressions in Women's Literature

At the end of the nineteenth century, namely at the time of the rise of first-wave feminism, writing became a viable professional option for women in Italy. Indeed the professionalization of women writers is among the most relevant cultural phenomena in turn-of-the-century Italy, and women writers begin to constitute for the first time during this period a veritable social category. Because they belong to that generation whose creative energy comes into its own during the positivist crisis of the late nineteenth century, writers such as Neera (1846–1918), Carolina Invernizio (1851–1916), Annie Vivanti (1868–1942), Ada Negri (1870–1945), Grazia Deledda (1871–1936), and Sibilla Aleramo (1875–1960), to name a few, contend with, accommodate, and/or displace the positivistic paradigm of women's intrinsic sexual and reproductive pathology. Their thematic violation of cultural and literary stereotypes goes hand in hand with linguistic transgression if, as Patrizia Zambon notes in a seminal article about the literary formation of Negri, Neera, Deledda, and Aleramo, these writers were reprimanded, by both contemporary and later critics, for the quality of their writings. These were judged to be ungrammatical, immature, slovenly: in a word, "feminine" (324). At the same time, with the exception of Aleramo, these writers do not display a feminist consciousness; on the contrary, they are often self-proclaimed antifeminists, despite the resolute criticism of the condition of women through much of their written production.

For the feminist reader, turn-of-the-century women writers' texts are fascinating because they both reproduce the stereotypes of womanhood and/as motherhood, begotten by patriarchal discourse, and conceive of alternative constructions. (Re)reading these pregnancy texts is fundamental if, as Oakley incisively claims, "just how reproduction has been socially [and, I would add, culturally] constructed is of prime importance to any consideration of women's position. It may even be in motherhood that we can trace the diagnosis and prognosis of female oppression" ("A Case of Maternity," 608). The importance of turning to the cultural representation and construction of pregnancy is also obvious if we keep in mind that the crisis of female sexuality—the conflict between social, cultural, and moral demands and the woman's own identity—does not necessarily coincide with sexual contact or even with the conception of a child, but rather can take place at any time during a cycle that includes pregnancy, childbirth, and breastfeeding (Accati, 45). Analogously, psychoanalyst Silvia Vegetti Finzi criticizes traditional psychoanalysis for seeing coitus as the culmination of sexual development and for not taking into account menstruation, childbirth, breastfeeding, the postpartum period, and menopause ("L'altra scena del parto," 187).

The interaction between pregnant mother and unborn child is problematic in the works of many women writers who were contemporaries of

Lombroso and Mantegazza. But the outcome of that prenatal bond in these texts is not, as was the case in the positivistic treatises, a predictable pathology, however torn apart by contradictions and paradoxes. Rather, the impressive maternal bond can multifariously lead to life or death, beauty or deformity, artistic ability or linguistic handicap. Many of these writers—Annie Vivanti, Ada Negri, Grazia Deledda, Neera, Sibilla Aleramo, Maria Messina, for instance—attempt to write of motherhood differently, an endeavor that is indispensable if, as Finzi claims, "there are no words for maternity, or at least no ready-made ones," because "maternity is located in a pivotal position . . . between the preverbal substratum and discursive formations. . . . between what is inside and outside" (*Mothering*, 116, 127). Finzi's is an especially appropriate definition in this context. The theory of maternal impressions is precisely a theory of the relationship between the outside and the inside of the maternal–fetal body. It is a codification of the interaction of the preverbal body and the discursive structures of desire. Because of its ritualization, its repetition, its shared nature, childbearing can also be inscribed within that "other female expression," or the "female expression as other" that Rasy posits as part of, and preceding, the relationship between women and literature: "This too has something to do (from afar, obliquely) with the relationship between women and literature; this too comes *before* that relationship, it must be experienced and worked out before a relationship with literature can be established" (*Le donne e la letteratura*, 11).

The production of late-nineteenth-century women writers, as Anna Santoro notes, is characterized by a will to comment on their surrounding reality, which makes it a privileged means of accessing, among other things, social customs and daily life (14). From a sociohistorical perspective, Gloria Chianese writes that we know little about women's own experiences of childbirth and breastfeeding in the past, and the little that we do know about the relationship between mothers and children is generic. These literary texts about the very early stages of motherhood, then, written by women who were also mothers, constitute precious, though also oblique and intricate historical-anthropological evidence, even as they energetically question the validity of the anthropological method prevalently employed, at that time, in scientific theories of womanhood (Chianese, 18). More generally, as Gélis points out, "It is often hard for us to understand the real experience of pregnancy in past times. Through modesty and through fear of doing harm to the child, the woman, be she from town or country, said little about her state: her hopes and fears and everyday attitudes are revealed to us only incidentally by doctors" (45). But these hopes, fears, and attitudes are also revealed less and less incidentally by women writers during the period that coincides with the development of openly feminist practices.

The association between maternal craving and filial body is reproduced in literary as well as in scientific texts, and one would naturally expect to find it more frequently in texts that appeal to and represent women and women's concerns. The works of Carolina Invernizio, for example, a popular and prolific writer in turn-of-the-century Italy, are permeated with references to such a connection; one can turn to her gripping novel *Odio di donna* (A woman's hatred, 1907). Annie Vivanti, among the most favored writers of that time, also deals with the risks of maternal impressions in her graphic novel *Vae Victis!* (Woe to the defeated! 1917). And Ada Negri, yet another author among early-twentieth-century readers' favorites, much of whose work centers on the figure of the mother, presents several instances of the effects of maternal impressions—as in the autobiographical novel *Stella mattutina* (Morning star, 1921, in *Prose*) and the short stories "Il suo diritto (in *Finestre alte*, High Windows, 1923, in *Prose*) and "La confessione d'Ignazia" (in *Oltre,* Beyond, 1946, in *Prose*).

But it is to a story told within Grazia Deledda's autobiographical novel *Cosima* that I turn my attention. Like many if not most of her colleagues, Deledda did not participate in the growing feminist movement of her time. Yet her work reveals an insistent attention to women's issues and, more subtly, to the questions of gender identity and sexual difference. These questions are placed in particular relief given the traditional, patriarchal community—turn-of-the-century provincial Sardinia—in which Deledda's stories unfold. *Cosima* first appeared posthumously in installments in *Nuova Antologia* in September–October 1936 and was then published as a volume in 1937; Cosima was Deledda's middle name. Thus, although the writer coincides with the protagonist of the story, she speaks of herself in the third person and changes, somewhat, her name: the signifier of self-identity slides from first name to middle name, from Grazia to the less direct Cosima.

Cosima narrates the protagonist–author's childhood and adolescence, repeatedly touching on the issues of motherhood and reproduction. The first important event in the narration is the birth at home of the protagonist's sister, a profoundly mysterious occurrence that elicits an unsatisfied curiosity in the little girl who still knows nothing of sexual reproduction. This uncanny reproductive event is the center around which the setting of the story is first presented. What Cosima quickly learns, however, are the deleterious effects of reproduction on mothers: on her own mother, first of all, withered and gray before her time, unknown and unknowable for

Cosima, a figure of absence and loss. Significantly, Cosima's mother remains anonymous: Her name remains unspoken, unlike her admired and beloved father's name, Antonio. Cosima also learns of the destructiveness of reproduction through its effects on her older sister Enza, who dies suddenly and alone from a miscarriage shortly after her marriage: fourteen-year-old Cosima herself finds Enza's lifeless body in a pool of black, foul-smelling blood.

The complex, ambiguously complicit effects of maternal impressions are at the very core of the narration of the story-within-the-story I now turn to; they constitute, in a sense, its punch line. The protagonist of this story-within-the-story develops a unique relationship with a mouflon, a Sardinian sheep who faithfully visits her every night "like a lover" (*Cosima,* 25). But the mouflon comes only when her fiancé and, later, husband, is not in town. The latter is described as being "strangely jealous" (25) of the anthropomorphized mouflon, though it is not made entirely clear to the reader whether it is he who finally kills the animal. Nine months after the mouflon's last visit, the woman gives birth to a baby boy. He was "beautiful, with copper-colored hair and large sweet eyes like the mouflon. But he was deaf and dumb" (27). Of the mouflon, the narrator had indeed noted the beautiful, striking hair and eyes ("with copper-colored fur polished by the cold, its big sweet eyes shining in the moonlight," 24), and, more indirectly, the surprising lack of voice: she "feels him quiver and pant. She almost expects him to speak" (26). Silence and the inability to speak proceed from the bond to the mother as the impressive and transgressive subject of desire.

This story-within-the-story has been aptly described by Anna Dolfi as "one of the most cryptic and suggestive passages in *Cosima*" (13). It is told by an old servant to his master's young children, among whom is the little girl Cosima; with its fairy-tale, even mythical aspects it is an instance of Deledda's anthropological interest in Sardinian folklore, her perhaps overemphasized regionalism. Yet the storyteller, and especially the audience—a group of children—preclude bestiality from becoming anything more than a vague suspicion. Because what causes the little boy's misfortune is not his mother's bestial pleasure but instead the perhaps equally transgressive silent, prelinguistic influence or impression that the pregnant woman's lifestyle has on the child she carries: that prenatal, semiotic connection that borders on a supernatural dimension, confirmed by the fantastic tone of the narration, and makes of the two one even as they paradoxically remain two. This same connection reproduces the shape of woman's desire onto the product of her reproduction. The story is in this sense an instance of the conflict between desire and interdiction that characterizes and is fundamental to Deledda's narrative at large. Thus, although Dolfi minimizes the reproductive role of female desire when she interprets the little boy's misfortune as a retribution for his father's alleged killing of a sacred animal, still she ends her analysis by pointing out that the mouflon is the attribute of the female figure used to represent Deledda's island, Sardinia (14–15). The mouflon, then, is explicitly associated with woman, as having a unique relationship with her, as with Sardinia—a region with a grammatically feminine name.

At the political level, the story of the mouflon, which appeared in print when Benito Mussolini's demographic campaign was well established, complicates without overtly undermining the fascist configuration of woman as ideally, as necessarily, as solely a mother. For despite its repeated dissidence, Deledda's representation of motherhood shares many traits with the fascist cult of the mother. This is perhaps to be expected if it is true, as Domna Stanton has written, that the "idea(l) [of the mother as a source of subversion] is always/already inhabited by, and accomplice to, the workings of contextual phallogocentric structures" ("Difference on Trial," 176; I return to Stanton's argument later in the book). Nevertheless the subversion inherent in the fascist rhetoric of virility, analyzed by Barbara Spackman (who draws on Michel Foucault's claim that opposing strategies are produced by the discourse of control), can also be read in the fascist rhetoric of motherhood: Deledda's construction of motherhood both recirculates the fascist myth of motherhood and produces a "reverse discourse" that challenges fascism's discursive regime. This story-within-the-story is one of those "dissonant notes," then, that allows us to realize "the contradictory ways in which women accommodated themselves to the gendering of power" (Spackman, 114). Indeed, Robin Pickering-Iazzi maintains that "Far from glorifying the culturally constructed image of the Mother, the many visions of motherhood authored by women throughout the 1920's and 1930's articulate a consciousness resistant to the essentialist ideology of the maternal as they refashion the terms and context of mothering" ("Unseduced Mothers," 37).

Appearing as it does in the reconstruction of her early formation as a professional writer (Deledda wrote over 30 novels and 250 short stories, and received the Nobel Prize for literature in 1926), the story of the mother and the mouflon resists fascist gender ideology by positing a powerful and dangerous alternative to the unfulfilled maternal figure. The latter is represented in this book by the author's own mother, whose intellectual and emotional barrenness directly proceeds from her adherence to the dominant values of female self-sacrificial dedication to husband and family. The protagonist of *Cosima* rejects these values and embraces instead the marginalization, exclusion, even the expulsion that is her only way out of the sacrificial system. As Susan Briziarelli notes, "Cosima alienates herself from traditional society, and her marginalization allows her a freedom she does not otherwise have" (24).

The mute boy who resembles the mouflon in both positive and negative ways breaks the matrilineal cycle that hands down the immutable monotony prevalent in the rest of the book. He does this not only, not even primarily, through his male sex, but rather as corporeal proof of the effectiveness of the mother's desire and its independence from her husband's, as well as through his association with outcast disability depicted elsewhere in the book: Fortunio, a young man who is aware of Cosima's poetic talent and participates in her erotic initiation through a kiss, is lame from birth. He is also an illegitimate child, excluded from that male genealogy so important in Cosima's world: for Cosima's brother Andrea, who rules the family after the father's death, Fortunio is "an absolutely inferior being, socially and physically" (86). Fortunio transgresses male genealogy even aesthetically, since his beauty is described as "feminine," "languid," and "caressing" (84). When their tryst is discovered, the scandalized villagers comment that "only Cosima was capable of such adventures with a cripple, a bastard, one rejected by fate" (92). A woman, an animal, a mute, a cripple: These figure otherness and marginality with respect to traditional society and a transgression of the production of utilitarian values at the basis of patriarchal economy. They are associated instead with a desire that transcends the useful, the profitable, and rejects dichotomization, dualisms, in favor of connectedness and continuities: between human and animal, between male and female, between health and sickness, normality and abnormality, mother and child. It is through relationship to the other that, for better or for worse, the self is constituted.

Philosopher and cultural critic Susan Bordo has rightly suggested that "a major paradigm shift has occurred over the past hundred years. Formerly, the body was dominantly conceptualized as a fixed, unitary, primarily physiological reality. Today, more and more scholars have come to regard the body as a historical, plural, culturally mediated form" (288). Certainly the impressive, impressionable bodies encountered in the preceding pages allow us to regard them as Bordo describes: not unitary or fixed, but rather multiple and moving, signifying beyond the discourse of physiology, mediated instead by numerous discourses, and firmly rooted in space and time. The theory of maternal impressions can be read as an attempt, on the part of discourses such as literature, folklore, and science, above all—disciplines that are indissolubly linked in figures such as Lombroso and Mantegazza—to bridge the gap between body and language, biological reproduction and the metonymic structures of desire. Yet the body constructed in the theory of maternal impressions is always a pregnant, hence a female body, and its scientific codification at the turn of the century is the construction of an often misogynous gaze whose objective was to cure a fabricated pathology rather than to care for a healthy body performing a biological function.

It is not necessary, nor is my argument sufficiently equipped, to make the dangerous leap from books to life, from the textual level to historical experience, in order to perceive the repercussions in our own time of the pathologization and medicalization of the female body at the close of the nineteenth century and the first few decades of our own. On one hand anthropological theories of womanhood such as the ones developed by Lombroso and Mantegazza provide us with a cultural background against which we can better understand the writings of authors such as Deledda, Invernizio, Vivanti, and Negri; this is a rather old-fashioned approach to the relationship between literature and science, certainly, and a productive, even prolific one. At the same time, however, these literary works imaginatively elaborate on the scientific theory of maternal impressions. In this process, the texts interact at a discursive level that contributes to the shaping and development of scientific ideas themselves. Thus, literature and science become each other's unspoken backgrounds, each other's unconscious, as it were. Furthermore, women's literature subtly yet effectively illuminates some of the medical anthropologists' unspoken objectives: their implications of bodily duplication in pregnancy as linguistic silence, the dangers to patriarchy inherent in the reproduction of women's desire, the humiliating and at times even lethal transformation of pregnancy into a supervised asceticism. These themes, implicit in Deledda's *Cosima,* recur throughout the works of her colleagues and contemporaries. With an opposite strategy, for example, narratives such as Negri's "Il suo diritto" and "La confessione d'Ignazia"—in which pregnant women influence in a positive way the children they carry—textually transform the medical-anthropological theories by reversing the social and personal value those theories attach to their findings. The meaning of the pregnant woman's desire becomes a celebration of her life-giving, molding ability rather than a deprecation of her neurasthenic, pathogenic influence. The woman's own subjectivity, pathologized and therefore silently edged out of the scientific treatises, acquires in much of the literature by turn-of-the-century women a central position that defies the simplistic classifications of positivistic anthropology by staging instead the complex workings of human desire and the paradoxical dimensions of maternal power.

Maternal Impressions and Feminist Theory

Obviously the theory of maternal impressions no longer occupies a place of relevance in cultural debates. Analogous discursive elaborations of the maternal, however, can be located in contemporary analyses of the relationship between mother and daughter. Crucial, for instance, to the little girl's development, the mother–daughter bond has been barely sketched by classical psychoanalysis—focused as it is on Oedipus's problems with the phallus as exemplary of subject formation. The mother–daughter relationship occupies instead a pivotal place in the work of influential feminist critics such as, most notably, Luce Irigaray and, more indirectly, Hélène Cixous and Julia Kristeva in France, Adriana Cavarero, Silvia Vegetti Finzi, and Luisa Muraro in Italy, and Adrienne Rich, Jessica Benjamin, and Nancy Chodorow in the United States. The mother–daughter relationship touches in many ways the maternal matters that arise when we consider the influence the mother has on the child she carries for nine months within her own body: the contradictory pulls of positive shaping and negative disfigurement; the insoluble issues of continuity and separation, connection and discontinuity, identification and rejection; the attempts to keep away from the two extremes of idealized perfection or pernicious destruction of the mother.

Significantly, the editors of an Italian collection of psychoanalytic essays on the mother–daughter bond, *Corpo a corpo: Madre e figlia nella psicoanalisi* (Body against body: mother and daughter in psychoanalysis—the title echoes Irigaray's *Le corps à corps avec la mère,* partially translated as "Body Against Body: In Relation to the Mother"), Gabriella Buzzatti and Anna Salvo, write in their introduction that "we can, in a certain sense, state that each daughter is the 'symptom' of her own mother. She, the daughter, carries with her—beyond any psychopathology—tortured, intricate, imperfectly released, repressed signs of her body against body relation (*il corpo a corpo*) with the maternal body" (40). Like a birthmark induced by forbidden or unsatisfied maternal craving, the physical relationship with the mother, beginning in utero with an imagined child, can be read on the daughter's own body: as in the economy of maternal impressions, the mother's desire is reproduced, and indelibly impressed, in the daughter's subjectivity.

Reproduction is of the body and of desire. But human reproduction is a misnomer, for birth always brings something, someone new into the world; it always engenders difference. It is never a repetition of the same. In the context of European feminism especially, difference is an indispensable concept. The impressive difference of the maternally inscribed body foreshadows the impressionability of the maternal subject in that Italian feminist theory known as *pensiero della differenza sessuale,* the thinking of and about sexual difference. The birthmark in literary texts prefigures in its very economy of desire the sexual difference theorized by thinkers such as Irigaray in France and Muraro in Italy: difference as excess, difference as the unthinkable and, at the same time, as that which must be thought in order for women to attain symbolic representation. In the words of Elizabeth Grosz, "difference is seen not as difference from a pregiven norm but as pure difference, difference itself, difference with no identity. This kind of difference implies the autonomy of the terms between which the difference may be drawn and thus their radical incommensurability" ("Sexual Difference," 91). It is important that Buzzatti and Salvo should stress in the passage I quoted above the phrase "beyond any psychopathology" in their definition of the mother–daughter bond. For what we witness in the spaces that unite and divide the theory of maternal impressions as elaborated by turn-of-the-century women writers and the mother–daughter bond as conceived of by late-twentieth-century feminists is a connection that is, inseparably, of the flesh as well as of the psyche and the spirit, a connection that is corporeal as well as symbolic, but which at the same time escapes, exceeds the medical paradigm that would tame and reduce it to an instance of pathology: a sickness, a disfigurement, a mistake. A birthmark. Which leads of course to a more inclusive issue: In the age of science and the heyday of medicine, can we talk about the body, especially the pregnant body, authoritatively yet beyond the medical reaches of pathology?

Let us go back for a moment to late-nineteenth- and early-twentieth-century Italy, a time and a place when maternity was not yet pervasively medicalized. Among women writers of that time and place, the mother–daughter bond was crucial in both fictional and autobiographical texts. In Deledda's *Cosima,* for instance, the protagonist's desire is shaped in contrast to her mother's destiny of defeat, even as it partially replicates it. In this way, the story of the mouflon encapsulates some of the contradictions of the connections between mother and child: difference in continuity, for example, and the necessary transgression of the father's law for the effective symbolization of the maternal. The mother–daughter bond is comparably important in the works of Neera and Aleramo, as we will see in chapters to come. In these writings, its centrality is all the more striking given that the mother–daughter bond has been traditionally underrepresented in the Western written tradition. Irigaray, a theorist to whom I return below, even goes so far as to state that the patriarchal regime has made the love between mother and daughter "impossible," and gives practical, political suggestions for ways of making this bond more visible in our society ("Each Sex Must Have Its Own Rights," 2). Similarly, the group of Italian feminists known as the Milan Women's Bookstore Collective claim that "In the social order thought up by men, there are no forms of symbolic bond between a woman and the woman greater than herself, who is her mother" (127). Italian turn-of-the-century writers' thematic and narrative choices, rich in autobiographical echoes, point to many intricate cultural, psychological, emotional, spiritual, interpersonal, and social issues concerning both this bond and its cultural and social invisibility; these issues find an echo in the writings of late-twentieth-century feminist writers and theorists. The texts I have encountered go well beyond those simplistic daughterly perspectives that see mothers as women identified and constructed in, collusive with patriarchy. Rather, what stands out in these accounts is a multifaceted, problematic identification of mother and daughter on the basis of a common, yet ever-differing sex, and the common (re)inscription into a female genealogy that patriarchal thought has, with varying degrees of success, attempted to ignore, repress, silence.

Among the most notable of these contemporary echoes is a rejection of the traditional antagonism between mother and daughter that permeates too many traditional literary and psychoanalytic texts alike. The mother–daughter relationship is threatening and only theorized/imagined, by psychoanalysis, in terms of pathological symptoms; for instance, hysteria is for Freud a form of pathological attachment to the mother. Or, in Muraro's feminist spin, the hysteric is the woman who, etymologically, remains attached to the maternal womb (*hystera*) and yet rebels against her real mother because she perceives her substitutive role in the maternal continuum, in the sequel of mothers—a role that can have no meaning in the symbolic order of patriarchy: "the hysteric interprets the female relation with the matrix of life. She interprets sexual difference" (*L'ordine simbolico della madre,* 60). And it is the hysteric's inability to acknowledge her debt to, her dependence on the mother, that makes her incapable of any subsequent social relationship. But if psychoanalysis insists on the Oedipus complex as a sine qua non of subject formation, then the girl's relation to the mother is going to be erased, and femininity censored into silence. It isn't until the work of Irigaray in the 1970s that the mother–daughter bond, the female passion for and of the maternal body, attains a place of relevance in the psychoanalytic field.

Although of Belgian origin, Irigaray figures prominently in the so-called "new holy trinity of French feminist theory" (Moi, "Introduction," 5), along with Julia Kristeva (Bulgarian) and Hélène Cixous (French-Algerian). Much has been written and said about this trio. For example, in *Maternal Pasts, Feminist Futures,* Lynne Huffer forcefully argues that "the concept of 'French feminism' has outstayed its welcome: it no longer works, so it is time to move on" (22). Although I agree with Huffer, I have nevertheless found it necessary, in my own reading of maternal impressions, to confront the formidable construction of the mother proposed by these three theorists; though I have also found it useful to recontextualize them in their European rather than exclusively in the much-maligned context of the Franco-American connection. The concept of difference, for example, which Huffer associates with French feminism, was also effectively theorized by Italian feminist thinkers such as Muraro and Cavarero with important differences—so to speak.

But let me begin with Irigaray. In her introduction to a volume of essays on Irigaray, Naomi Schor makes the resonant claim that "as the major French theoretician, Irigaray is actually Simone de Beauvoir's chief successor" ("Previous Engagements," 4). Irigaray's work has been both enormously influential and repeatedly criticized. Most vociferously, this theorist has been perceived by many feminists as an obscurantist paradigm of biological and psychic essentialism, even though, as Schor perceptively notes, "by the end of the eighties the very antiessentialism that had attacked essentialism for its universalism had assumed the status of a universal value" (7). The notion that identity is a construction destabilizes any comfortable embrace of essentialism, yet the need for a shared sense of identity in political and ethical action forces us to reconsider the value of essentialism itself. Italian feminism, for example, perhaps because of its emphasis on the political dimension of sexual difference, has traditionally been less suspicious of essentialist positions. Thus Teresa de Lauretis writes that "feminist theory is all about an essential difference, an irreducible difference, though not a difference between woman and man, nor a difference inherent in 'woman's nature' (in woman as nature), but a difference in the feminist conception of woman, women, and the world" ("The Essence of the Triangle," 1). In a 1999 review essay, noted Italian feminist philosopher Adriana Cavarero describes the role of essentialism in the language of feminism—several pages before even turning her attention to the French connection and Irigaray: "Although the naming of the female gender is an act of naïve mimesis triggering a series of contradictions, the naming of woman must in fact be read as the temporary gesture of a subversive strategy aimed at deconstructing the androcentric logic of the subject" ("Il pensiero femminista," 136). Indeed, Margaret

Whitford has posited Irigaray's essentialism as a strategic, rather than the final stage, in a process necessary for any philosopher unwilling to exclude the maternal–feminine. For the maternal is a central, often structuring element in Irigaray's impressive theoretical elaboration, one with which feminists engaged with maternity must grapple, and one which, I believe, ultimately works to radically dismantle the rather facile opposition between essentialism and antiessentialism. After all, binary thought has not traditionally served women well. I urge the reader to heed, then, Whitford's invitation to "engage" with Irigaray, rather than more simply and quickly dismiss or idealize her (25).

Irigaray is an especially appropriate theorist for my discussion because of her centrality in the contemporary Italian cultural scene. In Italy, Irigaray is not considered an abstract theorist, as she is in the United States, but rather a political thinker whose work attends to the actual contexts of women's lives. Rosi Braidotti notes that Irigaray's work was instantly translated and recognized in Italian culture and especially in the women's movement, while it took over ten years for her work to be translated into English ("Foreword," xiv–xv). And Naomi Schor speculates that "in national feminist contexts such as the Italian where heterosexual institutions have been subjected to a particularly thoroughgoing interrogation, Irigaray should be vastly more popular and influential than in cultural contexts where homophobia remains covertly rampant even among feminists" ("Previous Engagements," 10).

Irigaray writes about the relationship between women that "women must love one another both as mothers, with a maternal love, and as daughters, with a filial love. *Both of them*" (*An Ethics of Sexual Difference*, 105). This imperative disrupts the clichéd psychoanalytic descriptions of, for example, the daughter's antagonism toward the mother and the ensuing rivalry between women. So again today, as in the theory of maternal impressions of old, two interpretive strands emerge concerning the relationship between mother and daughter in psychoanalytic understanding: one, based on classical psychoanalysis, in which the mother's desire is a pathogenic entity—the origin of neuroses and of disfiguring birthmarks, or, in the Oedipal account, of a suffocating fusion that can only be staved off through the father's mediating intervention; and another, more complex strand, inaugurated by the work of Irigaray (herself a transgressor in the already-dissident psychoanalytic establishment of Jacques Lacan), whereby the mother has a molding ability with effects that cannot be reduced to a mechanistic pathology. "In a way," Irigaray reflects, "the daughter has her mother under her skin, secreted in the deep, damp intimacy of the body, in the mystery of her relationship to gestation, to birth, and to her sexual identity" ("Gesture in Psychoanalysis," 98). The vocabulary of the prenatal connection, a vocabulary of body and body fluids, of desire and need, of love and knowledge, links Irigaray's sentence to the tradition of maternal impressions, even as it evokes, "in a way," though, that biological essentialism with which Irigaray's reader is repeatedly and necessarily confronted.

Significantly, Jane Gallop's discussion of Irigaray's essentialism as construction also evokes a language of bodily connections and maternal impressions when she writes, about Irigaray's belief in a language analogous to the female body: "I determined to examine, precisely, the poetics of [Irigaray's] writing, to discover how she produces the imaginary impression of female analogy" (*Thinking Through the Body*, 93). Gallop's determination is to trace, through rhetorical analysis, the female desire that impresses itself in the body of the text. Like a birthmark, women's language, *parler femme*, proceeds from women's desire. Like an impressed body, language entertains with corporeality a relationship that is mutually constitutive and imaginary, presymbolic. The bodily impression of the imaginary, as well as the imaginary impression on the body (to paraphrase Gallop's line about the phallus/penis: same difference?) construct Irigaray's plural, multiple female body, be it maternal and/or daughterly, her sexuality, her difference. But this prototypical relationship between women remains unsymbolized in patriarchy, and its symbolization constitutes for Irigaray an urgent necessity. Without the symbolization of the mother–daughter relationship, women's symbolic identity must be limited to the maternal function and thus be residual and defective.

In the work of turn-of-the-century Italian women writers, too, mother and daughter are not simply oppositional terms, nor is the mother erased in a textual or other concern with the child as is the case in classical psychoanalytic theories of subject formation (in which the silent maternal figure is the background, the *object*, against or in relation to which the individual *subject* forms and develops). Rather, in the alternative models provided by these texts, mother and daughter share a complex relationality that defies the assumptions of subject formation according to Freud—succinctly and adversarially summarized as follows by Jessica Benjamin:

> that individuality is defined by separateness; that separation is brought about through paternal intervention (read authority); that the father's phallus, which forbids incest, is the prime mover of separation; that the girl's lack of the phallus relegates her to a passive, envious relationship to the father and phallus; that this position, in which the girl is deprived of her own agency and desire, is the hallmark of femininity. (82)

Against these assumptions, Benjamin's feminist psychoanalysis states, among other things, that little girls consolidate their sexual identity as females by identifying with their mothers, as numerous turn-of-the-century women's texts, for example, confirm. "Thus," Benjamin continues, "maternal identification theory leans toward the reevaluation of the mother, whose influence Freud neglected in favor of the father, and is less likely than the theory of phallic monism to emphasize the negativity of the female condition" (83). For Benjamin, that is, infants are not locked in a mother–child dyad that is impervious to the attractions of the outside world; rather, the primary bond between mother and child is already social, *intersubjective,* and the child's desire for autonomy is not dependent on the paternal threat.

Also for Irigaray the recognition of the bond between women, exemplified in the mother–daughter bond, is a necessary step in the development of a symbolic system in which the patterns of separation and subject formation would not be mediated, as in Lacanian psychoanalysis, by the Name of the Father (the Father's Law) and the primacy of the phallus as the signifier of desire. A change in women's position in the symbolic order (access to society, to culture, and above all to language) is what needs to take place, however, for women to avoid dereliction, the state of abandonment and fusion, the failure to differentiate and to separate that prevents one's emergence as a subject. This can only be achieved through the symbolization of the relation to the mother and to the mother's body because the nonsymbolization of this relationship to one's origins is what threatens women with psychosis. For if one's sex has no value, then what is the meaning of the loss of origins for the daughter? The mother–daughter relationship is unsymbolized insofar as the daughter is prevented from imagining, or symbolizing, her relationship to her beginning, her origin: her mother. This is so because, if the mother has no value in a system of representation that is phallic, the daughter cannot know her mother because she cannot represent her. Hence the non-differentiation, or in-difference, of mother and daughter, captured by Irigaray in her lyrical essay "And the One Doesn't Stir Without the Other," published in 1979 as "Et l'une ne bouge pas sans l'autre" and translated into English two years later.

The theme of "And the One Doesn't Stir Without the Other" is the complicated relationship flowing between a mother and a daughter, "the one" and "the other." Their common movement, beginning with birth and before, oscillates between paralysis and advancement, stasis and change. As in the writings of turn-of-the-century women writers, birth is in Irigaray's text forever linked with death, in a knotted relation that reveals the complicated structures of the mother's and the daughter's mutual desire: "When the one of us comes into the world, the other goes underground. When the one carries life, the other dies. And what I wanted from you, Mother, was this: that in giving me life, you still remain alive" (67). This is how Irigaray's meditation ends, with a poignant invocation, steeped in a uniquely female body language that is reminiscent of Sibilla Aleramo's passage from which the title of *A Woman* is derived: Can a woman be a mother and still remain "a woman," can she mother without abdicating subjecthood? For without female subjecthood, Aleramo claims, motherhood itself is bound to failure—especially for the daughter, incapable of finding in the mother a model and a source of authority. So also the daughter in "And the One Doesn't Stir Without the Other" experiences bodily paralysis as a figure of the broken bond to her mother. In place of verticality, in place of the needed genealogical link, the generational difference between mothers and daughters—broken, matricidally suppressed in favor of the son–father relation—patriarchy sees lack of differentiation and rivalry as paradigmatic of women' relationship among themselves. The phallic mother obsessively oppresses, suffocates even, her own daughter with her relentless love, choking her with milk that turns into paralyzing ice and boxes the mother into her function as nourisher. Dereliction, a state of dependence, ensues. The identities of both mother and daughter are confused; their continuity is deadly because their relation is not symbolized. The daughter is unable to recognize, in her mother, a woman.

In later texts, such as the lectures collected in the volume *Sexes and Genealogies,* Irigaray moves away from the paralysis of the mother–daughter bond produced by patriarchal logic. Identity remains sensuous and ongoing, thus still resolutely antipatriarchal, yet the mother and the daughter become able to act and to speak as women, to experience each other as women, by appropriating a space where their relation may be symbolized. But in "And the One Doesn't Stir Without the Other," as Carolyn Burke notes, "Painfully, Irigaray's prose embodies their knotted relations and the guilt-ridden structures of their mutual desire" ("Irigaray Through the Looking Glass," 39). Whitford observes, furthermore, that the fusion of the mother–daughter relationship "is shown to be, not a desirable and delightful state of fluid identity, but a pathological symptom of a cultural discourse in which the relation between mother and daughter cannot be adequately articulated" (82). Because of its potential for fusion, for dereliction, identification with the mother can be dangerous for women's identity; nevertheless, it is the only way for women to avoid hating, rejecting their mother. It is also the only way for women to avoid the bodily paralysis that figures the absence of a connection to the mother.

The articulation of a continuity between mother and daughter, a process intrinsic to the theory of maternal impressions, is also fundamental to Irigaray's theorization of the maternal body. Analogies can be discerned between the dangers of the mother–daughter bond—fusion as dereliction and therefore as psychosis—and its symbolic potential. The relationship with the mother is indispensable for the daughter's symbolization of her, and abandonment is not, cannot be the antidote to fusion. Mother and daughter can be together *and* separate, related *and* individuals. Irigaray's "Body Against Body: In Relation to the Mother," a 1980 lecture included in *Sexes and Genealogies,* is an impassioned plea for the recovery of the representation and the interpretation of the time spent in utero and an analysis of the trauma of separation from our mother's womb. Significantly, this is also the lecture where Irigaray makes the powerful suggestion that civilization is founded on an original matricide rather than a patricide—overtly contradicting Freud: that the unpunished murder of the mother's body is at the origin of the erasure of birth and mothering in Western culture. But, or perhaps therefore, the subject of maternity, of pregnancy and birth, is almost taboo in psychoanalysis, according to Irigaray, to the point that phallic language replaces the flesh and blood of the maternal womb. And it is painfully ironic that this language should be incorrectly termed "the mother tongue."

Among the consequences of this repression on the part of psychoanalytic discourse is a fundamental misunderstanding, or fantasy, of human need. Woman's sexuality, like the infant's hunger, is seen as insatiable despite bountiful evidence to the contrary. Another fantasy involves a misogynous perception of the woman as mother. For quite unlike the cut-up image of the mother offered by Freudian psychoanalysis—according to which mother is breast, mother is voice, mother is gaze, and so on, yet she is never whole—the integration of mother and child in pregnancy and their total bodily interaction in this primary experience underline that "mother and child are linked in a way that precedes all dissociations, all tearing of their bodies into pieces" ("Body Against Body," 14). Psychoanalysis fears the closeness of this link because of the potential fusion it implies of the subject with the mother as original matrix, as contagion, sickness, madness, even death. Hence the refusal of psychoanalysis to acknowledge the maternal bond and its consequent taboo status. But for Irigaray the clear and present danger is the opposite: The daughter's paralysis or self-destruction is the consequence of a lack of relation with the mother.

In "Body Against Body" Irigaray focuses on the mother–child rather than the more specific mother–daughter connection. Yet what Irigaray has to say is especially appropriate in a discussion of female genealogy because every woman spends the first part of her life in the body of another woman, and Irigaray challenges the economy of sameness dominating Western culture. I now turn therefore to the work of two Italian feminist thinkers, so as to underline continuities as well as divergences in the elaboration of difference itself. For unlike the by-now-ubiquitous writings of French feminists, Italian feminist thought is not well-known among U.S. feminist thinkers—and this in spite of the fact that, as Serena Anderlini-D'Onofrio points out, "in the 1970's the women's movement in Italy was one of the most intense in the world; that it produced a vast amount of works in the areas of theory, pedagogy, and social and political thought" (213). This body of work only began to be translated in the late 1980s, and some anthologies as well as single works are now available in English translation: for example, *Sexual Difference,* a collaborative work by the Milan Women's Bookstore Collective; the two anthologies edited by Paola Bono and Sandra Kemp, *Italian Feminist Thought* and *The Lonely Mirror;* Adriana Cavarero's seminal *In Spite of Plato* and, most recently, her book on autobiography, *Relating Narratives.*

The relationship to the mother informs the work of Silvia Vegetti Finzi, a professor of psychology at the University of Pavia and a practicing psychoanalyst. Finzi is an especially interesting figure for my discussion because, being a psychoanalyst, she diverges from the pattern according to which "Italian *pensiero della differenza sessuale* is less deeply rooted in psychoanalytic theory than its French counterpart, tending to draw instead on the idioms of philosophy, political theory and politics" (Bock and James, "Introduction," 5). As Finzi puts it in *Mothering,* one cannot explore maternity without considering first the figure of one's own mother, and from this consideration emerges "a comparison that hinges on some failing, some lack of vital nutriment" (116). At the basis of the mother–daughter bond, Finzi finds a lack, the absence of a crucial connection troped as an unappeased hunger, an impossible or unavailable food—an unsatisfied craving, to return to the language of maternal impressions. But this lack, this emptiness, reflects and is in turn reflected in the very possibility of pregnancy, of generation. The womb is an empty organ, much of the time, waiting to be filled. Both mother and daughter are marked by the ability to contain another as well as to be contained, so that female descendance is not only temporal but spatial as well.

Finzi refers time and again to the concept of female genealogy invoked by Irigaray and, through Irigaray, by Luisa Muraro—to whose elaboration of female genealogy I return below. The womb marks sexual difference by excluding, temporally (vertically, then) and spatially (or horizontally) the male child and males in general. The womb marks both emptiness, in its function as container, and fullness—partly through the same function: the vertical genealogies of the mother–daughter bond and the horizontal connections of sisterhood, to which males have no access. It is thus frequently through maternity, whether it is experienced physically or psychologically, that women negotiate a resolution in the relationship with their mother, for Finzi. Indeed, more often than by taking the place of the father, the daughter resolves her conflict with her mother by recovering "the mother in herself, containing her as she was once contained in her;" she receives in exchange, "through a secret metabolism, an inheritance of generative power" (63). Again, I must underline the analogies between Finzi's psychoanalytic expressions and the dynamics of maternal impressions. The physical contact between mother and child during pregnancy is perceived to determine the bodily and psychical development of the subject-to-be. For women can "be inside" as well as "have inside" (a double definition probably alluding to Lacan's distinction between having and being the phallus), and the possible conflicts between these two states emerge in the course of a woman's pregnancy, even as her problematic relationship with her mother faces a possible resolution.

The connection and continuity between mother and daughter in the work of Finzi are complemented by her theoretical elaboration of "the child of the night," a virtual child created by the mother's imagination, a child that is both very near, almost confused with her own body, and at the same time so very far; the Italian title of Finzi's book *Mothering* is *Il bambino della notte*, literally "the child of the night." This child provides another metaphorical space dividing and uniting contemporary feminist psychoanalysis and the literary imagination of turn-of-the-century women. For "the child of the night," a figure of maternal creativity, is in a sense a craving, a molding, an impression of the mother's own unconscious, aimed at filling the otherwise empty space of the womb as container—much like it happened for the fictional mothers in turn-of-the-century Italian women's writings. "Maternity, which does not begin with gestation nor end with childbirth, is a creative act at every moment," optimistically writes Finzi (*Mothering*, 159). The relationship between mother and child is one more way to imagine the transformation of the "thinking body" into its correlative, "corporeal thought," one more paradigm that may redefine the symbolic field and renegotiate social relationships, one more place where we may seek ordinary women's extraordinary capacity for innovation—and for the deconstruction of binary thought. The feminist focus on the relationship between mother and daughter is the most visible facet of that redefinition of the bond between mother and child necessary in a culture that considers that relationship as potentially dangerous as, in past centuries, the theory of maternal impressions saw the womb: disturbing because inaccessible and thus in need of limitation and control. Maternal affection is posited in classical psychoanalysis as the cause of neuroses and psychoses just as the mother's desire used to be identified in popular belief as the source of disfigurement. Instead, in Finzi's proposal, we find a call for the creative potential of motherhood and for the mother–child relationship as an ethical paradigm: the endless task that requires the mother "to move from possessing of the child to allowing for his or her autonomy, from control to trust, from imposition to responsibility" (*Mothering,* 175).

It is with maternal fullness that Luisa Muraro is concerned in her work. Indeed, maternal fullness is elaborated almost to the point of metaphysical fullness—and in this respect Muraro's work seems to go directly against the grain of poststructuralism and postmodernist philosophies of the fragment. Yet in Muraro's work the central concept of symbolic mother arises directly from her elaboration of the hysterical woman. The hysterical woman, at the origin of Freud's psychoanalytic edifice, is one of the primary figures of the split self in the twentieth century, thus complicating any notion of metaphysical wholeness. Muraro's theories are developed most fully in her best-known book, *L'ordine simbolico della madre* (The symbolic order of the mother, 1991). Influenced by the work of both Luce Irigaray and Adrienne Rich, this book has unfortunately not yet been translated into English. Before turning to *L'ordine simbolico della madre,* I will therefore approach Muraro's thought by way of an essay that has appeared in English, entitled "Female Genealogies." The word *genealogy* refers to the maternal continuum of birth through its etymology (*genea* = birth) and is thus linked to words such as *generation, gender, genesis.* Yet the concept of a female genealogy is almost a contradiction in terms, given that recognized genealogy was traditionally passed on through legitimate male descent.

Muraro is a professor of philosophy at the University of Verona, a member of the Veronese philosophical community Diotima, and a translator of Irigaray's work into Italian (she first translated *Speculum of the Other Woman* in 1975, ten years before it appeared in English). Muraro states near the beginning of "Female Genealogies" that "The mother-daughter relationship is always present in Irigaray's work, from *Speculum* onward" (317). But the basis of Irigaray's elaboration is patriarchy's violent destruction of the mother–daughter bond, figured by Muraro as the ultimate female genealogy from which her own essay takes its name. I say "figure" and not, more precisely perhaps, "define," because for Muraro it is impossible to define female genealogy in any traditional or conventional way. Like the mother–child connection in the theory of maternal impressions, the bond between mother and daughter finds itself at the intersection of body and language, or, in Muraro's own words, at "the border between the speakable and the unspeakable" (319). Our debt to the mother, in Muraro's reading of Irigaray, is both bodily and verbal. The genealogy based on procreation, that vertical female continuum that leads back from mother to mother up to the beginning of life, must be thought of in conjunction with a genealogy based on words—the history of women and of women's texts. In both cases, the verticality of the mother–daughter bond is a dimension that needs to be reinstated in order to symbolize that relationship and thus free it from both lack of differentiation and rivalry in difference. In both cases, and as Irigaray and Finzi also noted, sexual difference is inscribed from the very beginning, in the relationship with one's mother. Males are necessarily excluded from female genealogies.

Unlike its American counterpart, intimately tied to the academy, Italian feminist theory is most closely bound to political practice. Cavarero notes for example that "the Italian philosophies of sexual difference move in fact especially within political *practices* and speculate on these rather than on the canonical texts of philosophy" ("Il pensiero femminista," 138). Thus Muraro seeks a political reflection of Irigaray's theoretical discussion of the mother–daughter bond. She finds teaching to be Irigaray's principal political practice, and the concept of female genealogies to be its most important fruit. Although in the second part of her essay Muraro goes on to discuss Irigaray's turn away from the community of women-among-themselves and toward an ethical world of women and men together (a move about which Muraro, whose background is separatist, remains skeptical), I will remain instead with Muraro within the framework of female genealogies as women's alternative to being homologated into the patriarchal code, the framework of female genealogy as an instrument, a practice of sexual difference.

One way in which the possibilities inherent in the concept of female genealogies have been explored in the political context of Italian feminism is through the practice of *affidamento*, which could be roughly translated as entrustment. As a founding member of the Milan Women's Bookstore Collective, Muraro is associated with this highly controversial Italian feminist practice. Patterned in many ways on the mother–daughter bond, with its function of symbolic mediation to the world, *affidamento* is a mentoring relationship established between two women, one of whom is older or has more experience, privilege, power, status, than the other. The juridical meaning of *affidamento* in Italian is custody—of a child, a minor, a disabled person. Since the Italian system privileges females in these cases, the notion of *affidamento* is intimately tied to the maternal. Although it has been criticized for being based on hierarchy and subordination, the purpose of this relationship is liberation. As Anderlini-D'Onofrio defends it, "Entrustment does not institute the power structures in which women's relations develop; it recognizes their presence and reclaims women's power to inhabit them with other women like themselves" (223). This practice in many ways goes against the goals of egalitarian feminists, who see unequal power, theorized by Italian feminists as *disparitá,* as incompatible with women's mutual trust. But in *L'ordine simbolico della madre,* Muraro states quite plainly that, in order to be free, women symbolically need maternal power, just as they needed it physically in order to be born (9). In *affidamento,* women entrust themselves and recognize one another symbolically while avoiding both individualism as the rejection of solidarity among women on the one hand and the erasure of difference(s) from other women on the other. Through *affidamento,* the mediation between a particular woman and society is provided by another woman, in a contract that explicitly acknowledges the otherwise invisible debt to the knowledge and thus the power of other women and, particularly, of one's mother. Needless to say, *affidamento* was a controversial practice regarded by many feminists (including for example Finzi) as excessively rigid and programmatic.

Through a style that relies on political and autobiographical practice on one side and metaphysical philosophy on the other, and which draws liberally from the theories of Irigaray and, more critically, Kristeva, what Muraro passionately refutes in *L'ordine simbolico della madre* is the equation of womanhood with silence and the subject's need to separate from the mother in order to gain access to language and knowledge, to the symbolic order. For the mother is always-already in the symbolic order insofar as it is she who teaches language to the child, as Muraro repeatedly reminds us. Although there is a symbolic order that is not the mother's (as the patriarchal code in Lacan's elaboration), still the language learned from the mother is for the child the prime or archetypal form of knowledge—knowledge of love, of loving the mother: "I state that being able to love the mother is part of the symbolic order" (21). By "mother" Muraro means the matrix of life itself but also, she tirelessly reminds the reader, the literal mother, the woman who gave us physical and symbolic life. The two cannot be disengaged, just as we cannot separate life and language, body and mind, practice and theory.

In contrast with the Anglo-American distinction between sex and gender as indicators of the biologically given and the symbolic order, the Italian *pensiero della differenza* (thinking about difference) emphasizes the inseparability between bodily morphology and the imaginary. (This line of thought is also followed by American feminist theorist Judith Butler, for example, in her *Bodies That Matter*. Far from being an irreducible materiality, sex itself is for Butler a construction of gender, for matter is an effect of power and cannot be thinkable outside of culture.) For Muraro, disengaging the mother from the acquisition of language means relegating the female to the body and the male to the mind, and thus perpetuating the Cartesian dichotomy that *pensiero della differenza* actively seeks to overthrow.

It is the autobiographical experience of a conflict between her life choice of philosophy and her mother's authority that led Muraro to write *L'ordine simbolico della madre,* as she vividly describes in the first chapter of the book. But this disorder goes beyond the limits of personal autobiography, for according to Muraro "there is no doubt that the history of philosophy, like the culture of which it is a part, shows the signs of a rivalry with the maternal work and authority" (10). Significantly for the discussion I have developed throughout my own first chapter, the language used by Muraro is reminiscent of the vocabulary of maternal impressions, and sounds indebted to its economy. Muraro writes, for example, that "It is the experience of connection with the mother which leaves within us not a memory but an indelible trace, like a pattern for future experiences and the possibility of giving them a logical order. On its part, that experience remains unique and unrepeatable" (26). Instead of the colored mark left by the mother's impressive desire in tales of old, what the "unique and unrepeatable" experience of contact with the mother leaves the subject with is a less physical, yet no less lasting impression. Because, according to Muraro, our very relation to the world is molded on this, our first relation: the bond with our mother, founded on disparity and debt. And disparity and debt are precisely what the practice of *affidamento* wants to acknowledge: disparity between women, so we may derive authority from another, more powerful woman, and debt to the symbolic mother. This bond to the maternal persists in the subject not simply as memory but, like a birthmark, as "an indelible trace," the origin of language, theory, practice, as well as body. More prosaically, Muraro explicitly admits that she agrees with what "almost everyone thinks," namely that the most important experience in our lives takes place in our first months and years, "centered on the relation with the mother" (37).

The importance Muraro attaches to the preverbal stage of a subject's life is analogous to the turn-of-the-century emphasis on the prenatal, in utero experience. Psychoanalysis claims to have taught us that the infant (*in-fans,* literally, the one who is non-speaking, therefore pre-verbal) experiences itself as merged, as one, with its mother in terms of body, mind, desire. Yet in spite of much poststructuralist psychoanalytic discourse to the contrary, all of us learned to speak from our mother—or at least, Muraro concedes, from someone who functioned as our mother. And significantly the mother was at the time of that learning also our primary if not our exclusive source of authority. It is unbearably reductive of every mother's role, and of the symbolic mother, to conceive of her as nothing more than a ventriloquist for a patriarchal symbolic. Language acquisition, then, is not an accessory detail of infancy but rather a fundamental component of our vital communication with our mother—just as, against the assumptions of Freudian thought outlined above by Benjamin, the impulse for separation is present in the mother–child bond and does not require the father's outside intervention. The subject achieves a balance between separation and connectedness by differentiating and simultaneously recognizing the other. This is a model of growth into individuality, into selfhood, into subjectivity, as a process of nurturing into the capacity for agency *and* relatedness, rather than as a battle against one parent for the love of the other—the patriarchal, violent, antagonistic mode of individuation, of becoming a subject: the Oedipal. The mother's loss of authority in women's adult lives is related to this cut from the mother: Muraro refers to Kristeva's notion of the "thetic cut" as the historically determined expression of a patriarchal symbolic order (44–46). The thetic cut, which prevents the order of female genealogy, forms the basis, for Muraro, of our linguistic, symbolic incompetence, our sense of inadequacy to theorize: "I was born in a culture where women are not taught love for/of the mother. And yet it is the most important knowledge, without which it is difficult to learn the rest and to be original in anything . . ." (13).

Without disparity and debt, the mother's desire is not impressive, then, or at least we would remain unimpressed. A practice such as *affidamento,* on the other hand, impresses in us the need for a figure of female authorization and symbolic mediation, as well as our need to acknowledge our debt to her. As the Milan Women's Bookstore Collective puts it, "Authority is received originally from another human being, who has the authority to give it. But she cannot have it if the person who needs to receive it does not acknowledge it in her" (126). The debt acknowledged in *affidamento* is the debt to the mother, which can only be realized through the vertical practice of disparity. For horizontal, sisterly connections, while necessary, are unable to supply that female authority every woman needs: "Women need maternal power if they want free social existence" (127). And it is in the ability to translate into women's adult lives our ancient relation to the mother, biological and symbolic at once, in the choice of this impressive relation as our principle of symbolic authority, claims Muraro, that women may become able today to signify ourselves, to impress the mother on and in us, I would say, to overcome the silence, linguistic uncertainty, or meaningless repetition that ever threaten to become our lot in the symbolic order of patriarchy.

Spurred by the conflictual relationship between Simone de Beauvoir's *The Second Sex* as the mother-text to the daughterly group of contemporary French feminists, Gayatri Chakravorty Spivak has some harsh words to say concerning the Western feminist focus on the mother–daughter bond: "In *our* time-space of feminism, we have kept uncertainties at bay by binding mother to daughter in our theories and strategies. But we cannot make the whole world fit forever into that devoutly wished embrace" ("French Feminism Revisited," 59). Muraro's construction of the mother–daughter bond, however, deconstructs both the notion of "embrace"—for the purpose of the mother–daughter bond is the establishment, however untraditional, unconventional, of a female genealogy, hence of a vertical rather than a horizontal relation of sisterhood—and the "keeping at bay of uncertainties," which are instead productively unleashed. Working on and for the symbolic order of the mother, for the acknowledgment of our debt to her, is the very work of uncertainty, of disorder, above all of disparity and difference. As de Lauretis notes, the concepts and practices that articulate the theory of sexual difference, the *pensiero della differenza,* such as female genealogies, the symbolic mother, *affidamento,* disparity, "mark an epistemological rupture in the continuum of Western thought" ("The Practice of Sexual Difference," 13). In Muraro's words, "we cannot correct a social disorder without working on the symbolic order" (47), and in the words of the Milan Women's Bookstore Collective, "what is at stake is the revolution of a symbolic order" (123). In the elaboration of the theory of maternal impressions by turn-of-the-century women writers, the debt to the mother was acknowledged through the recognition of her symbolic power, intricately tied to her biological power to reproduce—or, more precisely, to produce anew. Although irretrievably bound up with the logic of patriarchal reproduction, and thus not an overtly, much less a univocally feminist text, Deledda's construction of the woman with the mouflon in *Cosima* points to the symbolic power of the mother beyond her sexual reproducibility. A certain order is disrupted throughout the eruption, in traditional genealogy, of an other, incommensurable order of desire. This order shapes the child's body according to itself, but also it shapes, or rather misshapes, the symbolic order of language into its own refusal through the maternal production of the child's muteness, his silence.

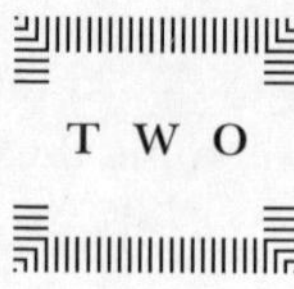

TWO

Quickening, or the Knowing Body

Impressions of Fetal Movement

Fetal Movement in Advice Manuals and the Gospel of Luke

"Three months for the blood, three months for the bones, three months for the flesh," is an old Venetian saying reflecting a popular theory on the formation of the fetus. So also today, in medical and popular texts, pregnancy is usually divided into three, more or less equal segments: first, second, and third trimester, each about thirteen weeks long. The mother's ability to affect the child in utero, her impressiveness, was, and, in some ways, is still believed to work its powers from conception to birth. But it is usually around the beginning of the second semester that the pregnant woman for the first time feels fetal movement. This event is poetically described as "quickening," or even, with an expressive metonymy, as "life." The feeling of fetal movement, although it changes in the course of the remaining weeks, is experienced throughout the rest of a healthy pregnancy. A first-time mother usually takes longer to identify such movements for what they are, often mistaking them for gas bubbles and thus confusing the reproductive organs for the gastrointestinal tract (a confusion reminiscent of Basile's Petrosinella, whose mother's food craving for parsley is contiguous, through the daughter's body, with the prince's sexual desire for the pretty parsley girl). Sooner or later, the pregnant woman learns to recognize quickening as the physical presence of an "other" living and growing and moving, and thus impressing her, within the center of her body. Usually romanticized as a uniquely joyful experience, the feeling of fetal movement can also figure the loss of bodily control experienced in pregnancy, the intrusion of an other, the uncontrollable growth of cells and tissues within oneself.

In this chapter I examine the feeling of fetal movement as emblematic of a type of knowledge associated with women and the uneducated, and thus relegated by traditional epistemology to the status of untrustworthy: for this knowledge, before all else, deconstructs the opposition between self and other, knower and known, subject and object, on which epistemological theory is founded. The dismissal of the feeling of fetal movement and, more generally, of the type of knowledge it implies can also be seen as analogous to the epistemological transition underlining the move of childbirth from home to hospital, and especially from midwife to doctor. For practical success alone cannot account for this crucial shift. Many factors were at play, for example, the consolidation of a medical establishment with a worldview closely aligned with scientific epistemology—a field dominated in turn by upper- and middle-class males. Thus, not only women, qua midwives, were discredited by medical imperialism, but also apothecaries and barber surgeons, usually men, as well as religious and other nonmechanistic interpretations of the body. While the knowledge embraced by medicine was and is a written discourse, a discourse assuming that all knowledge must be propositional and subject to theorization, midwives' knowledge on the other hand was orally transmitted and eminently pragmatic. Significantly, this experiential type of knowing is closely related to the knowing of the pregnant woman herself: Midwives relied heavily on their personal experience of childbirth for their ability to empathize and care. It is therefore not surprising that, along with the invalidation of midwives' knowledge, the pregnant and birthing woman's own knowledge should also have been discredited. The experiential knowing constituted by fetal movement is one fertile place to realize such invalidation, and perhaps it is also a place where we may recover other valuable ways of knowing.

"Fetal movement may be the greatest source of joy in your pregnancy, and lack of it the greatest cause of anxiety. More than a positive pregnancy test, an expanding belly, or even the sound of fetal heartbeat, the presence of fetal movement affirms that you've got a new life growing inside you. Its absence breeds terror that the new life is not thriving" (Eisenberg, Murkoff, and Hathaway, 159). Because quickening was used to detect pregnancy in the past, it bestowed a unique power on the pregnant woman. She alone could have a sensory contact with the unborn child, she alone could experience and thus establish the existence of a pregnancy. Knowledge of gestation, of the fetus, of her body, was hers, and hers alone to share. But the social, and to a lesser extent the personal impressiveness of quickening was largely lost with the advent of pregnancy tests and, especially, with the dissemination of ultrasound technology, which through the representation on a screen of both fetus and womb allows individuals other than the mother sensory access to what otherwise would be visually unrepresentable—including to the mother. Through ultrasound technology the invisible becomes visible and the secrets of pregnancy are revealed or extorted, and epistemological control is exerted.

This epistemic change occurs at the expense of the pregnant woman's reliability. She can no longer be trusted to accurately report or even understand her symptoms as well as, and as early as, the ultrasound machine and the technicians who know how to operate it. Michie and Cahn, for example, note that ultrasound "produces and is produced by a series of social assumptions: about mother-infant bonding, about the relation of technology and expertise to self-understanding, and about the power of the visible in an increasingly scopic culture"(79). Both times that my waters broke before the onset of labor, to tell a personal tale, further examinations, including ultrasound and microscope testing, was deemed necessary by my doctors to ascertain the nature of the fluid that was leaking out of me: as if I, or the doctor for that matter, could not tell the difference between familiar urine and mysterious amniotic fluid. A simple sniff on the doctor's part would also have sufficed since, unlike urine, amniotic fluid is odorless, as well as colorless. Yet that was out of the question because, in scientific terms, smell is ranked as the lowest, most animalistic of the senses. Therefore, testing, as in the case of ultrasound technology, had to be visual: performed by a doctor under a microscope, it emphasized the primacy of looking (the doctor's) over feeling (mine). For the feeling of an amniotic gush, utterly beyond one's control, is nothing like the flow of urine, which I could control with the muscles of the pelvic floor. Smelling and feeling are suspect senses because too animalistic (smell) and only perceivable by the self (feeling). As a consequence, I had to spend my last evening before my first child was born lying in a hospital bed waiting for someone qualified to scientifically legitimate the obvious. But I am not as antagonistic to the medical profession as I may sound. Do I even wish that things had been different, that I had planned, for example, a home birth—a possibility which in 1994 did not even cross my mind? I cannot say. If on the one hand I felt disempowered and ignored, on the other I was grateful for the thoroughness with which I was being cared for. I had chosen to put myself in the hands of doctors, and the doctors were doing their job. I gave birth to a healthy child.

As is the case with the theory of maternal impressions, however, forgetfulness of history leads cultural critics to read contemporary technology as providing a new (and for the first time, allegedly, a negative and disempowering) approach to women's pregnant bodies. Certainly ultrasound technology is a twentieth-century invention, yet the impulse to look inside the woman's body is not. So, for example, Rosalind Pollack Petcheski is well known and respected by many feminist critics for having criticized, in her essay "Fetal Images," the visually oriented cultural assumptions underlying fetal-imaging technology as an antifeminist attack concocted by right-to-life voyeurs with the intent of degrading woman into "maternal environment," or empty space, and with the effect of fetishizing the fetus as space-hero. But this scopic drive, the supposedly unsituated gaze of technology, is at the very least as old as anatomy itself. Even older is the association of nature with the female and especially the pregnant body: Both are dark and secretive. The pregnant body is the epitome of this epistemological opacity, knowable only to the pregnant woman herself (though knowable through a suspect because bodily type of knowledge), and inaccessible to everyone else. And yet its size announces the presence of a secret that science wants to ferret out. The threat of female interiority is dissolved by exposing it, by making it visible and therefore knowable to, and controllable by, others. As Evelyn Fox Keller has proposed:

> Well-kept secrets pose a predictable challenge to those who are not privy. Secrets function to articulate a boundary: an interior not visible to outsiders, the demarcation of a separate domain, a sphere of autonomous power. And indeed, the secrets of women, like the secrets of nature, are and have traditionally been seen by men as potentially threatening—or if not threatening, then morbidly alluring—in that they articulate a boundary that excludes them, and so invites exposure or requires finding out." ("Making Gender Visible," 69)

The scientific method, for Keller, is the strategy devised for dealing with this threat: by making what was previously invisible visible, the secrets of nature can be undone. "Scientific enlightenment is in this sense a drama between visibility and invisibility, between light and dark, and also, between female procreativity and male productivity" (*Secrets of Life, Secrets of Death*, 41).

This epistemological drive on the part of Western science can be discerned, for example, in the history of dissection, the iconography of which often privileges woman as the object of its gaze. In 1315 Mondino de' Liuzzi, the founder of the anatomical renaissance, brought into his Bologna classroom two female cadavers, chosen because they had been executed and because, according to some, women lacked a soul (Cosmacini, *Storia della medicina*, 31). The earliest known representation of dissection, dating from the early fourteenth century, portrays a prosector who has just opened a female body. Finally, the title page to the first edition of Andreas Vesalius' *De humani corporis fabrica* (1543), generally hailed as the first work of modern anatomy, shows the dissection of a woman—a prostitute. In the nineteenth century, this fascination with the dissection of the female body was made more prominent and dramatic in many cases by the addition of a fetus. Most relevant to this context is a poem by Italian author and librettist Arrigo Boito, entitled "Lezione d'anatomia" (Anatomy lesson), written in 1865. The lyrical "I" of this poem observes the corpse of a beautiful young woman who died of tuberculosis and who lies on the anatomist's table. As the poet looks on with pity, he fantasizes about the virginity of the woman's heart and body, and he bursts out, outraged, against the doctor and science itself for profaning her otherwise inviolate nakedness. But near the end of the poem a thirty-day-old fetus is unexpectedly discovered inside the cadaver, destroying the poet's reverie of feminine angelic purity and making the anatomist's crude representation prevail over the poet's idealized one (Mazzoni, "Is Beauty Only Skin Deep?").

According to Michel Foucault the corpse in general, during the nineteenth century, is transformed by medical discourse into "the brightest moment in the figures of truth"—a statement which in turn comments on the contemporary acquisition of knowledge on the part of medical discourse by making us reflect on its genealogy (125–26). More specifically, historian of science Ludmilla Jordanova has argued that the representation of women's dissection in the nineteenth century allegorized the acquisition of knowledge (58, 93). The female corpse is transfigured as the imaginary site where meaning and truth are engendered, embodied, made flesh. Woman's skin is a veil behind which lies truth; epistemology, in this context, is a process of unveiling until the truth is reached. It is out of this opaque body that knowledge must be teased, and dissection was for the nineteenth-century imagination the most literal, direct way of performing this quest. Late-twentieth-century ultrasound technology allows for a comparable epistemological move, much less violent, yet equally charged in terms of ideology.

Fetal-imaging technology, however, can only take place sporadically, while the pregnant woman is constantly and literally in touch with the fetus. In addition to real or construed joys, this relationship confers on her the ability to detect problems and prescribes the moral imperative to solve them. Pregnancy manuals reiterate such power, an early version of maternal–infant bonding, and the frightful responsibility it entails. In *Pregnancy*,

Birth, and the Newborn Baby we read: "Once you have felt life, if a whole day goes by without your having felt the baby move at all, you should notify your doctor—something may have happened to the baby" (Boston Children's Medical Center, 92–93). This is the advice generally given in pregnancy manuals: Women need to be reminded of the responsibilities entailed by pregnancy. But the authors of *What to Expect When You're Expecting* are considerably more demanding. They suggest testing for fetal movement no less than twice a day, beginning in the twenty-eighth week:

> Check the clock when you start counting. Count movements of any kind (kicks, flutters, swishes, rolls). Stop counting when you reach ten, and note the time. Often, you will feel ten movements within ten minutes or so. Sometimes it will take longer.
>
> If you haven't counted ten movements by the end of an hour, have some milk or another snack; then lie down, relax, and start counting again. If another hour goes by without ten movements, call your practitioner without delay. Though such an absence of activity doesn't necessarily mean there's a problem, it can occasionally indicate fetal distress. In such cases, quick action may be needed. (202)

I clearly remember scoffing at such a suggestion even in the course of my first pregnancy, when I had the leisure to take good care of myself and consequently (?!) of the son I was carrying. Of the many mothers with whom I have been tirelessly discussing pregnancy in the past decade or so, not one has followed (or, at least, has admitted to following) such advice/prescription to the letter. The degree of conscious self-awareness, self-control, self-policing necessary to carry out such a task reads like a caricature of Foucault's notion of the penetration of power and social control into our daily lives. Pregnancy is constructed as a reading assignment, and pregnant women need instructions in order to participate in their own pregnancy: being pregnant is not itself sufficient, and the communities of women of ages past—those mothers, grandmothers, older sisters, aunts—that used to teach us how to be pregnant cannot be assumed to be there for all of us.

But I must now admit that it is solely because of this impressive self-awareness, however serendipitous, that my third child, Sophia, is alive and well today. Would things have gone the same way had I not learned from books and doctors and midwives about the importance of being aware of, if not systematically checking for, fetal movements? Would I have "naturally" known that something was wrong with my child? The very act of asking these questions shows up the perceived, internalized conflicts between knowledge, nature, and the female body: If what is natural should come naturally, then the very need to learn it indicates a congenital deficiency in the learner. Or, in Ruth Ginzberg's words, women "are imagined already to know (innately?) whatever we need to know" (51). This assumption effectively excludes women from the production of knowledge, for our engagement in practices of knowledge production indicates either an extension beyond the female role—a quest for "access to 'nonnatural' (that is, male) spheres, to which we are not entitled"—or that "we are defective qua women in the first place, and we seek to learn that which women are already supposed to know; in other words, we are suspected of seeking remedial measures to compensate for our 'natural' defects" (Ginzberg, 51). The existence of pregnancy manuals, when combined with the association between birthgiving and nature, confirms this hypothesis, but it is destabilized if we reconsider, deconstruct, and ultimately reject the dichotomy between knower and known, knowledge and what contains it, epistemic quest and its target.

As Elspeth Probyn has powerfully argued, "emotions can point us in certain critical directions," for "an emotional foregrounding of the self [is] a way of critically acknowledging the ontological and epistemological bases of knowledge formation" (83). It is in this spirit that I weave one of my most agonizing experiences with the critical and theoretical reflections of this chapter. When I was eight months pregnant, mothering three-and-a-half-year-old Paul and two-year-old Gemma, and busily in the middle of a full-load teaching semester and the many other duties academics are well familiar with, I lay down with Gemma for a rest and it slowly occurred to me that I had not felt any fetal movement for a while: at least since that morning, perhaps longer. And, I had no recollection of the two previous days, either: what with birthdays parties, classes, lunch interviews, bathing kids, and making dinner, counting fetal movements was not exactly on my to-do list. To make a long story short, my daughter Sophia was born with an emergency cesarean section just a few hours later, after many tests. She had lost over two-thirds of her red blood cells through a faulty vascular connection in the placenta, hence her lethargic in utero behavior. Two transfusions and a brief stay at the Neonatal Intensive Care Unit (NICU) cured her and within a few days we were both home, thankfully. During the days and weeks following her traumatic birth, many pieces of the puzzle of what had happened gradually came together. "The major cause of stillbirths," is how placental insufficiency was described to me (the only comparably common cause is congenital malformation). "Even twenty-five years ago, when we started practicing at this hospital, your baby would not have made it," my normally reassuring pediatrician and the NICU nurse declared in unison. And, most memorably, "You saved your baby," is what the various midwives, obstetricians, nurses, and pediatricians I encountered at the hospital all seemed to agree on. I actually was not trusting my instincts and was inclined to minimize, fearful of my own potential hypochondria, reluctant to bother the midwives, hating the thought of leaving the house in the snowstorm blowing that February afternoon. But my husband urged me to call the midwife when the sugars from the baby-shower cake had not managed to get movements out of Sophia (as it turned out, that delicious frosted cake was the last thing I ate for the next two days or so: the dietetically obsessed authors of *What to Expect When You're Expecting* would have been appalled!). So I certainly did not save my baby alone; yet, without my bodily knowledge, technology and even my husband's impressive "maternal thinking" would have been powerless. The reverse is also true, alas.

Ironically, just a few weeks before Sophia's birth I had completed an article on the feeling of fetal movement. It was the first version of this very chapter, though a much more objective, detached, specialized account. And the center of my discovery was a sense of shared knowledge as it is developed through the bodily, psychological, and spiritual connections between pregnant woman and fetus. Far from repressing it, this knowledge openly embraces its corporeal genealogy, and it can never mistake itself for the ethereal product of a disembodied mind—how could it? Such a knowledge is among the chief reasons why quickening held and continues to hold a prominent place in writings that deal with pregnancy. Its thematic recurrence in late-nineteenth- and early-twentieth-century women's novels first alerted me to its centrality. The relationship constituted by quickening, hinging on body and intellect, sensations and emotions, links knowledge, power, and self, thus staging on the pregnant body, site of the convergence of life and death, some traditional, classical even, philosophical issues. At the same time, quickening destabilizes and deconstructs the binary opposition between the intelligible and the sensible that has historically characterized Western metaphysics, as well as, more subtly, some of the feminist epistemology that critiques science; this is the opposition that relegated woman to the domain of the sensible, a domain to be transcended if one is to attain the highest or the deepest reality. But this is also the opposition that is implicitly reinforced, as Toril Moi notes, in feminist critiques of science such as Evelyn Fox Keller's. Refusing to accept the subject/object division proposed by scientific ideology—which casts the knower as male and the known as female—Keller espouses instead a Chodorow-inspired feminist theory of science, a commingling of subject and object in which empathy and feeling prevent the reification of the object and encourage respect for its integrity. Moi critiques this solution not only for its cultural essentialism, but especially because "if the 'union' proposed reinforces the separate identities of subject and object, their grand vision of 'female science' promises no more than a certain elasticity of boundaries between separate, self-identical essences. There is no attempt here to question the logic that underpins patriarchal metaphysics, or to contest the very meaning of terms such as masculine/feminine, reason/emotion, and so on" ("Patriarchal Thought," 193). As an alternative example of a discourse truly disruptive of patriarchal opposition, Moi evokes at this point the work of Hélène Cixous, the theorist to whom I return in the last section of this chapter.

I would propose that another alternative to the binary thinking of both patriarchal and feminist science can be found in the kind of knowledge produced by quickening. Rather than simply reversing the historical privileging of the mental over the corporeal, quickening is an explicitly sexualized knowledge that stages a sexed corporeality as constituting and constituted by a particular subjectivity: the pregnant woman's. Knowledge, in this scenario, is intrinsic and unique to the mother's self, body and psyche, for in this union alone can she hold contact with the fetus. If the workings of a ubiquitous power can be discerned both in the woman's knowledge and in the uses society, through the medical establishment, for example, makes of such knowledge—hence the large social investment in monitoring the reproduction of the body politic and its asymmetrical power relations—still this impressed, impressive knowledge continuously splits sterile dichotomies apart. It does this, for instance, by insisting on the tenuous boundaries not only between body and psyche, inside and outside, but also between self and other. As knowledge about the self is obtained in relation to knowledge of the other, and if subjectivity itself depends on the other for its own coming into being, then how can we possibly establish clearly defined boundaries between other and self?

After presenting discursive prescriptions and describing a personal inscription, let me turn to a traditional narrative, the Visitation of Mary and Elizabeth from Luke's Gospel, which I propose to reread, to revisit so to speak, with the aim of reactivating two female figures buried under layers upon layers of masculinist readings.

> During these days Mary set out and traveled to the hill country in haste to a town of Judah, where she entered the house of Zechariah and greeted Elizabeth. When Elizabeth heard Mary's greeting, the infant leaped in her womb, and Elizabeth, filled with the holy Spirit, cried out in a loud voice and said:

> "Most blessed are you among women, and blessed is the fruit of your womb. And how does this happen to me, that the mother of my Lord should come to me? For at the moment the sound of your greeting reached my ears, the infant in my womb leaped for joy. Blessed are you who believed that what was spoken to you by the Lord would be fulfilled. (Luke 1:39–45 New American Bible [NAB])

This is the best-known narrative of fetal movement in Western civilization. (I admit that the competition is scarce.) It stars Mary of Nazareth, who in Luke's Gospel is an active participant in God's incarnation, a veritable theological agent: Luke's Mary cooperates with God in order to bring about the messianic event. Still unmarried and recently impregnated with Jesus by the holy Spirit, Mary on her own initiative travels in haste to a town in the hill country of Judea to visit her relative Elizabeth, herself six-months pregnant with the one later known as John the Baptist. Both women have conceived miraculously: Mary without sexual intercourse with a man, Elizabeth in her old age, after a lifetime of humiliating sterility. Both women are given in this text more prominence than their male partners: of Joseph there is little mention, and Zechariah, Elizabeth's husband, is struck dumb by the angel in punishment for his doubts. Both women are cast in a more favorable light than their partners as models of faith. Indeed, it is these two women, repeatedly humbled—Mary is an impoverished teenager who is pregnant out of wedlock, Elizabeth is an old woman who has suffered throughout her life the shame of childlessness—that are chosen as the first to greet God's embodied arrival on earth.

As something like a first encounter between Jesus and John the Baptist takes place, a more uncanny relationship develops in the course of the two women's meeting. And what is at stake, in this encounter, is theological knowledge: fetal movement is cast as epistemic awareness, on which the revelation and exaltation constituting the theological significance of this scene are predicated. Fetal movement reveals a secret, the secret above all of the archangel Gabriel's annunciation to Mary. The feeling of fetal movement, the infant leaping in her womb, impels Elizabeth to "cry out in a loud voice." (This experience, by the way, is echoed by the cry of some of the characters in the texts of late-nineteenth- and early-twentieth-century Italian women writers.) Her reaction in turn oversteps the bounds of the reasonable, of the orderly. Elizabeth, whose own voice is freed by her husband's speechlessness, is a prophet, the first prophet to recognize and acknowledge, thanks to her extraordinary semiotic abilities, the incarnation of God in another pregnant woman. It is she who prophesies the fulfillment of God's promise. Her words—"fruit of your womb," "mother of my Lord," "infant in my womb"—make palpable the reality of their two maternities, the physical embodiment of pregnancy on which its social and theological implications are founded. The word "fruit," in particular, acknowledges the work of motherhood, the product of the labor of reproduction. Importantly, Elizabeth's pregnancy had also remained a secret until now. It is revealed to Mary, as Mary's is revealed to Elizabeth, before it becomes public. The two women thus find themselves within a spiral of shared knowledge: of each other's pregnancy, of the religious and social significance of their status, and of their children's difficult future; this same Gospel speaks twice of Mary's knowledge of and her active meditation on the future of her son (Luke 2:19, 2:52 NAB).

Despite the importance of the meeting that was to become known as the Visitation, Luke's Gospel does not mention the reason for Mary's hasty trip to Judea, nor for the encounter in general between her and Elizabeth. Why does the narrator want the two women to meet? What is at stake in their encounter? Can we explain it as simply part of the parallelism Luke sets up between the parents of Jesus and the parents of John the Baptist? From a feminist as well as a theological perspective, what matters most is the effect of Mary's greeting, namely the fetal movement that in turn impels Elizabeth—who is initially the superior of the two women by social standards: a daughter of Aaron, the wife of a priest, the elder of the two—to praise Mary as superior to herself, as blessed among women, as a woman of faith, and above all as the mother of the long-awaited Messiah. It is not clear whether John leaps with joy at the encounter with Mary or with the child she carries, nor is it clear who it is that John, and, with John, Elizabeth, is acclaiming. But perhaps it does not matter; I would even suggest that this very uncertainty is emphasized because it productively deconstructs the perceived opposition between mother and child, Mary and Jesus. For in either case we can read in this passage an immense theological investment in the encounter between two pregnant women full of knowledge that erupts into spirit- and body-inspired speech—amidst the silence and ignorance of the others, including Joseph and Zechariah.

That knowledge and speech, and their mutual impressiveness, are central to this pregnant encounter between Elizabeth and Mary is exemplified by the issues raised by the "Magnificat," the often-prayed hymn (it is part of the daily office in the Catholic Church) that follows Elizabeth's words to Mary in the passage quoted above. It is significant that it has been questioned whether the author of the Gospel actually intended Mary to speak the "Magnificat," or whether it originally came from Elizabeth's mouth, as some manuscripts indicate. Moreover, very few scholars believe, if Mary was indeed intended to speak it, that she actually composed it. And ultimately, what does this hymn tell us about Mary? Most relevant to my discussion is the question of the speaker's identity because it highlights the issues of individuality and separation at work in the construction and representation of pregnancy. It can be argued, for example, that Elizabeth and not Mary spoke the "Magnificat" because this hymn is similar in several ways to the Old Testament hymn of Hannah (1 Samuel 2:1–10 NAB), a woman who like Elizabeth had a child after years of humiliating barrenness. Elizabeth and Mary, both pregnant through divine intervention, are confused with one another as speakers of a hymn of praise to God ("My soul proclaims the greatness of the Lord" Luke 1:46). Indeed, the connections between fetal movement and knowledge are further exemplified by this relationship between an older and a younger woman. The former reassures and confirms, with the help of her own pregnancy (her awareness of her leaping child, of the movements of and within her womb), the younger woman's understanding of her own extraordinary state.

That the first recognition of the incarnated word of God should be announced from a pregnant woman to another pregnant woman through a knowledge embodied in the uniquely female feeling of fetal movement is especially relevant for feminist theology. Through a hermeneutics of suspicion, seeking feminist traces in a phallocentric religious tradition, theologians such as Elizabeth Johnson and Elisabeth Schüssler Fiorenza have discussed at length the female face of God as Wisdom, or Sophia. God's Wisdom is a female figure present in biblical books such as Proverbs, Job, Ecclesiastes, Sirach, and, of course, Wisdom—books knows as wisdom literature. From this perspective, Jesus is seen as an earthly appearance of Wisdom, as her personification, as her incarnation (1 Cor 1:22–24)—a belief readily developed by feminist theology (for example, in Johnson's *She Who Is* and Fiorenza's *Miriam's Child, Sophia's Prophet*). This makes me wonder about the connections that quickening develops between divine wisdom and women's wisdom, both embodied in a womb, enfleshed in the knowledge of a leaping life. The wisdom of the body, like the wisdom of God, is born of relationality, of connection to the other (hence the analogies between motherhood and the Trinity, for example), of a subjectivity grounded in, or even arising from love as the ethical, but also the ontological bond to the other.

For what is finally the knowledge exchanged between these two oddly pregnant women in the hills of Judea—one a single teenage mother, probably no older than twelve or thirteen, the other postmenopausal yet also a mother-to-be? What is the significance, for these two women in occupied Palestine, of the arrival through the body of one of them, of the long-awaited Messiah? The "Magnificat," whether spoken by Elizabeth or by Mary, especially because it could have been spoken by either of them, offers a glimpse of this meaning, of this narrative, and it is not a piously comfortable story. We don't even have to read Luke's account against the grain to realize that it is revolutionary, really, what these two pregnant women come to realize through their meeting of mutual recognition: the "Magnificat" proclaims God's liberating action, it enunciates divine justice and well-being, it promises salvation, ultimately, to the humiliated and the downtrodden, those uncomfortably placed at the margins: God "has thrown down the rulers from their thrones but lifted up the lowly. The hungry he has filled with good things; the rich he has sent away empty" (Luke 1:52–53 NAB).

Given the bond developed in the Visitation between two women, a print of the Visitation by German artist Käthe Kollwitz (1867–1945) is the perfect gift, in Sara Maitland's novel *Virgin Territory* (1984), from a Catholic nun to her radical lesbian feminist friend. This picture, the nun reflects, "brought their two worlds together, close like the women in the lithograph" (146). But while Sister Anna sees the print as representing "two strong women leaning on to each other's arms," as the picture of women's spiritual and physical solidarity, her friend Karen interprets the Visitation as the "ultimate Dyke moment," because "when two women get together and in love proclaim their freedom, they sing that the personal is the political and from their love will come freedom for all the world" (146). Both Sister Anna and Karen are right, of course; in revisiting a traditional textual site of womanhood they discover, uncover, recover new knowledge claims, new meanings. And Kollwitz's visual vocabulary of progressive politics and feminism, successfully developed even within a masculinist and conservative setting, combined with Kollwitz's own stylistic conservatism, is well-suited to Maitland's literary choice of inserting radical feminism and socialist aspirations within her depiction of Catholic characters and institutions. Kollwitz and Maitland both achieve in this way a powerfully affective contrast—at the thematic, aesthetic, and ideological levels, be it through visual or narrative means.

Kollwitz's *Maria und Elisabeth* (1928) has rightly been called "one of the artist's finest achievements in the woodcut medium" (Prelinger, 168). This lithograph is both a traditional image, the Visitation, and a scripturally transgressive portrayal of the two women from Luke's Gospel: Elizabeth's wrinkles are prominent, as is Mary's youth and, more surprisingly, her pregnancy: At the scriptural three months, she is surely not supposed to be so big already. Kollwitz's work rarely refers overtly to biblical topics. It is significant and, given the rest of her production, not surprising that the chosen biblical passage should portray mothers, as it does here—

mothers, furthermore, whose children will prematurely die, as in several of Kollwitz's most poignant motherhood works. It also makes sense that Kollwitz, an artist renowned for her passionate commitment to social justice, should have selected an image dear to liberation and feminist theologians: the Visitation as, among other things, the prelude to that "Magnificat," in which God exalts the lowly and feeds the hungry while scattering the proud, sending away the rich, and putting down the mighty.

In Kollwitz's print, Elizabeth kisses Mary while her hand rests on the young woman's large belly, as if Elizabeth were feeling Mary's own child leap as well her own. Elizabeth's other hand sensuously caresses Mary's bare neck. Both women's eyes are closed, their faces are serious, solemn, even, as they savor a fleeting moment of physical closeness, mutual support, knowledge of self and/as of other—of the other woman, also pregnant, and of the children they bear. The dark form that surrounds the two enshrouds their shapes within itself, to the point that they seem to be one being, sharing one body. The boundaries between individuals are blurred between Mary and Elizabeth as they are between each woman and the child she carries. One of these children is, in the Christian faith, God made flesh, the divinity emptied out into human form and dwelling inside a woman's body. From a perspective that sees stories of fetal movement as epistemic narratives, in the Visitation episode of the Gospel of Luke, the divine is ultimately imaged, found, recognized, and announced as dwelling in a woman's uterus, without whose touching the continuity between humanity and divinity could not be envisioned, much less established in a covenant. Luke's narrative of the Visitation between Mary and Elizabeth—themselves impossibly pregnant—locates the divine in that space where the touch of two pregnant women mirrors the intrauterine touch between divine body and female body that constitutes the good news of Wisdom, Sophia made flesh.

Fetal Movement and the Science of Knowledge

Narratives of fetal movement confirm Iris Young's theory, inspired by Julia Kristeva's psychoanalytic work, on the messy, boundary-defying subjectivity of the pregnant woman: "The first movements of the foetus produce this sense of the splitting subject," because "pregnancy challenges the integration of my bodily experience by rendering fluid the boundary between what is within, myself, and what is outside, separate. I experience my insides as the space of another, yet my own body" (48–49). Some feminist theorists consider boundary challenges characteristic of female physiology, as the experiences of menstruation, pregnancy, childbirth, and breastfeeding illustrate. By stressing the irrevocability of the union of mind and body, these experiences defy the rigid separation between self and other—as the experience of quickening dramatizes. Quickening deconstructs the dualisms of subject and object, male and female, mother and child, body and mind, that dominate what Jacques Derrida calls "phallogocentrism" (an ugly term, no doubt, but one that expresses well the complicitous, specular centrality of phallus and logos as unexamined origin(s) of signification). Continuity prevails over dichotomy in ways that are also reminiscent, for example, of the theory of object-relations analysts such as Nancy Chodorow. In *The Reproduction of Mothering*, a feminist reconsideration of psychoanalysis, Chodorow claims that "girls come to experience themselves as less differentiated than boys, as more continuous with and related to the external object-world and as differently oriented to their inner object-world as well" (167). And yet this cannot be univocally celebratory: for while object-relations theory has indeed moved the mother from the wings of psychoanalytic thought to center stage, and many feminists have found cause to celebrate and revel in Chodorow's emphasis on the mother–daughter bond as fusion and/in separation, Chodorow's argument potentially reduces the mother to the origin of stereotypes of masculinity and femininity.

Prolific realizations of continuity in difference, of difference in continuity, have been evoked from other theoretical perspectives as well. These are useful in understanding the implications of texts such as the literary descriptions of women writers. From a phenomenological viewpoint, for instance, pregnant embodiment has been described by Drew Leder in *The Absent Body* as diverging radically from the habitual experience of one's body, as a transformation that prevents us from taking our body for granted, as being "in the *dys* state . . . doubled, away, asunder from itself," and "away, apart from the 'I' " (89–90). What Leder calls "instances of dys-appearance [such as pregnancy] demand attention," because they place a "demand for an affective and metaphysical wrestling with embodiment" (92). They are problematic but not dysfunctional, though they may also include dysfunctional moments. As a consequence, "our self-interpretation, importantly tied to the appearance and integrity of the body, is thrown into question at times of puberty, pregnancy, and aging" (Leder, 92). Rather than dismiss these times as pathological, one may find in them a new valuation of one's body, a renewed closeness to corporeality, an understanding of the flesh. Thus, Leder suggests that although these "dys" states are not hegemonic in terms of bodily awareness, nevertheless "there is something that sets them apart and renders them unusually significant"

(91)—a statement with which late-nineteenth- and early-twentieth-century Italian women writers would agree. For by placing a forceful, inescapable demand on bodily self-reflection, the experience of fetal movement, like that of other major body changes, compels self-awareness, heightens body focus, and productively throws into question our self-interpretation. There is therefore an existential character to this bodily demand for attention, for wrestling with embodiment.

Although discussions of quickening do not take place as often in turn-of-the-century scientific treatises as they do in late-twentieth-century pregnancy advice manuals, it is nevertheless significant that Mantegazza should begin the chapter on motherhood in his treatise *Fisiologia della donna* with a narrative of fetal movement imbued with the bourgeois stereotype of maternal womanhood. With his characteristic, flamboyant rhetoric, Mantegazza exclaims: "When the woman, blushing with joy and modesty, takes her husband's hand and placing it on her lap tells him: *don't you feel?* she experiences one of the most profound emotions of her life and in most cases (fortunately) one of its greatest joys" (2:53). Mantegazza's idealized woman blushes with joy but also, significantly, with modesty or even shame at her own pregnancy: "pudore," a term hovering between modesty and shame, is not coincidentally described by Lombroso as "the strongest of woman's feelings, after maternity" (*La donna,* 588), and by Mantegazza himself, in another book, as being one hundred times stronger in women than in men (*Fisiologia dell'amore,* 100). Indeed, in seventeenth- and eighteenth-century science, modesty was ascribed to all females, including apes such as orangutans and even, for some scientists, female insects (Schiebinger, 99–106). "Pudore" becomes embodied on the woman's blushed, reddened face, just as her maternal mission is embodied on her enlarged belly. Mantegazza's appeal to common sense, to his reader's daily experience, which underpins the arguments presented in his prolific production, is clear in the family scene he paints in this incipit, where the woman chosen as emblematic of the pregnant condition conforms to the ideal bourgeois woman of his time: wife and mother, sensitive, modest, dependent on her husband for support and protection. Yet what Mantegazza and his colleagues expected to derive from their discipline is a scientific knowledge that would replace with its experimental, numerical truths the uncertainties of common sense, and of maternal thinking, for example, derived from subjective interpretations.

Mantegazza's exemplary woman is almost ashamed, blushing, presumably because a pregnant belly is, short of a miraculous conception, an unmistakable sign of sexual activity; hence the woman's womb is euphemistically referred to by Mantegazza, who seems to be blushing himself, with the metonymy "seno." This is a common euphemism in Italian, culminating in the two interchangeable versions of the most popular prayer to the mother of Jesus, the "Hail, Mary." Thus, the Italian faithful may say either "benedetto il frutto del seno tuo, Gesù": discretely, "blessed is the fruit of your breast, Jesus;" or, more accurately, "benedetto il frutto del ventre tuo, Gesù," meaning "blessed is the fruit of your belly, Jesus." English speakers have the felicitously intermediate term "womb" to rely on instead—a term that is at once more precise than "breast" and less brutally anatomical than "belly." And I would venture to say that the same woman depicted by Mantegazza could also feel ashamed because her "profound emotion" and "greatest joy" must proceed not so much from the pregnancy itself but rather from its impact on her husband, as he places his hand on her quivering, expanded belly. Yet her attempt to share her physical knowledge of her pregnancy, of her body, of her child, is bound to fail: "*don't you feel?*" is what the woman asks her husband, significantly and presciently using the negative form ("*non senti?*" in the original Italian). For her husband does not, cannot feel what she feels, cannot be impressed by that which impresses her. The bump, the kick he can perhaps detect on the surface of his wife's belly is a perception wholly external to his body, and he is ultimately unable to experience the movement that is at once within herself and not herself, both continuous with and different from her own flesh.

As we read medical-anthropological texts, it is easy to entertain the suspicion that "at certain points in scientific discourse scholars unwittingly apply categories that are more the projections of their own way of being than the results of objective descriptions of female modalities; that, in short, their observations speak more of human beings and their fears than of woman, they are more the expressions of an author's spirit, of a culture and a period, than the conceptions and products of a controlled scientific elaboration" (Babini, 29). This is visibly the case in Mantegazza's *Fisiologia della donna* and Lombroso's *La donna delinquente, la prostituta e la donna normale.* Both of these prolix treatises project the image of a patriarchal culture afraid of losing its privileges and thus holding on tenaciously, desperately even, to unrealistic images of woman—romanticized by Mantegazza, animalized by Lombroso. The blushing of Mantegazza's exemplary woman is Mantegazza's own, it is a projection more than a description, a cultural expression more than a scientific elaboration. His image of blushing clarifies to what extent late-nineteenth-century European anthropological attempts to grasp female nature, the essence of femininity, mirror in reverse the issues raised at that same time by the women's movement. Mantegazza's book, like Lombroso's, aspired to a double function: scientific contribution to the knowledge of woman and direct intervention in a political and social debate, that is, woman's emancipation. The inseparability between the pursuit of knowledge and the attempt at social control is staged in these texts in an instructive manner, as their ostensible question "What is woman?" reveals itself to embed another one: "Is woman inferior to man?" I hardly need to answer it for Mantegazza and Lombroso, though the former insisted at least in theory on a functional complementarity that the latter did not even consider.

Another result of a study of these scientific texts is the somewhat frightful realization of their continuity with our own world, with our beliefs and practices—scientific as well as cultural. So, for example, despite turn-of-the-century scientists' efforts to naturalize woman as mother, an ironic effect of their increasingly numerous texts on the maternal function, nay mission, of women was precisely its denaturalization. Mantegazza, for example, devotes many pages and much thought-out rhetoric to the description of woman's bodily maternity as it is inscribed in her flesh and bones qua natural mandates—as I discuss in Chapter 1. Yet the effect of his text—and, even more, the effect of Lombroso's entire treatise on woman—is the alienation of woman from her own supposedly natural function and mission, the erosion of the normality of motherhood.

Above and beyond the importance of turn-of-the-century treatises on woman as the projection and expression of the thoughts, spirit, and fears of authors and cultures, and as a crystallization of a medicalized view of the maternal body with tangible consequences for our own daily life, these texts interest me because of their connection with novels and short stories written by women at roughly the same time period. That some of these authors, such as Ada Negri and Grazia Deledda, should continue to write and be successful well into the fascist era is only appropriate, given the continued popularity of and faith in both Lombroso's and Mantegazza's scientific work during that time. For what some of these scientific and fictional texts help us reconstruct is a little-known chapter in the history of the body. German historian Barbara Duden rightly laments the disappearance of quickening from both science and English usage, and its related absence in historiography: "The first stirring of the unborn is part of a whole set of experiences that lie outside the blinders of historiographers. Historians deal primarily with the visible remains of visible things" (80). Quickening belongs instead to the realm of the sense of touch, the history of which has been pursued even less than that of the other low-ranking senses, taste and smell, in part because it is a sense that is difficult to describe, and the traces it leaves are indirect, vague. "No wonder," Duden goes on, "that an inner touch experienced only by women has gone unobserved and unnoted," despite the fact that "the history of quickening is a key to a realm of the past hitherto closed to the historian: the study of perceptions that lie in the dark, inaccessible to notions, ideas, and styles of visualization" (80–81). Furthermore, touch entails a closeness between subject and object precluding the distance that sight, on the other hand, provides. Touch is simultaneously active and passive. The one who touches cannot touch without being, at the same time, also touched. Therefore, no clear opposition between subject and object can be posited through touch. Borders, in touch, are fluid, as they also are in pregnancy; indeed, pregnancy could be described, in a sense, as a nine-month-long touching.

"Observing" and "noting" quickening is the center of this chapter; Mantegazza's overture to what he must have regarded as the most important chapter in his own treatise on woman, the chapter on motherhood, that is, is an example of both the centrality and the elision of this uniquely female experience. Quickening opens Mantegazza's chapter on motherhood, yet quickening is described solely from the outside, as it is felt, though not quite, by the father and not by the mother, as it provokes a mediated reaction—the woman's joy is predicated on her husband's—tempered by modesty and shame. Nowhere does Mantegazza explore the possibility that fetal movement might be experienced instead as the ecstasy of a unique, empowering connection (as it is in, for example, Negri's short story "Confessione d'Ignazia," in *Prose*). Furthermore, the ghost of unwanted pregnancies is evoked in Mantegazza by the concession that only "in most cases" is the sharing of the feeling of fetal movement "one of the greatest joys" in a woman's life. "Fortunately," this is the case for Mantegazza, "fortunately" most women feel joy at being pregnant, "fortunately" . . . But what of those who don't? Where are they, in Mantegazza's treatise? Are they simply dispatched to his former friend, the more pathologically inclined Lombroso?

And where is knowledge located in Mantegazza's evocation of the feeling of fetal movement? Although the pregnant woman is posited as the source of "emotions" and "joys," it is significantly the husband who is the implied subject of knowledge—though ironically the negative used in "don't you feel" deprives him, too, of epistemological awareness. Emotions and feeling, connection and empathy, sexed as feminine, are interpreted as incompatible, in traditional Western epistemology, with the autonomous, dislocated, disinterested observer guided by rationality and objectivity who alone has privileged access to knowledge. Yet the putative neutrality of such a position has been harshly and justly criticized by feminist philosophers such as Lorraine Code, who powerfully argues in her essay "Taking Subjectivity into Account" that "ideal objectivity is a generalization from the *subjectivity* of quite a small social group, albeit a group that has the power, security, and prestige to believe that it can generalize its experiences and normative ideals across the social order" (22). This critique of male, white, middle- and upper-class epistemology has two important effects for my discussion of Mantegazza's work. First, we can use it to criticize his work at large as politically and epistemologically deceptive and even oppressive to the group he analyzes—women. Women's subjectivity and specificity is reduced to an observable variable, while the scientist's own subjectivity, as well as his accountability, are effaced as apolitical because rational and objective. Second, the implicit valorization of Mantegazza's method—positivistic epistemology—renders invalid every other way of attaining knowledge. The pregnant woman's knowledge of the child within her, for example, is reduced to an unthinking emotional outburst in need of validation by an external, detached observer: the husband. For the woman's own experience is too emotionally and bodily involved to get accorded the honorific status of "knowledge." It is just an impression.

The experience of quickening, and the feeling of fetal movement in general, is not only, as in Duden's discussion, a chapter in the history of the body—although that alone would be more than sufficient reason to study it. Rather, fetal movement is experienced as an exemplary acquisition of knowledge, and as such it also deserves a place in the history of epistemology. It is an experience that completes and corrects our perception of the maternal womb as a colored aura on the screen of an ultrasound machine, as a receptacle separate from the female body, as an organ in a frame that bears a child yet no connection to a human, feeling, thinking, knowing being. The obfuscation of this experience in official history, of the body as well as of knowledge, is certainly tied to what Vrinda Dalmiya and Linda Alcoff call "the delegitimation of traditional women's knowledge," an act that "is not only politically disturbing but also epistemologically specious" (217). Quickening would undoubtedly qualify as a "gender-specific experiential knowing" (229) not accessible to a male subject—Paolo Mantegazza, for example. Still men, by virtue of sharing a common humanity, would have some experience of it. If epistemology is truly concerned with the modalities of knowing, as it claims to be, then it needs to incorporate other knowledges, or ways of knowing that are other, epistemological paths that also allow, encourage, enliven the flourishing of every human being.

Fetal Movement in Women's Literature

When Italian women writers from the late nineteenth and the early twentieth century figure quickening—a description that takes place more often than one might imagine—the scene and its interpretation are at odds with, though culturally complementary to, Mantegazza's procreative fantasy. First of all, in these texts, otherness is embodied in the fetus and not in the husband. The woman's experience is not even recognized, at least at first, as fetal movement. And although it is certainly an emotional one, this experience is far from being univocally identified with life's greatest joy. Ironically, the one character I have encountered in whom fetal movement causes jubilation, to the point that her nurse makes her drink chamomile to calm her down, is the eponymous protagonist of Ada Negri's "La confessione d'Ignazia," a single woman who freely decides to bear and raise a child without a partner; Mantegazza would have been horrified! But more commonly, the visceral perception of fetal movement is the source of a puzzling, frightening knowledge: of the self, of the other, and of the continuity and simultaneous increasing differentiation between the two; of one's future and of one's present; and, at times, of the condition of women in society. This is the case in Grazia Deledda's *The Mother,* Annie Vivanti's *Vae Victis!,* Sibilla Aleramo's *A Woman,* as well as in Neera's work—to which I turn below.

But what can be the significance of narratives of fetal movement for a feminist cultural criticism? From a literary perspective, women's writings have been described as being both structurally and thematically imbricated in the difference-defying processes inherent in quickening: "the adherence, viscerality, and at the same time the almost omnivorous materiality which ties or contrasts every woman to her texts or to those of other women," writes Italian literary critic Biancamaria Frabotta, "twist around each other in a spiral which ends where sexuality begins, if not even where maternity begins" (141). From the viewpoint of cultural and psychological history, as Finzi underlines, nineteenth-century women's attitudes toward their own self-affirmation are at best contradictory: "the female imaginary is too large to let itself be compressed within the tight quarters of the bourgeois family; and at the same time it is too easily coopted to be truly alternative. In the female sublime I glimpse something great (the conviction of deserving more) and something base (the terror of losing everything)" ("Alla ricerca," 229). How do these narratives of fetal movement function to shape reproductive experiences and practices at a crucial time, between the late nineteenth and the early twentieth century, when pregnancy and childbirth began moving from the female space of the home to the male-dominated medical field? Can these pregnant bodies, so frequently silenced or ventriloquized in scientific treatises such as Mantegazza's and Lombroso's, act out and ultimately pronounce a language? And is such a language resistant to or complicitous with the homogenizing scientific view of woman as maternal carapace?

In the writings of Neera, Annie Vivanti, Ada Negri, Grazia Deledda, and Sibilla Aleramo, narratives of fetal movement insistently and originally explore the connections among the female body, its knowledge, and language, thus undermining the split between body and mind and the analogous division between "motherhood as experience and institution" decried by Adrienne Rich in *Of Woman Born.* Echoing Rich, in *Thinking Through the Body* Jane Gallop describes this split as that which "makes the mother into an inhuman monster by dividing the human realm of culture, history, and politics from the realm of love and the body where mother carries, bears, and tends her children" (2). But in many of the literary descriptions I have read, quickening conflates knowledge and body, history and love, by representing, for instance, the woman's first awareness of pregnancy. Although this is not a particularly early symptom, it was for a long time the most reliable one available. Quite often, it was by feeling a kick, a flutter, a bubble within her belly that the woman knew she was pregnant: hence a most basic psychosomatic connection between fetal movement and knowledge. Only the woman herself could detect and publicize her pregnancy, while today quickening simply confirms at a personal, internal level what the doctor had already verified from the outside weeks earlier.

Knowledge of pregnancy represents, metonymically, knowledge of one's body, as literary texts repeatedly imply: a problematic knowledge that can only be communicated to those who have experienced it themselves. Not husbands, then, as for Mantegazza, but other mothers, often embodied by an older, more experienced woman who, like Rapunzel's enchantress, helps the protagonist decipher the nature of her otherwise incomprehensible sensations. Bodily knowledge, pregnant knowledge is in these texts preverbal, semiotic, based on an internal touch. In phenomenological terms, it is an "interoceptive experience" (Leder, 61) that defies externalization and thus, to some extent, linguistic transposition. And yet the experience, because it involves otherness, is also an ethical one, an experience proceeding from identity and/in relationship. Narratives of fetal movement are therefore doubly central to the texts in which they appear because they may constitute a reflection, on the part of the author, on both the status of women (indissolubly biological and social, corporeal and linguistic) and on their use of language and/as the construction of identity. In tracing these narratives, I have tried to follow Elisabetta Rasy's advice to those who want to understand the relationship between women and literature, namely to privilege "clues, traces, details, more than general categories" (*Le donne e la letteratura,* 11). Maria Rosa Cutrufelli likewise insists that to critically read women writers' texts, one must note their thematic innovations and how these affect the textual structures of their works (241).

I believe that this recurrence of quickening is one of the thematic innovations to which Cutrufelli alludes. Quickening is, to borrow Rasy's words, a clue, a trace, a symptomatic detail that defies general categorization. It is a clue pointing inward rather than, as Mantegazza would have it, to the quivering surface of the body. Therefore, it is a peculiarly "female" detail because it is obtained from an exclusively female experience—an experience, furthermore, that imbricates the subject both in sexual difference and in the difference of otherness, the difference involving an ethical relationship to the other. Quickening as detail, then, may favor a different perspective onto the pregnant experience. This perspective might in turn defy the external observer's ambivalent attitude toward such a body, evidenced, in turn-of-the-century rural Italy, in the numerous prohibitions imposed on women during menstruation and pregnancy. Instead of being considered natural, as we sometimes romantically imagine, these times were experienced and regarded as dangerous and contaminating, with the effect of symbolically relegating women to the realm of nature as evil stepmother (Scaraffia, 207). Narratives of fetal movement are also precious clues for the articulation of a knowledge (maternal, female) all too often banished to the status of taboo, triviality, secrecy. It has been difficult for me, for example, to explain to colleagues who have never been pregnant, both women and men, that I was working on the epistemology of quickening: "Writers really talk about (read: bother with) that? Isn't it a bit specialized (read: trivial)?" I have seen only puzzled looks on the rare occasions when I have felt bold enough to even mention this topic. Nonacademic women who have been pregnant, on the other hand, had considerably less trouble understanding the compelling quality of this experience, and that it might be appropriate to study and to write about it.

Neera, the pseudonym of Anna Radius Zuccari, was "one of the most widely read authors of her day" (Wood, 32) and, "with Matilde Serao, the best-known and, let us say it, the most illustrious among the women writers of the last quarter of last century" (Pansa, 71). She is still a controversial, duplicitous figure among critics because of the striking split between her virulently antifeminist essays and the biting criticism of women's conditions characteristic of her fiction. This contradiction is not unique to Neera's work, since, as Antonia Arslan writes, "the majority of women writers at the turn of the century—Liala, Invernizio, Neera, Colombi, Vivanti—were, like most of their contemporaries, antifeminist and antidivorcist" ("Ideologia e autorappresentazione," 93). Arslan advances the hypothesis that an open commitment to feminism might have led to the loss of their women readers' approval, which was at that time the only legitimation for women writers (165). About Neera in particular, Bruce Merry claims that "the aggressively anti-feminist tone of her essays may be part of an attempt to keep her writing respectable and free of any bluestocking image" (288), while Sharon Wood believes that Neera's "exposure of the fallacy of romantic love and her depiction of the emotional desert of most bourgeois marriages is perhaps the stronger and the more striking for emerging from observation and experience rather than any *parti pris* or political ideology" (25). Thus, for Anna Nozzoli, Neera's "obscure female figures . . . become the bearers of an unavowed, resentful, repressed consciousness of their own enslavement" (5).

The literary and linguistic contradictions concerning the role and the value of motherhood, particularly of pregnancy and childbirth, are most apparent at a macroscopic level in the obvious separation between Neera's fiction and nonfiction, in both of which "the reproduction of mothering," to use Chodorow's phrase—namely the social-psychological process whereby "women, as mothers, produce daughters with mothering capacities and the desire to mother," daughters whose capacities and needs "are built into and grow out of the mother-daughter relationship itself" (*The Reproduction of Mothering,* 7)—occupies central though diverging positions. Indeed Neera's characterization of mothering makes us reflect on Kaplan's critical comment that, although they can be criticized for being a-historic and a-specific, Chodorow's "theories usefully describe the reproduction of white, bourgeois mothering in the period from 1860 to 1960" (*Motherhood and Representation,* 34). Neera's male characters are exemplary, sometimes even to the point of caricature, of Chodorow's theories: while women's mothering abilities are cyclically reproduced from one generation to the next, men are devoted to the impersonal, extrafamilial world of work and public life and are typically unable to entertain interpersonal, affective relationships, for their nurturant capacities and needs have been repressed. But while in Neera's essays this separation is exalted, her fiction shows that this division, which operates hierarchically, leads women to nothing but unhappiness and even, at times, self-destructive despair.

Neera's construction of fetal movement is also split between her theories and her fiction. Exemplary of this fracture is the essay "Tutte madri" (All mothers), in *Le idee di una donna* (The ideas of a woman, 1903). This collection has been described by Nozzoli as the "epitome of her antifeminism, a conglomerate of opinions and theses borrowed by the most traditional and reactionary literature on woman" (26). In "Tutte madri," Neera describes the feeling of fetal movement in enthusiastic terms, as a visceral experience of empowering difference for the pregnant woman: "when in the marvelous shiver that man ignores, from her own palpitating viscera she feels the voice of the *great mystery,* she will feel so lofty, so close to infinity that she will judge as petty every other undertaking" (*Le idee di una donna,* 145). Without the experience of pregnancy, Neera insists, woman "will never manage to grasp the profound meaning of life, because that quiver of a new being coming into the light has not passed upon her" (145). The religious overtones of Neera's description are vaguely reminiscent of the Visitation of Mary and Elizabeth in the Gospel of Luke. For Neera as for the Evangelist, the quickening womb is a knowing womb, whose knowledge is (physically? unexplainably? miraculously?) transmitted to the pregnant woman: just as Elizabeth correctly reads her body and decodes her child's unspoken message, so also the ideal mother as she is described by Neera "will hear the voice of the *great mystery*" (145; Neera's emphasis). It is not surprising, therefore, to read that *Le idee di una donna* "becomes the battle horse of the opponents of emancipation even outside national borders, gaining for its author a particular fame as antifeminist" (Pierobon, 31). Yet Neera's description qualifies the feeling of fetal movement as possessing an epistemic validity absent from, for example, Mantegazza's treatise. Man "ignores" such a quiver. Woman, on the other hand, recognizes it as she "listens to its voice." The experience is verbal, then, and not just bodily; it leads woman to "judge" everything else, it allows her to "grasp the profound meaning of life."

Notwithstanding its Christian evocations in her essays, Neera's empowering visceral quiver, troped as the univocal voice of a higher mystery, acquires a more complex and ambivalent epistemological function in her novels. Let us explore more in depth the novel *L'indomani* (The next day, 1890). *L'indomani* tells the story of a woman's progressive disillusion with a marriage that she formerly believed would be the pinnacle of her existence. In Anna Folli's judgment, Neera's entire novelistic production is characterized by the fundamental figure of "the woman who lacks love" ("Le arpe eolie," 118), and *L'indomani* is for Nozzoli a "gray metaphor of the marriage condition" (27). Marta's pregnancy in the second half of the novel shatters her illusions concerning love and marriage, and constitutes that crisis of female sexuality described by Accati as the conflict between social, cultural, and moral demands and the woman's identity (45). The feeling of fetal movement finally convinces Marta that her fate is likely to be similar to that of the local doctor's wife, whose five children and four miscarriages, ironically described as her husband's "annual fruits of love," have turned her into "a little woman who was neither beautiful nor ugly, with a flat chest and a protruding abdomen, the profile of a madonna prematurely aged" (*L'indomani,* 35). Maternity changes the doctor's wife into an unattractive woman whose husband continuously cheats on her with their young maids; she cannot hire older and thus less desirable ones because they would not have the energy necessary to handle her five young children and is doubly trapped by her motherhood. As Folli remarks, Marta is much like Neera's other heroines because she is a "passionate and sensual character and is therefore convinced that knowledge can be achieved through love and the body" ("Le arpe eolie," 105).

It is through her body that Marta attains knowledge of self. But this does not take place through the experience of a body-in-pleasure, as might be expected of a new bride. Rather, Marta achieves knowledge through the realization of impending suffering: those life-threatening labor pains described by the doctor's wife as "a really bad deal that the Lord has given us women. Men get all the good stuff, don't they?" (*L'indomani,* 41). Like Teresa's aunt in Neera's *Teresa* (her best-known work), who had sixteen or seventeen children without learning anything about sexual love and pleasure, the protagonist of *L'indomani* finds no pleasure in sex and, it seems, no pleasure in motherhood, either. Indeed Marta wonders, poignantly: "why should she give her own blood and her own flesh, and risk touching the threshold of eternity without knowing the threshold of pleasure?" (171).

L'indomani dwells on the first two times when Marta feels her child move. Quickening is perceived when the protagonist sees a farmer and his wife embrace with obvious love and sensuality; but we have already learned that Marta has never experienced sexual pleasure (171–72)—which would make her for Lombroso a "normal woman" since woman is "naturally and organically frigid" (*La donna,* 57)—and conjugal passion is here represented as the exception to the rules of marriage. Significantly, it is experienced by people belonging to a lower social class, two peasants figured as "other" to the middle-class protagonists of Neera's world. The following passage is the culminating point of the story, a fundamental step in Marta's complex transformation. As she views the peasant couple's display of passionate love, Marta

> had stifled a cry, as if struck to the heart; and in that same moment she felt her entrails swell up, she felt in her womb the movement of a being, and through her veins, through her flesh, she felt the anticipated throbbing, the revelation of another life, exploded with the revelation of love itself. Every veil was removed, every doubt was undone, her virginity fell at that point, she had become a woman. She understood, felt, desired everything. The im-

> pression had been so quick and violent that that man's presence, now, was hurting her. (183)

Love reveals itself to Marta not through a pleasurable physical contact with her husband, as one might expect of a recently married young woman, but through a disconcertingly painful voyeuristic episode: the sight of a happily married peasant couple's passionate kiss as it is viewed simultaneously with the tactile experience of quickening. It is through voyeuristic pain, and not through conjugal pleasure, that Marta loses her virginity, by her own avowal, and the veil, figure for the hymen of innocence and thus for the knowledge of good and evil, falls as she at once discovers the existence of love and her lack of it, the existence of an other inside her and her own womanhood, the impossibility of pleasure in marriage and perhaps in motherhood. Thus Folli interprets the expression "struck to the heart" used by Neera in this passage as indicating that "Marta is fertilized by her desperate desire for an ideal, severed and gone back inside her, according to Neera's elaboration of an exclusively female maternity" ("Le arpe eolie," 106). The heart, to which I return below, is sexed as female by being conflated with the uterus, with the effect of displacing the heart's association with the seat of consciousness and knowledge onto the uterus itself—redeemed from hysterical conversion, invested with linguistic ability.

Knowledge, and hence signification, is attained as Marta's pregnant body becomes conscious of its de-centeredness. Knowledge, "the revelation," is not located in her head nor even in her womb, but rather "throughout her veins and her flesh." In this process, Marta's body becomes aware of being splintered into self and other, "another life." This visceral consciousness, however, cannot be verbalized in a univocal manner, for it has one foot at the prelinguistic level. It is with a similar vocabulary, it is worth noting, that Lombroso, through biblical allusions, describes woman's loss of virginity as the acquisition of a knowledge of good and evil that is dangerous to her morality—and therefore to the social order: "the enchantment has disappeared, that veil which concealed the knowledge of good and evil is ripped open and in front of a suddenly-acquired knowledge, those women whose moral sense is not too strong and who have a bad rapport with society, easily decide to throw out all other regards, as well" (*La donna,* 584). The veil of knowledge is silently likened to the veil hiding woman's body and thus protecting her morality. Knowledge, then, rather than forming the basis of an ethical relationship with the other, doubles for women as an immoral enterprise.

Doubling, dys-appearance, wrestling with embodiment, self-change—

terms I discussed in the preceding section of this chapter—are intrinsic to Marta's experience of quickening. The corporeal realization of love—a love that she is denied, and not the *caritas* that pregnant Elizabeth and fetal John the Baptist immediately recognize and are impressed by—and of the other life in her womb, in her veins, and in her flesh, explode at once in the feeling of fetal movement. Quickening tropes what Neera metaphorically describes in "Tutte madri" as a "voice," hence a language, that would take woman close to "infinity," into a "violent," rather than a maternal, impression: a corporeal, prelinguistic, semiotic contact that strikes Marta to her "heart" (one with the uterus) and makes her "scream." Thus, she is compelled to revert to a state anterior to language, a state that effectively if symbolically isolates her from her own humanity and excludes the possibility of communication, of a significant and signifying relationship to the other.

The de-romanticization and especially the "desymbolization" of quickening is completed when Marta experiences fetal movement for the second time. The occasion is a conversation with her mother, which darkly emphasizes Chodorow's "reproduction of mothering" as self-destructive more than productive of otherness. Marta's mother is trying to convince her unhappy daughter that love does not exist and that what Marta witnessed between the two farmers was but a fleeting moment of physical passion. Just as Marta admits to her mother and to herself, "Then . . . there is nothing," the perception of a movement in her womb makes her certain of the presence of an-other within her, a visceral presence that, in a perspective doubted by the text itself, is expected to fill the gap left by the disappearance of love's illusions and by her loss of bodily integrity: "The same sensation that had startled her the previous day in the two peasants' little house was coming back. She felt her organs move under the impulse of a living person, and the strange revelation of another being within herself. It resembled a little hand beating on her breast, a little hand that seemed to say: Open up, I am love and truth" (197). This same sentence is repeated on the following page, the second to last in the book: "But meanwhile the little hand repeated, insistently: Open up, I am love and truth" (198).

The apparent and clearly superficial plenitude evoked by the unborn child's movement, tear-jerkingly metonymized into a little hand, signifies the plenitude of the woman's body. This body is finally filled with a child, filled with meaning: love, truth. But does the text really mean for us to buy this, to be deeply impressed by it? It is painfully ironic that for Marta the sensation of fullness should come about through the realization of a primordial lack: of Marta's lack of a love that others instead have, in the first experience at the farmers' house, and ultimately of the universal lack of such a love. It is no accident that love should be posited by Marta's own mother as the deluded construction of the female imagination. Marta becomes in the course of *L'indomani* an increasingly empty container, she "dys-appears," to use Leder's phenomenological term, despite the growing physical fullness brought about by her pregnancy. Fullness and emptiness are paradoxically experienced almost at once, in a fantasy of autonomous generative power that ambiguously alternates, according to Finzi, with the pregnant woman's identification with an empty container waiting to be filled from the outside ("L'altra scena del parto," 190). The child will supposedly fill this gap constitutive of the female imaginary body, in *L'indomani,* with its "love" and "truth," qualities that echo the religious overtones of "Tutte madri." But it is too late, and the final optimistic words of the novel cannot dispel in the reader the lasting impression that Marta, exemplary of women's condition in marriage and pregnancy, is likely to fare no better than the doctor's wife: deformed and cheated. The apparent plenitude of the pregnant body only hides the emptiness of a signifier which, like the body that has lost its integrity, has already exploded and cannot be recovered. The knowledge Marta attains is not simply enriching; rather it is a step toward the internalization of the cultural prescriptions of motherhood. As gynecologist Muzio Pazzi put it in 1913, and as *L'indomani* with sadness confirms, "pregnancy constitutes a sacrifice tolerated by the individual in favor of the species" (in Babini, 60).

For Marta, then, the new relationship with her body through a discovery that, according to Maria Minicuci, characterizes many women in their first pregnancy—who for the first time discover their own body as both familiar and mysterious (57)—entails the interoceptive consciousness of symbolic emptiness, or loss, together with that of corporeal and semiotic fullness. *L'indomani* thus conforms to the ending characteristic of many turn-of-the-century women's novels: an ending which, according to Arslan, even as it echoes the debates around the question of woman, nonetheless reconfirms the return to the status quo through the protagonist's inevitable defeat and subjection ("Ideologia e autorappresentazione," 169). And yet, for Wood, in *L'indomani* "Neera could hardly come closer to condemning the emotional and sexual frustrations foisted on women by a self-serving, male-centered culture and sexual economy, ably assisted by the sugary dreams of romantic literature" (37).

At the same time, Neera's repeated, though also ironic emphasis on truth embeds her representation of fetal movement within an epistemological quest. There is a striking parallel between turn-of-the-century women's representations of fetal movement and the chapter entitled "Subjective Knowledge: The Inner Voice" in the controversial 1986 book

Women's Ways of Knowing, by Mary Field Belenky, Blythe McVicker Clinchy, Nancy Rule Goldberger, and Jill Mattuck Tarule. For example, one of the interviewees in this chapter states that knowledge is "like a jerk or something inside you," while another said: "I just listen to the inside of me and I know what to do" (Belenky et al., 69). The authors' generalizations in this book describe truth for subjective knowers as "something experienced, not thought out, something felt rather than actively pursued or constructed. These women do not see themselves as part of the process, as constructors of truth, but as conduits through which truth emerges" (Belenky et al., 69). As is also the case for Neera's characters, knowledge is understood by some of the women interviewed for this book as located somewhere in their body, regardless of the scientifically established centrality of the brain in our thought processes. Thinking, knowing, truth-production are perceived by some women, rather holistically, as the outcome of experiences that involve more than one's brain or disembodied mind. But while *Women's Ways of Knowing* posits a hierarchy in the acquisition of knowledge according to which it is primarily white affluent women who pass beyond the early stages, Neera's works establish connections between the various modes of knowing within women of her same social class, the educated upper-middle class. The representation of quickening as a way of knowing can thus also be compared to what the authors of *Women's Ways of Knowing* describe as "connected knowing," drawing on the work of Carol Gilligan and Nona Lyons. Indeed this sense of connection and interdependence is dramatized in the figure of quickening, where knower and known inhabit the same, and yet also a paradoxically different body.

In spite of her collaboration with Paolo Mantegazza in 1881 on a popular manual, the *Dizionario d'igiene per le famiglie* (Dictionary of hygiene for families; intended as a guide on how to live a healthy and happy life, but not nearly as successful as the two authors' other separately written publications), and in spite of an epistolary friendship between Neera and Mantegazza that displays mutual admiration, Neera's characters in no way resemble the blushing yet somewhat smug pregnant woman who ushers in Mantegazza's chapter on motherhood in *Fisiologia della donna.* I must therefore disagree with Rasy, for whom Neera downright incorporated Mantegazza's devaluing theories of women's physiology into her works (*Le donne e la letteratura,* 124). This may seem to be true of Neera's essays, but it is certainly not the case for her novels. Indeed, the full maternal metaphor so prominent in Neera's essays is effectively displaced by the metonymic lack that maternity constitutes in Neera's fiction. Particularly, Neera's narratives of fetal movement propose an alternative, problematic reading of women and/as mothers. For the context-bound nature of metonymy, based on contiguity, as Domna Stanton argues, "exposes specific cultural values, prejudices, and limitations," even as it "would promote the recognition that the mother cannot symbolize an untainted origin" ("Difference on Trial," 175–76). With its emphasis on contiguity, and its inability to be displaced, fetal movement posits maternity as metonymy, rather than metaphor, of women's condition. It is a trope that always demands relationality and the presence of another: the fetus and the pregnant woman, the pregnant woman and her husband (as in Mantegazza), the pregnant woman and the other woman who helps her read the signs of her body. And in this relationality one may certainly find joy, but that is not what Neera's reader will be left with at the end of *L'indomani.* The relationality of Neera's women's feeling of fetal movement rejects symbolization in favor of the metonymic realities of pregnancy as it implicates the subject into a system in which women are, ultimately, destroyed.

Narratives of fetal movement push hard against that symptomatic "opaque nucleus" which, in Finzi's analysis, is the result of the cultural repression of the internal representation of pregnancy: "There is in every pregnancy a symptomatic opaque nucleus. It seems to me that one of the greatest repressions carried out by our culture is the one that removes from us every internal representation of pregnancy and childbirth. The images all come from the outside and are projected onto a darkened screen, unable to transcribe endogenous sensations" ("L'altra scena del parto," 186). If one of the results of this cultural repression is the woman's inability to read the signals of her own body (at a time when a girl's sexual education was more often than not left to the hands of fate—or to those of her impatient new husband), another result is the writer's difficulty in expressing the pregnant experience without the silences, stammerings, and ambiguities brought about by the clash of language with the "darkened screen" of a culturally repressed experience. Hence the metonymic displacement from the uterus to the heart, for the heart is a more acceptable, somewhat less sexed organ (this displacement takes place in several narratives of fetal movement: Giovanni Verga's "Nedda," Annie Vivanti's *Vae Victis!* as well as Neera's *L'indomani,* for example). Roland Barthes compares the heart to the (obviously male) sex, because in his view "The heart is the organ of desire (the heart swells, weakens, etc., like the sexual organs)" (52). Of course the uterus also swells and weakens, but I doubt that was what Barthes had in mind. More interestingly I think, and with a more complex sexualizing trope, Hélène Cixous—the theorist of sexual difference and of *écriture féminine* to whom I return below—has described in an interview the heart as "what the sexes have in common," as "the most mysterious organ there is, indeed because it is the same for the two sexes. As if the heart were the sex common to the two sexes. The human sex"

(*Hélène Cixous, Rootprints,* 31). Between Barthes' phallic heart and Neera's pregnant heart is this optimistic convergence that eschews sexual difference even as it invites dialogue and a common ground.

But can sexual difference be so easily set aside? As a culturally pregnant image, the heart has been consistently identified in Western culture as the seat of intellectual thought and of all deep feelings, as the origin of vital forces and interiority, as the center of decisive things such as conscience, morality, and the law. Against the tumescence of Barthes' male organ and the utopia of Cixous' androgynous one, and through their organic association of the uterus with the heart, Neera and other writers perform a metonymic move counter to the appropriation by male writers of the maternal metaphor. Rather than co-opting childbirth imagery to describe masculine creativity—conceiving a book, giving birth to ideas—some turn-of-the-century women writers explore instead the possibilities inherent in figuring and reproducing maternal thought and work—in this case, pregnancy—by metonymically moving along culturally pregnant images: such as the heart. At the same time, their texts develop ways of speaking the body as it traverses difference (corporeal, existential, moral, sexual, and so on) without turning it over to pathology. Even as they reject a mechanistic view of the human body as machine, these texts nevertheless figure pregnancy as it transforms the world by radically changing a woman's sense of self and autonomy, her relations with others, her habitual sense of space and time. The uncanny, visceral interoception of an otherness within the self is a fracture merging the otherwise irreconcilable dualities generated by quickening: power and surrender, knowledge and ignorance, choice and fate, fullness and emptiness, words and silence. Impressiveness and impressionability. Quickening becomes an interrogation of the moral boundaries between self and other as well as between mind and body, autonomy and responsibility, subjectivity and ethics. With its emphasis on the fetus's otherness, quickening effects a break between mother and fetus that allows the emergence of the pregnant woman as a thinking and knowing subject separate from the fetus that makes a mother of her. This is the break necessary for language and the constitution of the subject, and it is also the break indispensable for the development of a maternal ethics.

Fetal Movement and Feminist Theory

Among the best-known examples of the representation of pregnancy in contemporary Italian culture is journalist Oriana Fallaci's successful short book *Lettera a un bambino mai nato,* first published in 1975 and translated into English as *Letter to a Child Never Born* a year later. It is the story, told in the first person and directly addressed to the child she is carrying, of an unnamed, unmarried woman pregnant with the child of an estranged lover. The protagonist decides not to have an abortion despite her former lover's and her feminist best friend's encouragements not to keep the child; yet her child dies in her womb when she refuses to remain in bed for the duration of her pregnancy as her doctor ordered after an episode of severe bleeding. At the end of the book, it is implied that the protagonist–narrator, who had refused to have the dead child removed from her womb, is also about to die.

The child's problematic second-person identity becomes subtly bound up with the reader's. As the narrator states toward the beginning of the story, her own life is due to the fact that she kicked her mother in utero for the first time just as her mother was about to swallow an abortifacient medicine: "She drank it faithfully until the night I moved inside her belly and gave her a kick to tell her not to throw me away. She was lifting the glass to her lips when I signaled. She turned it upside down immediately and spilled the fluid out. Some months later I was lolling victoriously in the sun" (*Letter to a Child Never Born,* 10). Although it is a comparably dramatic event, this scene contrasts sharply with turn-of-the-century representations of quickening as knowledge of pregnancy. For in Fallaci's passage the same event, quickening, is thematically utilized as the victory of life (as in "pro-life") over the death caused by the narrator's mother's unsuccessful abortion. A further form of knowledge, of bodily knowledge again, is actively represented in this passage, one that is not addressed in any of the late-nineteenth- and early-twentieth-century texts I have read (because, I suspect, it is implied and never even questioned): the knowledge that the object of pregnancy, the fetus–child, is alive and kicking, so to speak. This added dimension, on the other hand, is to be expected in a book on an unplanned pregnancy written in the 1970s in Italy, at the time, that is, of the struggle over the legalization of abortion. (In 1977 the Italian Parliament approved a bill on abortion, which was finally legalized in 1978.)

Aware of her own in utero movement, presumably from her mother's oral repetition of this story, the narrator anticipates a comparably dramatic affirmation of the life she herself carries. Although she has not yet experienced quickening ("You've sent me no answers, you've given me no signs," 11), the narrator has nevertheless established early on in her pregnancy an epistemological connection with her child that allows her to affirm its existence, to positively know its being, in spite of the doctor's scorn: "I'll go back just to show him he's an ignoramus. All his science is not worth my intuition; how can a man understand a woman who claims before it is time that she is expecting a child?" (14, translation modified). When the perception of movement finally arrives, it is a caricature of quickening, a painful experience brought on by the sudden encounter with her former lover. He lets himself, uninvited, into her apartment and she reacts: "The first thing I felt was a pang in the belly. Not the usual knife stab but a pang: almost as though you were frightened to see him and had grasped me with your fists to take shelter and hide behind my womb" (59). The mother's fear becomes the child's, their reaction to an unexpected and unwanted presence (the unwanted being, ironically, is not the child but the father) is one and binds them together in a shared suffering—foreshadowing their common death. As the lover stays on and demands paternal rights, the narrator continues, "the pain in my womb was so bad I could hardly bear it" (61). This is not quickening, of course, but its painful perversion caused by the intrusion of another into the mother–child couple, already filled, it seems, with as much difference as it was able to withstand. The intrusion of "another other" is corporeally, emotionally, and intellectually unbearable.

True quickening significantly takes place when the narrator has decided to sign herself out of the hospital despite her bleeding, for although she wanted her child she was not willing or able to spend the remaining months of her pregnancy confined to a hospital bed. As the doctor leaves her bedside in a fit of rage for her selfish, antimaternal disposition, the narrator realizes:

> And just at that moment, you moved. You did what I had waited for, yearned for, for months. You stretched yourself, perhaps yawned, and you gave me a little blow. A little kick. Your first kick . . . like the kick I gave my mother to tell her not to throw me away. My legs turned to marble. And for several seconds I sat there breathless, my temples throbbing. I also felt a burning in my throat, a tear that blinded me. Then the tear rolled down and fell on the sheet making a little plop. But I got out of bed all the same. I packed my suitcase all the same. Tomorrow we leave. By plane. (73)

Quickening occurs at a moment of crisis, the moment when the narrator decides to take her life, and her child's, into her own hands, when she decides that her personhood will not, cannot be sacrificed. Like Sibilla Aleramo's narrator, she must remain "a woman" if she wants to survive as a mother. Her experience and her own mother's, then, to which she openly compares it, are opposite. Quickening impels her mother to set aside her intention to abort and to accept the pregnancy despite its costs—the child's bodily movement causes the mother's moral change—whereas the narrator's quickening takes place after she has made a fateful decision. It is the child who is affected by the mother's choice, and reacts to it, rather than the other way around. And the narrator's choice is opposite to her mother's, for it is the conscious, moral decision to risk her child's life in order to remain, as Aleramo, again, would say, a person, *a woman.*

As a consequence of this choice, however, the narrator's experience of quickening, in addition to being her first feeling of fetal movement, is also her last, and the narrator's knowledge as it develops out of her pregnant connection turns from life to death, from the exaltation of pregnancy to the mourning of a miscarriage perceived even as it is taking place: "With the same certainty that paralyzed me the night I knew you existed, I now know that you're dying" (84). The narrator's arguments against abortion, then, are tempered by the identical effect—miscarriage, therefore fetal demise—brought about by her choice to continue, yes, her pregnancy but not at all costs. Not at the cost of forgoing personhood. That is perhaps why *Letter to a Child Never Born,* despite the author's official stance against abortion outside of the book, has been appropriated by "pro-life" and "pro-choice" representatives alike. Like the writings of late-nineteenth- and early-twentieth-century women such as Deledda and Neera, productive tensions and contradictions characterize the ideological position of Fallaci's narrative, making it a fertile point of contact between her literary predecessors and her more theoretically inclined contemporaries.

The concept of otherness faithfully recurs in both theoretical and literary texts of pregnancy, marking the pregnant body as the place of a splitting and as the ultimate origin of subjectivity—but also of loss of subjectivity. "The pregnant subject," as Young notes from a phenomenological perspective, "experiences her body as herself and not herself. Its inner movements belong to another being, yet they are not other, because her body boundaries shift and because her bodily self-location is focused on her trunk in addition to her head" (46). Young draws repeatedly from the work of Julia Kristeva, who similarly writes, from a psychoanalyst's standpoint, that "A mother's identity is maintained only through the well-known closure of consciousness within the indolence of habit, when a woman protects herself from the borderline that severs her body and expatriates it from her child" ("Stabat Mater," 255). This identity or self-location, this closure of consciousness, is perceived as needing a sort of protection, for it is constantly threatened by the infiltration of an other through the prenatal connections established between woman and fetus. Yet the mother's lack of unitary meaning reflects and refracts the instability of linguistic signification itself: conflict, contradiction, antithesis mark the pregnant body even as they characterize maternal language. This unstable construction affirms the human form of the maternal and posits the gestating woman as a place of difference, a place that questions categories, in contrast to her traditional reduction to a bourgeois metaphoric idealization of maternal plenitude—with its unavoidable flip side, of course, her animalization, her reduction to gross mat(t)er.

Maternity texts repeatedly disclose that neither the pregnant woman nor the fetus are ever a totally autonomous self, both of their bodies being open, heterogeneous, impressive and impressionable, "grotesque," to use a definition given in a different context by Mikhail Bakhtin. The womb is grotesque because it is ambivalent, inspiring both terror and delight, suggesting both destruction and regeneration. Nancy Chodorow, for instance, retells the maternal heterogeneity with respect to the masculine, and its homology with the daughter, when she observes that a woman may symbolically return to her mother precisely "through her identification with the child who is in her womb" (*The Reproduction of Mothering,* 201)—rather than, as man more literally does, through coitus as a physical return to the womb. Indeed, Chodorow notes, "because of their mothering by women, girls come to experience themselves as less separate than boys, as having more permeable ego boundaries" (*The Reproduction of Mothering,* 93). While the sexual difference between mothers and sons precipitates the latter's early separation, the sexual sameness between a daughter and her mother encourages a continued identification which then goes on to characterize the woman's connections with others (including, presumably, the fetus she carries, the child/ren she bears) as marked by continuity and the need to establish a sense of self through relating to others. This concept of maternal permeability is also evoked, from a political perspective, by Carole Pateman, who argues that unlike the male body, "tightly enclosed within boundaries" and thus the model of civil order and political right, "women's bodies are permeable, their contours change shape and they are subject to cyclical processes" (96). Yet the distinction between self and other, problematic in the pregnancy literary texts I have been reading, is fundamental to the constitution of a recognizable linguistic system of signification. Language as we know it, most notably from Ferdinand de Saussure's linguistics, is explicitly and essentially based on difference: the recognition of difference, that is, is the condition of language. The pregnant body threatens the differential structure of language and therefore threatens language itself—though in threatening language it also ironically confirms it.

French-Algerian writer and critic Hélène Cixous has articulated at length in her fictional and nonfictional writings the permeable connections between sexuality and textuality, between difference and writing, between language and the mother's body—and, most pertinently, between pregnancy and knowledge. In Cixous' case, too, autobiography is implicated, for during Cixous' adolescence, her mother trained and then became a midwife, introducing Cixous early to the world of pregnancy and birth; Cixous said that she "could write a thesis on the theme of giving birth in texts by women, it would be fascinating. It's a metaphor which comes easily to women, dictated by their experience" (*The Hélène Cixous Reader*, xxvii, xxxiii). With Irigaray and Kristeva, Cixous figures in the holy trinity of French feminism that many critics have attacked as, for example, being neither French nor feminist. No attack has been more pointed, in my mind, than French feminist Christine Delphy's. In her article entitled "The Invention of French Feminism: An Essential Move," Delphy attacks the Anglo-American construction of French feminist thought around Cixous, Kristeva, and Irigaray as an imperialist fabrication that allowed its inventors to attribute their own essentialist and psychoanalytic agenda to foreign thinkers—the so-called French feminists: "French feminism was invented in order to legitimate the introduction on the Anglo-American feminist scene of a brand of essentialism, and in particular a rehabilitation of psychoanalysis, which . . . questions the very bases of what defines a feminist theoretical approach" (216). Delphy dismisses Cixous as "antifeminist," Kristeva as "*pre*-feminist," and Irigaray as "feminist by her own definition," (220, n.37). More forgivingly, Peggy Kamuf notes that the imprecise and hasty categorization as French feminist has been particularly hasty and imprecise in the case of Hélène Cixous, since her characterization as theorist was and largely still continues to be based on just two essays published in English translation in the feminist journal *Signs*: "The Laugh of the Medusa," published in 1976, and "Castration or Decapitation," published in 1981 (70). Despite accusations such as Delphy's, though, Cixous' work on maternity, like Irigaray's and Kristeva's, has been so influential that it would be impossible, as well as irresponsible, for me not to face it.

In what is perhaps her most popular book in this country, *The Newly Born Woman*, written in collaboration with Catherine Clément and originally published in 1975, Cixous calls for a rethinking of the maternal. She criticizes some feminist denunciations of the oppressiveness of motherhood (in contrast with her exaltation of its impressiveness), such as Simone de Beauvoir's in *The Second Sex*, and the patriarchal inability, or unwillingness, to see a woman as mother. In masculine mythology, the mother is virgin, the mother is desexualized—as if sexuality were not inherent in motherhood, I would add, regardless of the mode of its inception, as if sexuality were restricted to coitus alone. "If there is a specific thing repressed, that is where it is found: the taboo of the pregnant woman (which says a lot about the power that seems invested in her). It is because they have always suspected that the pregnant woman not only doubles her market value but, especially, valorizes *herself as a woman* in her own eyes, and undeniably takes on weight and sex" (*The Newly Born Woman*, 90). Cixous' evocative, hyperbolic language brings together cultural repression and self-empowerment over the pregnant body, whose physical increase and therefore visible sexuality add value rather than shame and/or modesty to the eyes of the (self-)beholder. It is repression, cultural repression, that has symptomatically exchanged the positive value for a negative one. The taboo surrounding pregnancy is the token of the repression of its power—hinting, perhaps, at Irigaray's theory of the original matricide at the basis of civilization. In the words of Michelle Boulous Walker, "Patriarchal systems of representation repress the (carnal) knowledge that the mother's body is a sexual one" (136). In this repression lies one of the many paradoxes of maternity: although maternity is impossible without sexuality (and traditional patriarchal thought could not envision contemporary techniques of artificial reproduction nor could it articulate perhaps the sexuality inherent in the experiences of pregnancy, labor, delivery, breastfeeding), this constitutive sexuality is a blind spot in the horizon of maternal perceptions, perceptions of the maternal.

Although she is quick to note the essentialist overtones of Cixous' representation of the maternal, Gayatri Chakravorti Spivak prefers to focus, far more productively than Delphy I think, on the ethical imperative flowing from Cixous' selective use of the name "mother" as "paleonymy," as a traditional metaphysical term that can be used in new, potentially transgressive ways. For Spivak, Cixous' sense of mothering is ultimately a relationship with the other woman—not, then, with a child of her body. If this shift of interlocutor seems to contradict the thrust of my book—I focus on maternity as the process constituting women as mothers via the intermediary, though not the only intermediary, of the female body—it also paradoxically confirms it. For unlike the figuration of metaphorical motherhood, coupled in Western culture with the real mother's political and cultural disempowerment, the very figuration I strive to avoid in my argument, Spivak's elaboration of Cixous on mothering avoids any narrow use of the maternal, the motherly, the matronizing. Rather, Spivak's Cixous formulates a demand for the effortful responsibility of practice: the selfless love instantiated in the mother is to be inscribed in the woman's relationship with the other woman, through a practice that, again paradoxically, we cannot grasp, a practice that constitutes "the undecidable in view of which decisions *must* be risked" ("French Feminism Revisited," 68). Later Spivak refers to "Cixous' impossible dimension of giving woman to the other woman" (72); this dimension, despite its perceived impossibility, beckons toward the ethical as the space from which, in which women may negotiate their subjectivity. As the ethical implies a relationship with the other, the ethical as the maternal functions as the space and time of a radically different contact with otherness and with subjectivity—a connection that is both internal (the child) and external (the other woman). This ethical contact is characterized by a relation in which the other and the self are enabled to exist; it is a relation, furthermore, that is sex-specific, marked, like pregnancy and childbirth, by sexual difference. Because women are able to become mothers and because women exist at the margins of masculine culture, they can more easily than men accept the bond to the (m)other, can more willingly experience the risky disruptions to subjectivity brought on by this bond as an encounter with otherness. Thus Braidotti also notes the ethical dimension of Cixous' work when she writes that "Cixous defines the ability to accept otherness as a new science, a new discourse that is based on the idea of respectful affinity between self and other" ("Of Bugs and Women," 133).

The taboo of pregnancy is interpreted in the Cixous passage from which I quoted earlier as being based on the cultural denial or repression of an unbearably powerful woman: one whose body and sex do not tolerate concealment, demanding instead to be seen and to become known. Hers is a body in relation to which writing is produced and understood. Furthermore, it is the inscription of the maternal body and its ongoing impact on our adult use of language that inform and unsettle the official patriarchal language we speak and write. This is part of Cixous' evocation of *écriture féminine*, or a feminine, female practice of writing that cannot be theorized or encoded. Cixous first wrote of *écriture féminine* in her essay "The Laugh of the Medusa," and, as Toril Moi notes, "it is largely due to the efforts of Hélène Cixous that the question of an *écriture féminine* came to occupy a central position in the political and cultural debate in France in the 1970s." (*Sexual/Textual Politics*, 102). In fact, despite its inability to be theorized, both Cixous and feminist critics indebted to Cixous have repeatedly attempted to describe what *écriture féminine* is. In part, Cixous' analogy between body and writing in *écriture féminine* works also thanks to what Spivak calls Cixous' "somewhat unexamined belief in the power of poetry and art in general" ("French Feminism Revisited," 66). Lisa Walsh, more substantially, writes that this *écriture* "refutes the exclusive mastery of the paternal Symbolic and opens into the possibility of an inclusive connection with a maternally inspired expression of a self always already indebted to her (m)other" (348). Through this return to the notion of the debt to the (m)other expressed in writing, *écriture féminine* links Cixous' thought to the concept of female genealogy and the Italian feminist development of the mother's symbolic order as the place of maternal impressions and maternal knowledge.

Like Elisabetta Rasy's "nurturer's language"—a concept developed by an Italian feminist critic and writer of fiction (like Cixous) but which draws extensively from contemporary French feminist theory—Cixous' *écriture féminine* challenges the masculine symbolic by including the maternal body in writing: writing is de-phallicized, is associated with, even analogous to, pregnancy and, more generally, with female sexuality and with sexual difference as the subversion of the binary scheme of thought characteristic of the logocentric tradition. It is worth remembering, however, that *écriture féminine* does not mean writing by women. Ironically, Cixous' work consists of both creative pieces of theater and fiction (instances of *écriture féminine*) and of critical readings of avant-garde male poets and theoreticians, in whose texts the feminine is seen to emerge. Women, on the other hand, have for Cixous largely been writing as "men," even though women today, Cixous admits, have a privileged relation with, and access to *écriture féminine* (witness her own prolific production). But, as Morag Shiach poignantly wonders, "Can we really feel that a writing practice is meant just for us, when it seems to be done so much better by Genet or Kleist?" (159).

Also controversial is the link *écriture féminine* evokes with essentialism. If on the one hand *écriture féminine* deconstructs binarism in the name of difference, which underscores that meaning is a process of deferral à la Derrida, on the other hand, as Moi notes, this deconstructive impetus "is opposed and undercut by a vision of woman's writing steeped in the very metaphysics of presence [Cixous] claims she is out to unmask," a vision constituting "a full-blown metaphysical account of writing as voice, presence, and origin" (*Sexual/Textual Politics*, 110, 119). Diana Fuss analogously points out that the much-discussed concept of *écriture féminine* is the most sophisticated expression of notions such as "the autonomy of a female voice and the potentiality of a feminine language," whose claims are underwritten by essentialism (2). In her lyrical-theoretical elaborations, Cixous consciously takes the risks of essentialism to emphasize that in our culture women must come to writing through the maternal body, itself a metaphor of writing; and whenever the maternal is invoked by a feminist, I have come to realize, paradox and contradictions, leading to implacable (self) criticism, are just around the corner. Yet, although it is culturally embedded and thus never immune to the infiltrations of patriarchal discourse, the maternal is potentially a privileged place for women to reformulate the cultural and the epistemological through their own sex-specific writing practice. Against Lacan's theory of the subject's complete separation from the mother with its entrance into the patriarchal symbolic order, *le Nom/Non du Père*, the Name of the Father as the Father's Law, Cixous' theory of *écriture féminine*, like Kristeva's notion of the pre-Oedipal, hysteromorphic, semiotic *chora*, the preconscious womb, argues for a continued impact of the mother's body, of its rhythms and articulations, on the speaker/writer.

Cixous does not delineate precisely how women could write differently, how we could subvert language without at the same time using it to express ourselves. *Écriture féminine*, she insists, cannot be theorized or defined, for it escapes traditional linguistic borders. Still her insistence on the role of the body in writing (writing as an activity of the body and the body as a source of imagery, as a way of understanding the world) is a fertile one especially in the context of pregnancy and childbirth. These images significantly recur in Cixous' *The Newly Born Woman* and in her work in general. For pregnancy and childbirth, with their challenges to bodily boundaries and to self-definition, physically illustrate the disruptions of the self that are entailed by the encounter with an Other, with difference—and thus, I would claim, with ethics and the invitation underscored in Spivak's reading quoted above: "How could the woman, who has experienced the not-me within me, not have a particular relation to the written? To writing as giving itself away (cutting itself off) from the source?" (*The Newly Born Woman*, 90). The experience of the not-me in me is most strikingly figured, I believe, in the experience of quickening, the physical as well as intellectual and emotional awareness, the "dys" state, brought on by pregnancy. And at the same time the maternal provides a framework (a risky one, no doubt, given its proximity to biologism and prescriptive motherhood) to think openness to the other, to practice enabling the other rather than violently appropriating her/his difference for uniquely self-fulfilling purposes. So for Cixous *écriture féminine* is characterized by a proximity to the voice; the voice is that which binds language to the body and, I would add, that which connects our prenatal relation to the mother with our linguistic relation and debt to her. The sounds and rhythms of the mother's voice point both to the interference of the semiotic into the symbolic (or to the unconscious in language) and to the prenatal perception of language as maternal, as the mother's attribute and gift. Again there is an analogy between what psychoanalysis terms the pre-Oedipal and the economy of the prenatal in texts of childbirth and pregnancy. Both are times and places in which the rhythms and articulations of the mother's body are inscribed in our subjectivity. The inclusion, in the process of writing, of the maternal body, entails lifting it out of repression, implies acknowledging that bond (Italian feminists would call it a debt) to the mother, hence to the presymbolic (and I would add prenatal) relation between self and (m)other—in contrast to the alienating loss and separation predicated by discourses such as traditional psychoanalysis.

In her 1976 essay "Coming to Writing," where the action described in the title is posited as maternally motivated and thus displacing phallic dominance, Cixous revels in the description of the birthing woman as sensuous and desirable, powerful and resourceful. Her words evoke an event of the body and of the spirit, an event in which the flesh is never erased in the communion with its other. And yet at the same time Cixous is also speaking of giving birth to oneself, of breastfeeding oneself, of mother's milk as inebriating ink—and vice versa: "Writing: as if I had the urge to go on enjoying, to feel full, to push, to feel the force of my muscles, and my harmony, to be pregnant and at the same time to give myself the joys of parturition" ("Coming to Writing," 31). The female body is in these pages the place from which the self begins, and from which the other begins as well; births are organic and metaphoric, no matter, because more than that, they are ethical. The female body is the place from which the inside—a child, a text—travels to the outside; it is the place and time of this travel, and thus the place and time when and where the two are one and the binary is broken. The body, the female body, the maternal body, emits writing even as it incorporates it. Far from being foreclosed or denied, this body is celebrated and identified with; one's continuity with it is in turn productively acknowledged and embodied.

Late-nineteenth- and early-twentieth-century women writers, however, are not as exultant as some of Cixous' texts in their reinscription of the maternal body within literary (re)production. If Deledda's unnamed woman transgresses the limits imposed on female desire by loving a mouflon, in silencing the male offspring of patriarchal genealogy she also silences, painfully, her own child. And Marta in *L'indomani,* as we have seen, finds in the experience of quickening knowledge, yes, but knowledge of a lack. These writers' ambivalence conforms to Stanton's advice, in her detailed analysis of French feminists' images of maternity and the dilemmas they pose, that "the moment the maternal emerges as a new dominance, it must be put into question before it congeals as feminine essence, as unchanging in-difference" ("Difference on Trial," 174). Certainly the maternal–feminine can be used heuristically, as "enabling mythology," in Stanton's words, to rework images and meanings in a way that negates and subverts "paternal hierarchies" (174). But Stanton's caveat is against Cixous' threatened return to a metaphysics of identity and presence. Stanton's fear is that Cixous' exaltation of the maternal may ultimately lead us back to the myths of natural motherhood and biological certainty that women have fought so hard to overcome. And Stanton's invitation is to question the metaphor of maternity and the concept of difference in favor of metonymic deferral, which, although dangerous because itself a traditional feminine posture, may be, in Stanton's colorful conclusion, "the most desirable course for diverse female explorations than excessive, tumescent metaforeplay" (177).

Stanton reads Irigaray's, Kristeva's, and Cixous' constructions of maternity as fundamentally metaphorical and thus anchoring women to materiality and corporeality. Although she appreciates these three thinkers' expansion of the traditional conceptions of the maternal, Stanton remains unconvinced that their maternal metaphor is capable of inventing a different language, be it poetic or theoretical. Rather, in Stanton's view, the maternal–feminine remains a metaphoric reproduction of the Law of the Father. The way out of this impasse is for this critic the rhetorical movement afforded by metonymy. Unlike metaphor, metonymy moves away from the condensation between woman and the maternal to underscore instead difference—including differences among women: "for if all women are maternal, where's the difference(s)?" Stanton pointedly asks (175). Her evocation of metonymy as the trope without a name, though, as a multiple supplement, as suggestive of lack of being, however seductive, is itself an idealization; in its phobia of essentialism, Stanton's essay subtracts from the knowledge inscribed into and inscriptive of maternity texts (her critique of maternal metaphors briefly extends to American feminist constructions of maternity as well, such as Ruddick's, Rich's, Chodorow's), in order to then place this residual knowledge in an imaginary metonymic text that is nowhere to be found. Unfortunately, the effect of Stanton's argument is to once again silence maternity in the name of something greater that is nowhere—literally utopia, the same utopia, perhaps, of which Stanton herself accuses the French and American feminists she considers.

Like Italian feminist philosopher Luisa Muraro, Cixous insists on the mother's gift of language as opposed to her relegation to a silent pre-Oedipal world, on the first voice as the mother's voice, on the continuing impact of the mother's body in adult life—an impact acknowledged more easily by women than by men. She does this most emphatically in *Breaths* (*Souffles* in French, 1975), one of Cixous' most difficult texts: breath is related to rhythm, flow, a recurring motion, a pattern of sounds and movements like voice. *Breaths* was significantly published in the same year as "The Laugh of the Medusa," though not nearly as promptly translated into English; we cannot thus speak of an intellectual progression. More likely, the two are different recastings of some of the same issues: the maternal, the mother–daughter bond, and their representation in language and culture, for example. Here, in the course of her repeated returns to the mother's body, Cixous is not afraid to invoke the destructive aspects of our relationship to it. I use the word "afraid" carefully, for the criticism of feminist exaltations of the maternal, like antiessentialist criticism in general, is plagued by a troubling fear. The association of womanhood with motherhood, and the valorization of the latter, is perceived by many feminist critics as dangerous. Claire Kahane, for example, writes that the yearning of writers such as Cixous "to make reparation to the mother, to undo the devaluation of the feminine by restoring to the mother her lost respect and authority through the body, is seductive, but *risky* to the feminist project" (83, my emphasis). Lynne Huffer speaks of "Irigaray's later meanderings into *dangerously* amniotic and even heterosexual spaces" (*Maternal Pasts,* 24, my emphasis). The title of Teresa De Lauretis's famed essay on the essentialism debate is indicative of this pattern: "The Essence of the Triangle, or Taking the *Risk* of Essentialism Seriously" (my emphasis). More examples can be found by perusing the pages of much feminist theory. Why so much fear, I ask, and why so much fear of exalting the maternal, when there is so much else to be afraid of? Why not be afraid, more productively, of the debasement of women's contributions to our world—including our contributions as symbolic as well as biological mothers? This emphasis on risk and danger reminds me of an encouraging statement by Derrida on Lacan: "To have courage, here, would be to read Lacan, among others, and to respect the difficulty and the heterogeneity of his works. It would involve isolating the layers in which he repeats phallogocentric presuppositions while giving him credit for having opened up a closed system elsewhere in his writings" (14). A comparable approach may be helpful as we read texts of maternity, an approach founded on respect and credit, as well as on the isolation of phallogocentric layers, an approach based on the courage to face the reading of difficulty and heterogeneity: "And so courage, in this context, consists of saying, 'Well, things are not simple' " (Derrida, 14).

Maternal things are not simple indeed. In *Breaths,* Cixous' dreamlike meditation on the desire to possess and to abase the mother's body, especially as this body displays pregnancy, at once exorcises the daughter's ambivalence toward the mother and indicts the masculine desire to appropriate woman's secret—a desire we encountered earlier in this chapter, a desire paradigmatic of the scientific method and encoded, for example, in some uses of ultrasound technology. Cixous writes about the mother in *Breaths*—the heavy breathing of labor and childbirth, the labor of speech and writing: "I wanted her pregnant: I need her full up. And slowed down. No interest in the contents: girl, honey or gold, it makes no difference. Pregnant, with a pregnancy which possesses and divides her" (54). The mother is always-already split; she is not a whole, unitary referent. Against traditional psychoanalysis, for example, Cixous sees the maternal body as the subject and not the background. Its contents, for once, are not what matters. She has no interest in them, they make "no difference." But pregnancy makes the mother, which the anonymous first-person female narrator is about to attack, more vulnerable, for she is "slowed down" and even "possessed," "divided" by her pregnant state. The narrator continues: "I need her in the right condition, when towards the seventh month her swollen belly becomes difficult to control and the occupant turns against her" (54). It is then that the mother, "overtaken, inhabited," is "more vulnerable," is "more than herself so less than herself" (54). It is at that point in time—toward the seventh month—that, for the narrator, the mother is "beautiful," and it is then that we read: "I have given orders that your secret be torn from your body alive" (54).

The underlying connection between pregnancy and writing prevents the silencing of the maternal body, its reduction to matter, for the maternal body in this text is always also a writing body—not just a written one. We could think as well, for example, of the stories generated by pregnancy and childbirth among communities of women, the endless conversations, chatter, narratives of pregnancy and childbirth that mothers never tire of producing. So language, the mother tongue, must be learned from the mother's body, her voice, her song—at the cost of stealing it, at the cost of tearing it away from her. It is true that the mother in this passage is physically full, yet we can hardly describe this fullness as metaphysical, as the sign of unified presence and univocal meaning. Nor are we in the presence of that privileged unity of mother and child vehemently criticized by feminist critics. And it would be disingenuously literal to interpret this passage as conveying, in Kahane's words, "the idea that the mother has some sort of unitary meaning for her daughter" (85). Nor does this passage support Kahane's critique that "feminist idealizations [like Cixous'] of maternal plenitude merely confirm the fantasmatic mother, the good breast, and by denying ambivalence promote the repression and thus consequent perpetuation of her other, fantasmatically destructive side" (85). If *Breaths* had appeared in English in 1975 instead of "The Laugh of the

Medusa," would the unity of French feminism over the subject of the maternal been so easily constructed, celebrated, attacked?

Once again, it is in a paradoxical construction of maternity that meaning is engendered. Paradox is indeed an appropriate, although imperfect word to describe the palpable contradictions inside and between Cixous' maternity texts. Rather than pushing us to quickly dismiss Cixous' readings, these contradictions reveal the inscription and suppression of the maternal in patriarchal as well as in feminist discourse. These contradictions and paradoxes place Cixous' work right among the many maternity works we are encountering, as well as within a characteristically contemporary discursive, self-transforming, culturally disruptive approach to the question of reading: "the diachronic emergence of the unthought, of the initially unreadable," as Robert Con Davis describes it. Davis maintains that Cixous's interpretive strategy, which he identifies as "oppositional reading," ultimately "fails," yet this failure itself—which can be productively compared to what I have identified as the failure to pin down maternity, to read it unequivocally—is "a cultural mode of 'reading' ideologically that we are only beginning to situate as an historical practice, a kind of 'reading' that, in fact, as Cixous hoped, would move us out of linear and oppressive masculine patterns" (279, 282). I conclude with this quotation because it extends in ways that I do not feel qualified to do my argument about the impossibility of speaking of maternity univocally and reasonably. It expands, that is, the notion of the unrepresentability of maternal discourse into the wider cultural and political system inside which, in turn, that impossibility was conceived, developed, and delivered.

Deledda's and Neera's texts, like those of many of their contemporaries and of our own, impel us to ask the questions formulated in a different context by philosopher and cultural critic Susan Bordo, and they may also help and encourage us to find multiple, polyvocal answers. In *Unbearable Weight,* Bordo wonders: "Is pregnancy merely a cultural construction, capable of being shaped into multitudinous social forms? Or does the unique configuration of embodiment presented in pregnancy—the having of another within oneself, simultaneously both part of oneself and separate from oneself—constitute a distinctively female epistemological and ethical resource?" (36). Late-nineteenth- and early-twentieth-century literary texts and contemporary theoretical elaborations often answer "yes" to the latter question: a painful yes, a qualified yes, for too easily is this epistemological and ethical resource silenced, misunderstood, turned against itself, or worse yet ignored. Still, pregnancy and, particularly, quickening can constitute for women a valuable experience, understood most profitably perhaps within an epistemological and ethical framework. Through the feeling of fetal movement writers can represent, literally as well as metaphorically and symbolically, the woman's ability to know the other and/as the self, and to act responsibly on such a knowledge. Yet these representations easily risk being obfuscated in a worldview that has relegated all senses other than seeing or hearing to a secondary status and defined all knowledge that is not disembodied and abstract as useless.

This is especially true of what Italian feminist psychologist Letizia Comba describes as a *sixth sense*—that is, proprioception, or the internal perception of one's body, of one's self. Comba, a member of the philosophical community Diotima, connected to the University of Verona and founded in 1984 by a group of feminists including Luisa Muraro, appropriates proprioception for a feminist understanding of the body. Although it is the newborn's first sense, in relation to which all other senses develop, proprioception is not considered reliable in our culture because it cannot be verified by eyesight. What Comba sets out to do, following a lead of early-childhood psychoanalyst Melanie Klein, is to explore the ways in which the inside of the mother's body—and of women's body more generally—contributes to the constitution of "the perceptive, affective, intellective, relational universe in which we live as women" (158). The inside of the mother's body is "the originary site of projection, and therefore a starting point for the investigation of the female imaginary" (157). A feminist appropriation of proprioception, then, would go beyond, for example, the bodily self-representation, the imaginary anatomy that psychoanalysis places at the basis of hysterical symptoms. Comba starts her analysis with the fact that women's sex is not visible, and not with the issues raised by pregnancy, yet her argument repeatedly returns to the mother's body, and more specifically to the "maternal cavity"—with which women, qua potential mothers themselves, necessarily entertain a different relationship than men do. But because of the masculine primacy in invention, science, art, and communication, it is men who have constructed the rules that describe women's imaginary. Multiple exceptions to this can be cited, I would add, beginning of course with the texts I discuss in this book, yet Comba's point is critical. An obvious example is the primacy accorded to the penis or phallus in psychoanalysis on the basis of its visibility, and hence its verifiability. The same can be said of women's pleasure, of women's orgasm: It cannot be seen, it leaves no trace and thus no evidence of ever having taken place—unlike men's. Most significantly, however, women's very existence could be considered unverifiable: "Who could verify if I tell the truth about what I feel, if I feel what I am?" Comba poignantly asks (158). From a scientific perspective, proprioception does not exist (which is not that far from Lacan's controversial and well-known assertion that woman does not exist).

Although it mentions labor and delivery, Comba's text does not explicitly discuss the experience of pregnancy. Nevertheless, her reflections are relevant to our present discussion of feminism, textuality, and maternity. They can be extended to the experience of quickening as exemplary of the significance of proprioception in the constitution of subjectivity, and in turn they extend this unique psychobiological experience to the experience of sexual difference of women in general—and not only pregnant ones. Comba's thrust, nevertheless, is not to bring out the inside, to turn what is internal into an external, for to do so would after all reinforce the very dichotomy she seeks to overthrow: the inside, associated with the subjective, imaginary, confused, emotional, and the outside—figured instead as visible and therefore objective, real, intelligible, orderly. Rather, a new articulation between these two spaces needs to be established, one that would do justice to the ways in which women experience and describe what they feel and what they see. A new articulation that would not rob women, in Comba's words, of "the root of our feeling, which is internal" (158). This new articulation encompasses the mind–body continuum expressed in late-nineteenth- and early-twentieth-century women writers' representation of quickening. How can we describe, without a tradition to help us, a corporeal version of subjectivity, or, alternatively, a psychological corporeality—without falling into dualism all over again? Feminist theorist Elizabeth Grosz, for one, argues in a vein analogous to Comba's for the development of metaphors and models of the body, models that "must demonstrate some sort of internal or constitutive articulation, or even disarticulation, between the biological and the psychological, between the inside and the outside of the body, while avoiding a reductionism of mind to brain" (*Volatile Bodies,* 23).

Also analogous to Comba's discussion of women's proprioception is Irigaray's emphasis on the "mucous," or mucosity, in her 1984 book *An Ethics of Sexual Difference.* The nontheorized mucous is "that most intimate interior of my flesh" (170), it belongs to the inside of the body, it is "experienced from within," it may even "perhaps take the place of the soul for women" (109), and it is significantly referred to in the context of a chapter that discusses intrauterine life, "The Invisible of the Flesh," and in one on the relationship between women—especially mothers and daughters ("Love of Same, Love of Other"). A figure of tactile proximity, the mucous can be associated with Irigaray's more general emphasis on fluidity as a marker of sexual difference: the connection between the fluid and the feminine is predicated on the difference of the female body, of which the mucous is an instance. (As a sexed bodily secretion, the mucous also reminds me of Cixous' figuration of mother's milk as white ink, as an important metaphor for *écriture féminine* in Cixous' writings.) For although it is known by both sexes in the prenatal bond, the mucous "is far more important in setting up the intimacy of bodily perception and its threshold for women"—the threshold, that is, that ensures passage between the inward and the outward, that very passage evoked in Comba's discussion of proprioception as the rupture of this binary. Irigaray elevates the importance of the mucous to the point of stating unequivocally that "Any thinking of or about the female has to think through the mucous" (*An Ethics of Sexual Difference*, 110) because "women are interiority and also exteriority," as Comba also suggests, and yet "often they lack the power to experience the inward and the outward, more particularly because they live their lives as a *threshold* that ensures passage between the two" (*An Ethics of Sexual Difference*, 106–7). The dichotomy between inside and outside, then, can be overcome thanks and through what the female body can teach us, show us, lead us to. It is indeed the debt to that most primordial of spaces, the maternal body, the uterine cavity, which phallogocentric thought has attempted to systematically obliterate.

Irigaray stresses the materiality of maternity with an etymological play that underscores the maternal foundations of materialism and, conversely, the material, bodily foundations of maternity itself as an expression of female sexuality and thus of sexual difference. As Braidotti notes, central to Irigaray's project "is the quest for an alternative female genealogy, by immersion into the maternal imaginary. For Irigaray this takes the form of the exploration of images that represent the female experience of proximity to the mother's body" ("Of Bugs and Women," 123). Thus in *Elemental Passions* the mucous is mentioned in relation to the womb and in a meditation on the maternal–fetal connection (14). With its emphasis on otherness and relationship, the mucous—a pregnant image for our discussion of quickening—may be compared to that other, better-known image of Irigaray's project: the lips or labia that star in "When Our Lips Speak Together," an essay later included in the book *This Sex Which Is Not One*. The lips figure female sexuality as indissolubly bound to the *parler femme* and to the relation to the other. Female lips, or labia (in English the pun does not work, as vaginal labia prudishly retain the Latin name for lips), signify woman and her sexuality as at once one and two, singular and double, as really "the sex which is not one." Like pregnancy, like the mucous, the lips are a plural figure critiquing the phallogocentric, universalist subject as a patriarchal illusion of total being. Like her lips, woman is not one, she is traversed by difference. Essentializing, perhaps, yet it is through this strategic essentialism that phallomorphic binary thinking (which includes the putative opposition between essentialism and antiessentialism), can be effectively reversed and displaced. Like the mucous, like quickening, the two lips point to a continuous touching that disrupts the primacy accorded to sight. This is the sensory primacy on which phallic primacy is after all predicated. Female sexuality and female identity are both not one and inaccessible to sight alone.

The maternal space then symbolically comes to stand, in Irigaray's discussion, for the contributions of women in general. The masculine universe, as well as masculine subjectivity, are built on the erasure of the maternal space. Masculinity permeates for Irigaray that supposedly neutral, sexually undifferentiated epistemology that instead displays an isomorphism with the male body—culturally correlated with the mind, eagerly forgetful of its own corporeality. The body in pregnancy and childbirth seems to me an especially apt figure for Irigaray's epistemological elaboration. It is in the expression of the experience of quickening, I might add, that interiority, as figured in the mucous, for instance, or even in proprioception, takes epistemological precedence over the normally normative exteriority—the world of sight, the world of the detached, the verifiable, the objective, the real. Although mucous and language at first may seem incompatible in Irigaray's text, the mucous corresponds both to sexuality and to speech; I would even say that the mucous emerges time and again in the linguistic attempts, literary as well as theoretical, to body forth proprioception and thus to establish a woman-centered, or difference-centered epistemology and, analogously, the *parler femme* that could be translated into "speaking (as) woman" (Burke, "Irigaray Through the Looking Glass," 37). This speech, thought, knowledge, this theory, should not be all too easily conflated with essentialism, even a strategic, temporary essentialism, because to do so would be to ignore, in Burke's words, "Irigaray's suggestion that female writing may be produced in analogy *with* the body and her awareness that it does not simply flow from it" (51). *Parler femme* is the basis of Irigaray's powerful images of woman's subjectivity and sexuality—and, conversely, these images constitute the pillars of *parler femme.* The literal, metaphorical, cultural, social links between language and body, while disturbing perhaps to some American feminists, are ever recurring in the written production of French and Italian feminists alike. Yet, as Diana Fuss notes, "The debate over Irigaray's essentialism inevitably comes down to this question of whether the body stands in a literal or a figurative relation to language and discourse" (62).

In the course of the ensuing pages of *Essentially Speaking,* Fuss proposes a reading of this connection as, instead, metonymic—that is, neither literal nor metaphoric, but rather deconstructive of the linguistic and psychoanalytic binary of metaphor and metonymy. This reading is particularly useful within my context of maternal impressions and quickening, for a sort of metaphorical metonymy is indeed the hybrid trope that best expresses the maternal–fetal connection on which the epistemology of quickening is founded. (And we have seen how for Stanton, too, metonymy as deferral is crucial for a productive reinscription of French feminists' construction of motherhood and for our present exploration of feminist alternatives.) Contiguity, the rhetorical movement of metonymy, is intrinsic to both *parler femme*—the two contiguous lips or labia touch each other without replacing each other or woman—and to a representation of pregnancy that escapes both the orders of medical pathology and bourgeois idealization. Metonymy is intrinsic as well to the construction of a pregnant woman who is neither metaphorically condensed into the child she carries nor symbolically assimilated to the eternal feminine. And yet, insofar as these pregnant women are (in) literary texts, they are always necessarily metaphorical as well, displacing other possible representations and standing in for an embodied female position within the patriarchal order of turn-of-the-century Italy, for example.

Sources in past and present writings can be found, and ought to be found, in order to better construct the articulation between internal and external dimensions and thus dismantle their seeming, and, for some, ideologically convenient opposition. It is in this deconstructive process that one may perhaps find theoretical elements to help heal that split within feminist theory—between equality and difference, between reclaiming identity and displacing it, between American feminists and French and Italian feminists (and without minimizing the differences within each of these terms). The literature of pregnancy, I would claim, forms an impressive body of texts in the development of the story of women's proprioception, in turn part of the larger history of the human body. These figurations, these reproductions intertwine the voice of language, language as it is physically (re)produced, with a reproductive body that constitutes itself and/as the other. They represent the procreation of subjectivity at its carnal inception, even as they posit a peculiarly female, singularly unvisualized knowledge of selfhood, otherness, and their constitutive inextricability. If the body can represent the procreative effort of discursive practices, it also always proceeds from physiological tissues and mechanisms, so it seems pertinent, necessary even, to ask again: Can pregnancy be a place, a space, a time of knowledge—a knowledge that, barring unforeseeable scientific discoveries, must remain the prerogative of women? And can such knowledge then be turned into words and actions? Or does/must it remain within the space of silence, however pregnant? In the quotation from *Fisiologia della donna* with which I opened the second section of this chapter, the pregnant woman's husband as described by Paolo Mantegazza "non sente." He does not feel, he will not hear, he cannot sense. He is not impressed, we could say. But that does not mean that we should not be.

Maternal Metamorphosis, or the Changing Body

Impressions of Deformity

Maternal Deformity in Advice Manuals and Freud's Schreber Case

During the second trimester, pregnant women are often said to "bloom." Morning sickness is usually gone by this time, some energy returns—and with it, "moods lift and spirits rise" says one manual, "skin and hair seem to improve noticeably and the abdomen is usually large enough so that people realize that you're pregnant and not just a little overweight" (Feldman, 70). But in the third trimester mother troubles start again, what with massive weight gain, the mask of pregnancy, and stretch marks—to refer to aesthetic changes alone. Because, in fundamental ways, the aesthetic identities of pregnant women are multiple, contradictory, making the theorization of motherhood, in a very real sense, impossible. Even within the relatively narrow confines of the Western world, even among the white, educated middle class, the interpretations and self-interpretations of the pregnant and maternal body, by which I mean the body as it is changed by the bearing of children, vary dramatically. What is perceived by some as a curvy, sensual body is seen by others as unsightly, obese, even grotesque. In a fascinating book about the maternal experience of animals, primatologist Sarah Blaffer Hrdy asserts that "Pregnancy and motherhood forever change a woman. I do not merely mean depletion of maternal resources like calcium, a stretching and redistribution of her tissues, or alterations in her hormone profile" (94–95). As if these were not enough, Hrdy describes changes in the mother's immune response, the presence of fetal cells in the mother's body for as long as twenty-seven years, pathological reactions to these foreign cells, alterations of the brain and of certain sensory capacities: "When a new mother says (as I did) that the birth of her first baby transformed her, she is not speaking just metaphorically" (94–95). Maternal transformations reach into the recesses of biology and psychology, body and spirit, ethics and aesthetics. They are impressive indeed.

Maternity clothes reflect to some extent the wide spectrum of interpretations of this self-transforming maternal body: some attempt to hide it, though usually that cannot last long; some heighten to the point of ridicule, displacing desire from the viewer by calling attention to the wearer as container, for example; while other clothes, mostly expensive ones, accentuate the sexy aspects of the pregnant shape. Maternity clothes matter, for they underline the boundary between self and nonself that dress itself, as threshold, forges. If dress, that is, traces a line between our body and the other, maternity clothes point at the same time to the presence of the other within the body, to the broken margin between self and other, subject and object, inside and outside. The very need for other clothes, and specifically for maternity clothes, points to the pregnant body as the place of a crisis in women's sexual identity, a crisis each woman must learn to face one way or another: a crisis that goes well beyond aesthetic differences from her prepregnant self, a crisis that involves varying degrees of self-transformation as a metamorphosis or as a deforming anamorphosis perhaps, guided by myriad factors. One of these factors in contemporary America is the reading of pregnancy advice manuals.

The looks of the pregnant and maternal woman, wherever one places them in the spectrum of aesthetics and sexual desirability, are inextricably bound today to one particular transformation: weight gain. But the issue of weight gain during pregnancy, usually paired with that of weight loss after the pregnancy is over, has itself gone through dramatic changes in the past few decades. "Perhaps no question is asked by more newly pregnant women than 'How much weight should I gain?' " we read in one advice book (Fenlon et al., 16). In 1971 the Boston Children's Medical Center handbook stated that "the average woman will lose fifteen to twenty pounds during the first couple of weeks following delivery. Consequently, your weight gain in pregnancy should not exceed this amount," further warning, rather ominously, that "any extra weight gained in pregnancy is likely to stay with you for the rest of your life" (78–79). Fifteen years later, in 1986, the American College of Obstetricians and Gynecologists (ACOG) recommended "that women of normal weight gain 22 to 26 pounds during pregnancy" (Feldman, 52). In the late nineties, on the other hand, we read references to "the normal 25 to 30 pounds," and that "the sensible and safe weight gain for the average woman is between 25 and 35 pounds" (Curtis, 288; Eisenberg, Murkoff, and Hathaway, 147). Indeed, according to *What to Expect When You're Expecting*, current research indicates that a weight gain under 20 pounds leads to increased premature births, babies too small for their gestational age, and growth retardation in the uterus (Eisenberg, Murkoff, and Hathaway, 147). Significantly this same manual is absolutely obsessed with food; it even has a companion book entitled *What to Eat When You're Expecting*, so similar in title, layout, and general appearance to the original manual that the bookseller and I, confused by the cover, both thought at first they were two editions of the same book.

Breastfeeding, strongly encouraged again in the nineties after a period of formula-feeding frenzy, is supposed to aid in losing much of the excess poundage left over after delivery. But it is a fact of life (or is it?) that women, and particularly mothers, lose shapeliness and desirability with age, and I find myself wondering what types of connections can be theorized between the temporary "deformity" of pregnancy and the more lasting "deformity" with which motherhood is associated. What cultural pressures define maternal shapes as shapeless, the mother's form-ation of the self and of her child as, ultimately, a de-form-ation? And on the other hand, where and how can we read the massive weight gain of pregnancy as appealing in an age that values thinness as the paragon of beauty? Is the pregnant body attractive or grotesque? Or, to couch the question in the pervasive medical vocabulary, is the pregnant body healthy or sick? Is self-transformation necessary for a successful pregnancy? A transformation into what? Is pregnancy a teratogenic cocoon that metamorphoses woman from beautiful butterfly into unsightly caterpillar?

These questions haunt many pregnant women at a time when aesthetic canons prescribe almost-anorexic thinness. In this respect, the authors of *What to Expect When You're Expecting* are kind and optimistic: "in the eyes of many beholders, a pregnant woman isn't just beautiful inside but outside as well. Many women and their husbands consider the rounded pregnant reflection to be the most lovely—and sensuous—of feminine shapes" (Eisenberg, Murkoff, and Hathaway, 160). Not just pregnant women and their husbands feel this way if it is true that, as Yvonne Knibiehler writes, in the nineteenth century "pregnant prostitutes were particularly sought after by the customers of brothels" ("Bodies and Hearts," 332). But then, is being attracted to the maternal shape equated to a perversion? More realistically, Penny Simkin, Janet Whalley, and Ann Keppler acknowledge the paradoxes of pregnancy when they note that "While one woman may feel ripe, beautiful, and sexual, another may feel clumsy and fat . . . One partner may feel anxious about the woman's health or turned off by her changing appearance, while another relishes the entire process" (138). Tracie Hotchner's *Pregnancy and Childbirth* devotes a more in-depth section to the pregnant woman's fear of loss of sexual attractiveness, focusing on the changes of body image that occur during pregnancy and comparing these changes to those experienced at puberty. But life is an attitude, the author optimistically implies, when she encourages her readers as follows: "Try to view what is happening to your body as a wondrous transformation. If you stop thinking of your bulging belly as fat, you will begin to see it as globelike, shining, and uniquely beautiful. A pregnant belly is a sensual, sensuous object; have you noticed how people want to stroke it?" (231).

I don't know many women who like their belly, pregnant or not, to be stroked by "people," so rather than answering the question about the aesthetic value of the pregnant body the above quotations point out its embeddedness in questions of sexual identity and subjectivity, of body and culture, of self and other. Throughout these pages, I assume the body to be both a biological and a cultural entity, a signifier that is at once corporeal and linguistic. As Susan Rubin Suleiman has written, "the cultural significance of the female body is not only (not even first and foremost) that of a flesh-and-blood entity, but that of a *symbolic construct*" ("Introduction," 2). This double role of the body is especially evident in the case of the gestating woman, whose change of bodily shape also entails a change of meaning: like the pregnant belly, the signifier of pregnancy, be it literary or scientific, must swell in order to accommodate otherness and change. Significantly, the Italian dictionary definition of the verb *deformare* (to deform) is dual, literal and figurative, and underlines the epistemological link between physical shape and language, between morphology and semantics: "1. To change the shape of something. . . . 2. fig. To change the meaning of something" (Zingarelli, 476). The pregnant shape, that is, undergoes an alteration that is both bodily and linguistic. In this process, it challenges metaphysical imperatives to unity, sameness, oneness. Aesthetic distaste, as well as repugnance and even horror, are the palpable effects of such alteration: from object of desire to reproductive apparatus, from shapely to shapeless, the pregnant woman in the texts I consider in this chapter is repeatedly constructed as deformed, disfigured, at times even disgusting. Her heterogeneity, expressive and impressive at once, challenges coherent meaning and univocal sense.

Throughout the literature of pregnancy, we encounter pregnant women viewed as unsightly or grotesque, in the throes of profound transformations or metamorphoses. Rather than add similar descriptions at this point, let me turn to a different grotesque, transformative representation of pregnancy: A male body that perceives itself to be female and pregnant. I am referring to Daniel Paul Schreber in Sigmund Freud's case study *Psychoanalytic Notes on an Autobiographical Account of a Case of Paranoia (Dementia Paranoides),* first published in 1911. This is the only one among Freud's five major case studies to be based on a text written by someone Freud had never met, Daniel Paul Schreber's *Memoirs of My Nervous Illness* (1903). Schreber's *Memoirs* were made up of the scraps and notebooks kept by its author during his nine-year stay at a public asylum, and this fact is repeatedly mentioned to show the reciprocity of psychoanalysis and literary criticism: all interpretation, including psychoanalytic therapy, is a textual exercise.

In his *Psychoanalytic Notes,* Freud interprets Schreber's madness as paranoia generated by his strenuous rejection of homosexuality, as a psychosis brought about by Schreber's inability, that is, to neither accept nor effectively suppress his own homosexual desire. Freud describes, with abundant quotations, the story of this formerly respectable man whose bodily integrity is shattered as he is transformed by God into a female body through a laborious, miraculous process Schreber expressively calls his "unmanning." Thanks to Schreber's attractive feminized nerves, God has been drawn closer to the earth, turning the world, in Schreber's psychosis, into a miracle-filled scenario. Schreber's slow transformation into a woman preludes his redemption of the world, in this psychotic's view: Schreber's fate, which at first horrifies him but to which he finally becomes a willing participant, is to become God's chosen bride, God's wife, through his acquisition of female nerves and his miraculous unmanning into a female body. It is out of his nerves that "a new race of men will proceed, through a process of direct impregnation by God" (*Psychoanalytic Notes,* 17). And indeed Schreber notes that "the further consequence of my emasculation could, of course, only be my impregnation by divine rays to the end that a new race of men might be created" (*Psychoanalytic Notes,* 21).

Freud, however, gives little emphasis to the reproductive aim of Schreber's sex change; perhaps that would imply giving unprecedented attention to the role and the authority of the mother, to the womb as full source of power rather than as lack desperately beckoning to be filled with a penis (envy). Thus, Schreber's mother and his own mothering fantasies play a minor role in the case study, with Freud dwelling instead on other aspects of Schreber's unmanning—above all, the heightened pleasure, or "soul-voluptuousness," of Schreber's new female persona. It is to a footnote that Freud rather dismissively relegates Schreber's pregnancy fantasy:

> Something occurred in my own body similar to the conception of Jesus Christ in an immaculate virgin, that is, in a woman who had never had intercourse with a man. On two separate occasions (both while I was in Professor Flechsig's sanatorium) I have possessed female genitals, though somewhat imperfectly developed ones, and have felt a stirring in my body, such as would arise from the quickening of a human embryo. Nerves of God corresponding to male semen had, by a divine miracle, been projected into my body, and impregnation had thus taken place. (*Psychoanalytic Notes*, 32)

Mistaking, as is all too often the case, the Catholic dogma of Mary's immaculateness as a description of her virginity in conceiving Jesus, rather than of Mary's own "immaculate conception" in her own mother's womb (unlike the rest of us, Mary was conceived in Anne's womb without original sin, hence she was "immaculately conceived"), Schreber can identify with that woman who, like him, never had intercourse with a man. Married to a woman with whom he had sexual intercourse, the man Schreber was not a virgin in the traditional sense. Nevertheless, he was a virgin like Mary because like her he never had sex with a man. Since God is clearly, in his delusion, male, then Schreber's body is, like Mary's own, virginal, pure, especially apt at containing God's offspring. He is immaculate and he is pregnant. (It is perhaps symptomatic that, in his discussion of the Schreber case, Jacques Lacan devotes a paragraph to the Virgin Mary without however noting that Schreber himself had compared his situation to hers, 279.)

The discourse of the psychotic can be deciphered and understood. This is Freud's breakthrough in his analysis of Schreber's *Memoirs.* According to Freud, Schreber abandoned his desire for the mother and yet identified himself with her position, under threat of castration by the father. His is a negative, inverted Oedipus, then, since it is the father who is the object of Schreber's passive homosexual desire. For Lacan, who dedicated his third *Seminar,* entitled *The Psychoses,* to the Schreber case, the foreclosure of the symbolic, of the Name of the Father, of the Father' Law, is the lot of the psychotic. Thus, Schreber's personality is missing an unconscious key signifier. Schreber is fixated on the real father's function of generation, and attempts to capture it through his delusional, imaginary proliferation of little Schrebers; these are figured as spermatozoa. Both Freud and Lacan depend on the Oedipus and its paternal metaphor for their discussion of psychosis. Yet, in either case, Schreber's fixation on reproduction is so pronounced that it seems unimaginable to me not to dwell more at length on his reproductive fantasies as they figure him, and refigure him, reshape him, maternally. (Lacan does refer to the involvement, in the Schreber case, of the feminine function at the level of procreation, but his interpretive method, based on the play and, especially, the absence of paternal signifiers, precludes maternity from entering the case in a significant way, 86.) Schreber's emphasis on his experience of quickening, for example, figures the imaginary as that connection between mother and child before the latter gains access to subjectivity (for Lacan, in the mirror stage, starting at about six months). The imaginary relationship is one of identification and alienation, of aggressive rivalry and erotic attachment. But in this scenario, where the figure of the mother as significant agent is erased, the imaginary connection envisioned by the analyst is not between mother and child, even if both are the protagonists of psychotic fantasies. Rather, it is Professor Flechsig (Schreber's physician) and God who are at once erotic objects and agents of persecution.

For Freud, Schreber's procreative fantasies are proof of the patient's unconscious homosexual desire—itself the cause of his psychosis. Hence their secondary status. They are mentioned in passing so as to buttress the evidence of the true etiology. They are explained as having been produced by the anxiety caused by the threat of castration that is implicit in homosexual desire. The procreative fantasies are not central to psychosis. Could it be argued, though, as it certainly seems plausible, that Schreber's transformation into a woman is necessary to fulfill his procreative fantasies, his desire for example to be pregnant and to give birth? That, etiologically, procreative fantasies—a term wider than pregnancy fantasies—come for Schreber before sexual inversion? Could maternity, womb envy, woman's ability to give life as object of desire and of scorn because bodily rather than spiritual, could all this be what is at the bottom, so to speak, of Schreber's psychosis? That is how I read the argument of Ida Macalpine and Richard A. Hunter in two articles, "The Schreber Case" and "Observations on the Psychoanalytic Theory of Psychosis," published in 1953 and 1954, respectively, in the prestigious *Psychoanalytic Quarterly* and the *British Journal of Medical Psychology*. Lacan, by the way, criticizes these authors (though he only mentions Macalpine by name)—who are the English translators of Schreber's *Memoirs*—for their insistence on birth fantasies and their questioning of Freud's Oedipal scenario of interpretation, with its prevalence of the paternal function (311–16; Lacan refers to Macalpine's and Hunter's discussion of the case located at the end of their translation of the *Memoirs*, which is a reprint of their article "The Schreber Case" from which I quote). For Lacan, it is impossible to understand the Schreber case at the level of Schreber's birth fantasies (106), though in *The Psychoses* Lacan repeatedly returns (unconsciously? the return of the repressed?) to phenomena such as pregnancy and childbirth fantasies, the couvade, procreation—phenomena that establish the importance of motherhood in Schreber's *Memoirs* (170–71, 179–80, 211–13, 279, 292–93, 306–9, 311–14). (*Couvade* refers to both full-fledged male hysterical pregnancy, a condition that is widespread among certain preliterate peoples, and to milder symptoms, fairly common in our own society, whereby the partners of pregnant women develop pregnancy symptoms such as morning sickness, food cravings and aversions, weight gain, backache, and so on.) Macalpine and Hunter claim that Freud selectively overemphasized Schreber's unconscious homosexual desire, which for these authors is a symptom of paranoia and not its cause, at the expense of his "archaic, pregenital, asexual procreation phantasies"—fantasies, that is, that originate before there is an awareness of sexual differentiation, of the different role of the two sexes in procreation ("Observations," 176). The deepest, most destructive layer of these, which constituted Schreber's greatest suffering, were his somatic delusions. These were disregarded by Freud in favor of Schreber's mental symptoms, with which they have a complementary relationship. Macalpine and Hunter note that impregnation fantasies are so destructive as to be incompatible even with psychotic mental life, especially for men, and thus are rarely uncovered, while homosexual wishes are more superficial and thus more easily reported ("Observations," 188).

Are pregnancy fantasies always secondary to homosexual wishes, as Freud claims, or do they exist independently as archaic procreation fantasies? Macalpine and Hunter believe that it is when these archaic fantasies receded that Schreber's condition improved; that these fantasies exist quite apart from relationships with other persons (Schreber's homosexual desire for his father/his doctor/his God) and from fears of castration. Schreber identifies with the mother's body, and his desire to give birth is the core of his psychotic manifestation. But unlike the girl's penis envy, the boy's envy of childbearing has received little attention in psychoanalysis. Macalpine and Hunter speak with precision of "parturition envy" as well as of pregnancy fantasies in both men and women ("Schreber Case," 340–43). After all, Schreber's wife had been unable to bear children, for her multiple pregnancies all resulted in miscarriages;

their happy marriage was "only clouded from time to time by the oft-repeated disappointment of our hope that we might be blessed with children" (*Psychoanalytic Notes,* 13; quoted again in a footnote, 57–58). Freud explicitly wrote that Schreber "may have formed a phantasy that if he were a woman he would manage the business of having children more successfully" (*Psychoanalytic Notes,* 58). So that, as Macalpine and Hunter persuasively put it, "his psychosis was a quest to procreate" ("Schreber Case," 343). Schreber's change into a woman was effected in order to permit him to bear a child. It is enlightening at this point to ponder over my colleague Robbie Kahn's assertion that "Freud thinks that a baby is a penis to a woman, but, on the contrary, a baby can stand for exactly the opposite. A baby may show a woman—in doubt of the worth of her body compared to a man's—that her body is complete already" (Kahn, 42). It is this very completeness that Schreber's psychotic quest sought to materialize, to enflesh.

Michelle Boulous Walker's *Philosophy and the Maternal Body,* a brilliant book that traces the silences and silencings of the maternal body through Western philosophical texts, convinced me of Schreber's importance for my discussion. Walker writes: "Schreber's psychosis is fundamentally a masculine form of the desire to give birth. In his somatic hallucinations we observe a hysterical identification with the potency of the maternal body" (62). Schreber's psychosis, we might say, is to displace the mother by becoming her. If we privilege rather than displace, silence, repress, as Freud does, Schreber's fantasies of generation and self-generation, it is the mother, the powerful mother, who seems to be foreclosed in his psychosis. This interpretation is at odds, of course, with traditional psychoanalysis as founded on the Oedipus, and with Lacan's belief that the most problematic form of the signifier of procreation, for Schreber, "isn't the form *being a mother* but the form *being a father*" (292). Being a father is what is unthinkable without the category of the signifier, for Lacan, and it is the signifier that is missing in Schreber. Thus the mother is doubly foreclosed and returns, like Freud's repressed, to haunt Schreber's fantasy life as hallucinations of pregnancy and childbirth, and to haunt even those interpretations of Schreber that would themselves foreclose her function. Which leads Lacan to assert that "To all appearances President Schreber lacks this fundamental signifier called *being a father.* This is why he had to make a mistake, become confused, to the point of thinking of acting like a woman. He had to imagine himself a woman and bring about in pregnancy the second part of the path that, when the two were added together, was necessary for the function of *being a father* to be realized" (293). Lacan's interpretation has an internal logic that I find impressive, daunting, and frightening. My reading of it is comforted by Jane Gallop's assertion that Lacan's text is "impossible to understand fully, impossible to master," and so it necessitates "a violent reduction of the contradictory plurality and ambiguity of that text" (*Reading Lacan,* 20). But what it is *not* impossible to understand, nor unfortunately to be mastered by, is the impression that once again, in a major text of contemporary culture, the function of motherhood is depreciated, reduced to a grotesque caricature of itself performed in the service of replicating a paternal order in which failure to father in patriarchal ways constitutes madness. The brilliancy of Lacan's reading must lie, I hope and at the same time fear, in his counterintuitive interpretation of *couvade* as the inability to be a father rather than in its more obvious appearance as the desire, on the part of a man, to be a mother. The corollary of Freud's and Lacan's interpretations seems to be that motherhood is not worth aspiring to, for it offers no power, no signifier, no law in accordance to which language, culture, desire can be elaborated. In fact, if anything, even woman's main aspiration in motherhood is penis envy, as the child comes to replace that organ she does not have and wishes she did have. Under these circumstances, how can we even conceive, so to speak, of such a thing as womb envy?

And yet Freud was not unaware of the psychological importance of the uniquely female processes of gestation and childbirth. When he discusses the definition of culture in *Civilization and Its Discontents* (1930), he selects the use of tools, control of fire, and the building of dwellings as "the first acts of civilization" and describes the last of the three, "the dwelling-house," as "a substitute for the mother's womb, the first lodging, for which in all likelihood man still longs, and in which he was safe and felt at ease" (37–38). This powerful archetypal description of the maternal womb fits well with another one in Freud's essay "The Uncanny" (1919) in which the title adjective is most memorably used to describe the "female genital organs" because "this *unhemilich* place . . . is the entrance to the former *heim* [home] of all human beings, to the place where everyone dwelt once upon a time and in the beginning" (51). Female genitals are uncanny because they recall for man his former home inside the mother's body. They are frightful reminders of the castrating possibility of his return there. They signify life, yes, but also death as the reversal to matter. Indeed Freud rather sweepingly generalizes that, whenever someone dreams of a place as being familiar, "we may interpret the place as being his mother's genitals or her body. In this case, too, the *unheimlich* is what was once *heimisch,* home-like, familiar; the prefix 'un' is the token of repression" ("The Uncanny," 51). The cultural and psychological import of the pregnant body, as well as its marginalized and yet at the same time central place in some of Freud's theoretical elaborations, is undeniable. The pregnant body is at the root of one of the fundamental acts of civilization. As the former home of all human beings, it is a collectively shared though unconscious memory, a common human geography whose recurrence shows up in dreams—the royal road to the unconscious—and is so prevalent as to allow for a univocal reading of otherwise disparate locations. Repression masks the status of the body, of the potent, full, fertile female body, as a place of nostalgia for the homesick man, who can deny what he sees yet cannot prevent its return—in dreams or, for the psychotic Schreber, in somatic hallucinations.

Freud had indeed already discussed much of this in his *Interpretation of Dreams* (1900): "In some dreams of landscapes or other localities emphasis is laid in the dream itself on a convinced feeling of having been there once before. (Occurrences of *déjà vu* in dreams have a special meaning.) These places are invariably the genitals of the dreamer's mother; there is indeed no other place about which one can assert with such conviction that one has been there once before" (*The Interpretation of Dreams*, 399). "Invariably," then, the universalized maternal body moves along the order of dreams as a paradoxically familiar and mysterious geography that is at once bodily and psychological. More generally, in dreams "boxes, cases, chests, cupboards and ovens represent the uterus, and also hollow objects, ships, and vessels of all kinds" (354). We also know how Freud was obsessed with statuettes of mother goddesses, those archaic pregnant symbols of fertility that posited the female body as the ultimate and sole origin of life. And yet, in the Schreber case, Freud effectively silences these associations he makes elsewhere. The maternal body, the female body in its potent incarnation, is analytically excluded, neurotically repressed, psychotically foreclosed. The patient's homosexuality posits an endless return of the masculine self, and motivates the relegation of the knowing and growing pregnant body to a footnote. Many have criticized Freud's insufficient concern with the maternal. Among these is Julia Kristeva, who has written in "Stabat Mater" that "among the patients analyzed by Freud, one seeks in vain for mothers and their problems. One might be led to think that motherhood was a solution to neurosis and, by its very nature, ruled out psychoanalysis as a possible other solution" (254). More specifically, if the desire for motherhood is a transformation of penis envy, then there can be no such thing as womb envy, or a male fantasy of pregnancy. Walker even sees "Freud's articulation of the Oedipal complex (and psychoanalytic theory itself) as an elaborate psychotic hallucination"; by refusing to register the mother, Freud appropriates the generative principle and "gives birth to himself in the form of his own brain child, i.e. psychoanalysis" (55). In Freud's silencing or foreclosure of the maternal body, in the Schreber case as in his other works, must we then see an attempt to deny maternal power while appropriating the power of birth by taking it away from mothers, and bodies, and sexual identity?

Maternal Deformity in Turn-of-the-Century Science

The tensions and contradictions of the pregnant experience, the bodily and linguistic splitting proceeding from gestation, become especially visible if we allow a dialogue between the literary texts of late-nineteenth- and early-twentieth-century women writers and scientific treatises of that time (again, Cesare Lombroso's *La donna delinquente, la prostituta e la donna normale* and Paolo Mantegazza's *Fisiologia della donna*). These treatises would constitute themselves as matrices of motherhood, thus producing, as well as regulating, a proliferation of reproductive stories. In reading these, we should keep in mind what Jennifer Terry and Jacqueline Urla describe as a "now almost commonplace axiom" in feminist and cultural studies of science, namely that "the modern life sciences and medicine—and, indeed, popular perceptions to which they give rise—have not merely observed and reported on bodies; they *construct* bodies through particular investigatory techniques and culturally lodged research goals" ("Introduction," 3).

Let me begin with a concrete example. If Ada Negri's poem "Eliana," in the collection *Maternità* (1904, in *Poesie*), indicts at one level its pregnant protagonist's abortion, it also contains a subtle sympathy for her fears that is at odds with the official, scientific, and legal interpretation of her behavior—not only having an abortion but, more generally, the avoidance of bodily mothering as a whole: pregnancy, childbirth, breastfeeding. These behaviors are seen as dangerously deviant in, for example, Lombroso's *La donna delinquente, la prostituta e la donna normale,* where those who behave in such a way are called "moral madwomen" and locked inside insane asylums. But, as Nancy Harrowitz rightly notes about Lombroso's research, "what happens when the female criminal is studied is that her two sisters, the prostitute and the normal woman, become unmasked as well" (31). A scenario set forth as typical of these "moral madwomen" portrays newly married women who selfishly avoid pregnancy and/or breastfeeding: "in order to avoid pregnancy they show an open distaste for their husband; if they have children . . . they lightheartedly hand them over to the first available wetnurse so as not to alter their beauty" (*La donna,* 606). The reasons why a woman might want to avoid pregnancy (and therefore sexual relations with her husband, given the unreliability of the methods of family planning available at the time)—such as, not unreasonably for that time, fear of death and/or disfiguration—are never mentioned by Lombroso. He assumes motherhood to be even more than a social duty, or, in Mantegazza's word, a "mission." Motherhood is for Lombroso a physiological need of all women, in the absence of which disease is inevitable.

This focus on women's physiologically determined maternal "instinct" is exemplary of Lombroso's method. As David Horn outlines in *Social Bodies*, a study of the body was for Lombroso a way out of the idealism and metaphysics of the classical school of criminology that preceded his own innovations (29). And Lombroso's insistent, even obsessive emphasis on the body as the privileged site of difference was shared by other nineteenth-century texts, scientific as well as literary and political. A particular case Lombroso describes provides an instructive insight into his methodology. He speaks quite plainly of a woman considered mad because lacking in maternal instinct. Thus, although she is "pregnant, she wants to get rid of it so as not to lose her beauty and, with it, her partner, for if he left her she would kill herself" (*La donna*, 607). The problem is not man's, and society's, excessive, exclusive attention to a woman's beauty, loss of which might result in abandonment. Rather, since motherhood is a physiological need, its absence indicates or entails pathology. So, too, the fact that prostitutes do not usually have children is seen by Lombroso as yet another proof of their degeneracy, of which a lack of maternal feelings is the unambiguous symptom: "If the *cocotte* is so preoccupied with her graces as to sacrifice motherhood to the preservation of her beauty, that is a sign that she has very weak maternal feelings" (532). Lack of maternal feelings is indeed described by this author as "a new and gravest symptom of moral madness" (531). But his pronouncements reveal more about the deleterious effects of unrealistic aesthetic codes and of women's sexual exploitation, at home as well as on the streets, than they do about women's mental health. And in the process of equating healthy womanhood with motherhood, the scientific text also indirectly establishes the incompatibility of desirability and the pregnant/maternal shape. A swollen belly expresses sexual unavailability rather than impressing the viewer with its attractiveness.

Healthy women are much more difficult to find for Lombroso than degenerates of all kinds. Pathological practices occur on a regular basis, for example, among what Lombroso defines as savage cultures, where their perceived normality reinforces the distinction between the higher and the lower races. The latter are for Lombroso biologically closer to disease. In his discussion of abortion and infanticide, Lombroso notes that the causes of these crimes are often "the care of one's own beauty and jealousy" (*La donna,* 201). The examples he adduces constitute, according to his logic, irrefutable proof:

> The women of the Abiponi people in Paraguay, since they cannot have intercourse with their husbands during the breastfeeding period, kill the child so as not to see their husband with other women. . . . certain Indian women of the Orenoco, convinced that beauty is altered after frequent childbirths, have abortions. . . . in Persia women try to abort when they see their husbands, during pregnancy, run after other women. . . . In New Caledonia, in Haiti, in Hawaii, women abort so that their beauty may last longer. . . . Even Roman ladies used to abort so as not to become ugly. (*La donna,* 201)

Lack of maternal feelings, which impels them to choose their own beauty over the life of their child, associates born criminals and prostitutes with savages and members of earlier, less civilized cultures. This is what Lombroso calls "atavism," a key concept in his science: women are for him atavistic, for they resemble savages and animals more than men do. Yet nowhere does this author attempt an analysis of the cultural and/or social forces that help motivate the behaviors he so abhors, behaviors that he convincingly transforms into perversions of healthy womanhood. By incorporating social assumptions into a vocabulary of physiology, Lombroso underlines woman's atavistic tendencies—and, therefore, her solid link to criminals, prostitutes, and savages. At the same time, however, he also reveals a major contradiction in his argument. This same contradiction more generally informs nineteenth-century scientific discourse on woman: Lack of maternal feelings is posited as a sign of degeneracy, but it is precisely maternity that prevents woman from achieving man's higher stage of development.

Yvonne Knibiehler rightly notes that, in the nineteenth-century view of female beauty, "value was . . . ascribed to signs of the natural reproductive function: round hips, ample breasts, well-fed flesh" (326). In his 1880 *Fisiologia dell'amore,* Mantegazza had analogously written: "If certain curves have such a strong and sudden power over us, it is because we seek in them, without wanting it and without knowing it, a woman capable of bearing and breastfeeding children" (91). Mantegazza develops this theory further thirteen years later, in *Fisiologia della donna.* For example, at the very beginning of the chapter on breastfeeding, we read: "Woman's breasts are among her greatest beauties, and they are beautiful precisely because they are assigned one of the reproductive functions, breastfeeding" (*Fisiologia,* 2:81). And earlier in that book the author had admitted that even "The most modest and chaste of men, when he first sees a woman, turns his eyes to the three points which define her as female: her breasts, her waist, and her hips" (1:220). Most unambiguously, Mantegazza develops an aesthetic theory based on the outward signs of female fertility, a theory worth quoting at length because directly related to this author's double-edged perception of the pregnant body:

> The basic features of female beauty are all genital, and I divide them into *upper* and *lower.* The latter are more important because they indicate a good mother, while the former indicate a good nurse. Without a wide pelvis, without round and generous hips, woman cannot nourish for nine moths the fruit of love, she cannot give birth. Without firm and abundant breasts she won't be able to give her child the milk of her blood. *To give birth* and *to breastfeed:* these are the two functions of woman's sexual life; and they are marked on her basic aesthetic features. (*Fisiologia,* 1:315)

The female body is in this passage clearly divided into two parts, upper and lower, breasts and hips, physically separated by the waist, thin or pregnant, and functionally divided by a watershed event: childbirth as the expression of a mission fulfilled.

The practical value of Mantegazza's aesthetic theory is at least debatable according to the views of today's science as they trickle down into maternity advice manuals: "All combinations of breasts and nipples have the capacity to dispense milk—the quantity and quality of which are not in the least dependent on outward appearance," we read in *What to Expect When You're Expecting* (Eisenberg, Murkoff, and Hathaway, 266). Still Mantegazza's words echo the beliefs of many of his colleagues and contemporaries. While the jurist Lino Ferriani saw in outward beauty a reflection of inner goodness, following the dictates of Lombroso's anthropometry, his colleague Vincenzo Mellusi saw the beauty of the female body as indicative of its maternal mandate—above all in its fleshiness: the woman's body seems "built to sit with a child on her lap, so enormous is the development of its hips, its lap" (in Babini, 70–72). And Mantegazza's aesthetic theory of sexual attractiveness has been recently confirmed "scientifically," as an article that made the cover of *Newsweek* in the mid-nineties affirms (June 3, 1996). Beauty, equated with sexual attractiveness, has allegedly been shown to be directly related to the outward signs of reproductive ability: facial and bodily symmetry, which is genetically associated with health and resilience, and, above all, the ratio between women's waist and their hips. Outward signs, in this study, are especially crucial in the case of women because women's attractiveness, according to the findings discussed in

Newsweek, is more important for men's sexual selection of a mate. Thus, we read, "almost anything that interferes with fertility—obesity, malnutrition, menopause—changes a woman's shape" (Cowley, 65). Just as Mantegazza had claimed, and just as reductively, the claims of popular science attempt to confirm a stereotype by reproducing scientifically the connections between fertility and sexy attributes.

Mantegazza's work on woman, although amply reductive and misogynistic, lacks the continuous sense of revulsion at the female body as a body that is always about to become deformed, debased, savage—a revulsion one reads throughout Lombroso's work. And while Mantegazza, along with other scientists, "justifies" woman's weaknesses and extols her qualities in the name of her maternal "mission," Lombroso never dabbles in the rhetoric that exalts maternity and woman's sensitivity. Thus we can usefully compare the above definition of woman's beauty given by Mantegazza with the following by Lombroso, whose theory of woman's innate frigidity ("woman being naturally and organically frigid," *La donna*, 57) is anatomically confirmed by her lack of veritable sexual organs:

> woman's sexual organs are more complicated and numerous (vulva, uterus, ovary, etc.), but for the most part they are not genital but maternal. This is especially true of the secondary sexual organs, breasts, hips, the Hottentot women's cushion, etc.; all these organs, unlike those of males, are necessary not for intercourse, but for the nutrition and development of the new being. And breasts, hips, etc., are erotic instruments only for that man with a refined eye and touch, because they indirectly excite him to coitus. But in themselves they do not have such a function, as we can see by scanning the biological ladder. And even our savages' . . . breasts, so often reduced to a long and flaccid pouch thrown over the shoulder, although they benefit the child, they certainly do not excite the lover. (*La donna*, 125)

In some ways Lombroso and Mantegazza, as well as *Newsweek*, agree. The outward signs of fertility and, more generally, of maternity determine woman's ability to attract a mate. But Lombroso goes one step further and denies the very existence of woman's sexuality by progressively transforming her genital organs into exclusively maternal ones. At first "for the most part," then "all" her organs are intended for the "nutrition and development" of her child and not for sexual intercourse. The author is unwilling to concede any intrinsic beauty to the female body (even her breasts, icons of sexual attractiveness for Mantegazza, are made repulsive by breastfeeding in Lombroso's view), as woman's puzzling organs are so "numerous" as to require three "etceteras," so strange as to deserve the adjective "complicated" (compared to the simplicity of what?), and thus frightful because ultimately unknowable. But also, such strenuous denial of women's sexuality clearly reveals a preoccupation with a desire that, if separated from its maternal aim, would jeopardize the tenuous bourgeois family order under attack at that time.

The scientifically established connection between beauty and fertility is confirmed by an article in which Neera herself deplores the new canons of feminist, androgynous beauty: "Maternal attributes, the main source of pride of ancient female beauty, now give place to an androgynous ambiguity. . . . No more breasts, no more hips. In a few generations, our descendants will be perplexed before Titian's *Venus,* wondering what kind of women those used to be" (*Le idee di una donna,* 69). Neera's prophecy has come true, as the fleshly opulence of Titian's Venuses is hardly compatible with our culture's admiration for the anorexic look of today's fashion models and actresses. We have gone even further than Neera could have predicted if, as Sandra Lee Bartky puts it,

> under the current "tyranny of slenderness" women are forbidden to become large or massive; they must take up as little space as possible. The very contours a woman's body takes on as she matures—the fuller breasts and rounded hips—have become distasteful. The body by which a woman feels herself judged and which by rigorous discipline she must try to assume is the body of early adolescence, slight and unformed, a body lacking flesh or substance, a body in whose very contours the image of immaturity has been inscribed. (141)

How well contemporary feminist discourse can reinforce the fears of turn-of-the-century antifeminists—or the other way around. Bartky's arguments for the appreciation of the full, mature female body can be applied to the maternal body as well; for if it remains unclaimed by feminists, the value of motherhood, and of the sexually mature/maternal body, risks being erased in the aesthetic exaltation of female immaturity.

Maternal othering and saming perform a damning dialectical dance in texts of motherhood. Mantegazza, champion of difference as the mark of inferiority, chose to theorize, before woman's beauty, her ugliness—not without some comical effects: "Woman and man have a different type of beauty, and when they deviate from it and approach that of the opposite sex, they become ugly. A thin woman, with a pelvis narrower than her shoulders, without breasts, without hips, with short hair, with a beard, is a monster" (*Fisiologia,* 1:305). Cesare Serono also writes: "little by little woman is acquiring a shape similar to man's: her pelvis gets narrower, her chest disappears, hair grows on her face. Women thus shaped become unable to breastfeed" (33–34). This is again rather amusingly, or perhaps I should say frightfully, confirmed by the *Newsweek* cover story, over one hundred years later. With the exception of hair length, the features mentioned by Mantegazza differentiate men from women, in the contemporary scientific understanding of the body, in terms of hormonal production. The imaginary masculine woman Mantegazza describes is a "monster" because she exhibits the effects of androgens rather than estrogens—the latter being necessary for female fertility and thus for sexual attractiveness. As *Newsweek* journalist Geoffrey Cowley wittily notes, "the tiny jaw that men favor in women is essentially a monument to estrogen—and, obliquely, to fertility. No one claims that jaws reveal a woman's odds of getting pregnant. But like breasts, they imply that she could" (65).

Woman's beauty is precariously suspended between two poles: The less fertile she looks, the uglier she is. Yet, paradoxically, the more fertile she is, the uglier she is going to become—not to mention stupid, as we have seen in Chapter 1. Because ironically, once the promise of these fertile signs of beauty is realized—that is, once the potentially pregnant and therefore beautiful body is actually pregnant and, later, maternal—the effect on the viewer is revulsion rather than attractiveness. Mantegazza himself must admit that "Maternity and breastfeeding quickly ruin many of woman's most fleeting beauties" (*Fisiologia,* 1:307), and woman's beauty can only last until she is thirty-five years old, "until maternity comes to touch the most beautiful petals of her roses" (1:324). But then, Mantegazza quickly discovers a socially expedient solution to this dilemma, when he describes as "not the least of her glories the sacrifice, on the altar of motherhood, of her primary treasure, beauty" (1:307). Maternal love is the emotional replacement for sexual attraction, and the sacrifice of her beauty is the proof of woman's competence in mothering. Motherhood and sexual attractiveness, as is clearest in pregnancy, are incompatible.

One way of softening the deforming double-bind in which Mantegazza and Neera, among others, place the woman as mother, is to read their descriptions as sympathetic indictments of woman's excessive burden in childbearing—which they are to some extent. Thus, in his chapter on the deformities of woman, Mantegazza blames the premature ugliness of young proletarian and peasant mothers, made more vulnerable by childbearing and breastfeeding, on their exploitation in the work force: "In many poor social classes, especially in the countryside, we allow woman, who has weaker muscles and the terrible labor of maternity and breastfeeding, to work harder than man; and therefore premature old age makes her ugly and exhausted and shortens her life" (*Fisiologia,* 1:205). At the risk of political incorrectness, I must agree. For many women, pregnancy ("baby-making" as a friend of mine calls it) is hard work. I have never felt so thoroughly exhausted as in the evenings of my pregnant months, and I cannot imagine working in a factory or in the fields in addition to the work of baby-making (though I can imagine fatigue itself to be a construction of my soft, bourgeois upbringing, or even an unconscious indoctrination into feminine frailty). Later in the volume Mantegazza extends this charge of exploitation to involve a larger number of women, all working mothers, in fact, and not just the poor: "Giving birth, breastfeeding, and working, all this is an excessive and cruel labor; and man is punished for his tyranny because, after just a few years of love, he holds in his arms a woman who, though still young in age, has an already decrepit body" (1:308). More explicitly, Serono demands: "the work of a married woman outside the walls of her home should be forbidden, at least for the entire duration of maternity and breastfeeding" (37–38). No matter that work in the home is often more brutal and exhausting than work in, for example, an office. (As he admits in a footnote, Serono did his proactive part in this plan by promptly firing all the women employees in his institute as soon as they got married, 92–93.)

Mantegazza adds the factor of man's exploitation of woman in the workforce to the causes of that loss of beauty which is nevertheless primarily the consequence of bearing children and breastfeeding them. But this is hardly the result of man's tyranny, given Mantegazza's own exaltation of the maternal functions as woman's primary destiny and mission: "Maternity is woman's first and essential mission" (2:78), a claim repeatedly made throughout his *Fisiologia della donna.* Interestingly, however, physical undoing, which goes beyond ugliness and refers instead to downright pathology, is portrayed in this passage as being primarily man's problem rather than woman's. It is he who suffers and is punished for his abuse by not being able to hold in his arms a desirable body. All he can embrace, instead, is a still-young yet already-decrepit one, impressed by maternity with the marks of old age. Thus, in her analysis of women's conditions under fascism, historian Victoria De Grazia poignantly and rightly notes that the photographical evidence of prolific mothers "presents an aesthetically disturbing scene: the youngest women, at forty, look ancient" (213).

In all of these texts, however, the woman's feelings about her own body and shape remain unspoken and need to be looked for elsewhere, in other writings, in other genres. Sensitivity for woman's fate is in Mantegazza—as in Neera, though in a more ambivalent way—paradoxically coupled with a distaste for the ungainly bodily shape that unfailingly results from maternity, which is for both authors, problematically, woman's primary, indeed her essential, defining function: "Maternity is woman's first title of honor, and when she gives it up she undermines the foundations of human society and stops being a woman" (*Fisiologia,* 1:123).

But woman is trapped by motherhood, and her biological destiny includes psychological imbalance as well as physical disfigurement. Instead of hurting others, woman's instinct, necessarily maternal within the bounds of normality, in the logic of positivistic medicine, turns her against herself. Turn-of-the-century Italian gynecologists define motherhood as woman's paradoxical destiny. If the refusal of pregnancy entails a multifarious pathology, so does its embrace. As Valeria Babini summarizes, "even when woman follows her own natural destiny she encounters risks and dangers no less terrible than when she opposes it. If in the latter case she is already sick, in the former she could easily become sick: it is not at all rare—and it is a gynecologist who says it—that she should fall sick, go crazy, be delirious, kill" (58). Just before stating that "maternity is—we might almost say—itself a moral vaccination against crime and evil," Lombroso categorically affirms in two consecutive sentences the indissoluble bond between woman's instinct and her very undoing: "Maternity, as we said, is woman's most intense feeling. This is confirmed by the fact that maternity is one of the most frequent causes of madness" (*La donna,* 337). As Harrowitz notes, "Woman's salvation, and, at the same time, her damnation, is physiology" (32)—and more precisely, in this case, biological maternity. Lombroso continues by conflating as usual the normal with the pathological, for the latter is the logical consequence of the atavistic nature of the female body: "One of the characteristics peculiar to the mad criminal, which is however only an exaggeration of a normal state, is its intensification during menstruation, pregnancy, and menopause" (*La donna,* 593). The normal changes incurred by healthy female bodies are interpreted as diseased when measured against the relative constancy of the temporarily healthy body of adult and not-yet-old males. "In sum," as Horn puts it, "woman was constructed as both normal in her pathology and pathological in her normality" ("This Norm," 121).

Maternal Deformity in Women's Literature

The novel *L'innocente* (*The Innocent,* 1892), by Gabriele D'Annunzio (1863–1938), contains one of the most misogynous perspectives on the pregnant body in Italian literature. In this novel, the horror caused by the changes in his wife Giuliana's shape is doubled by the hatred the husband–protagonist, Tullio, feels toward her unborn child. As soon as he learns of his wife's adulterous pregnancy, Tullio begins to imagine her as being "deformed by an enormous belly" (190), and although his mother describes her daughter-in-law's physical growth in positive terms as "a progress" (284), Tullio sees his wife's bodily expansion as pathology: "a monstrous disease," "the deformed part of the incurable illness" (262), "the ignominious lower deformity," "her deformed shadow" (272), a figure that "was getting as deformed as that of a dropsical woman" (265). His gaze keeps falling on her "swollen belly, the result of another man's excretion" (269). Tullio, in many ways an emblem of decadent aestheticism, sees Giuliana's reproductive ability, her fertility (she conceived a child after just one extramarital encounter), as a sign of inferiority, an animalistic prerogative of lower-class "hot females" (11). The fears dictated by possessiveness toward his wife and above all toward his name, which Giuliana's son would inevitably usurp in becoming his heir (Tullio and Giuliana have two daughters but no son together), are couched in a pseudoscientific medical language of pathology that depicts the adulterous pregnant woman as diseased and therefore as doubly distasteful. Pregnancy is in this novel a deforming mold impressing on woman the shape of repulsion.

Indicative of the inextricable conjunction of scientific and literary discourses, D'Annunzio's descriptions reflect and refract the problematic cultural reproduction of the pregnant body. Almost three decades after his novel, for example, the changed looks of the protagonist of Maria Messina's *Alla deriva* (Adrift, 1920) mark her as "sick" (131), and a rebellion against such pathologizing views is a part of the discourses constructing pregnancy and childbirth today. Because of the pervasiveness of the medical paradigm in our daily perception, the beautiful is seen as healthy, the ugly as unhealthy; this is true of contemporary popular science and aesthetics as well as of that of a century ago. In terms of a possible medical aesthetics of pregnancy, two examples of contemporary rehabilitations should suffice. The authors of *What to Expect When You're Expecting* self-confidently state that "the concept of pregnancy as an illness, and of the pregnant woman as an invalid . . . is as dated as general anesthesia in routine deliveries" (Eisenberg, Murkoff, and Hathaway, 189–90). Similarly, in a 1996 issue of the Italian magazine for new and expectant parents, *Io e il mio bambino* (Me and my child, July 1996), we read that "pregnancy is not an illness" (Piazza, 94). Analogous quotations abound in the literature of pregnancy and childbirth. The irony, of course, is that most of these publications burst with all sorts of medical advice and lifestyle norms for pregnant women, confirming what one of the numerous misogynistic proverbs claims: that "The life of women is one long illness" (Amerighi, *Proverbi delle donne*).

D'Annunzio's repulsed descriptions of Giuliana are perhaps the misogynous zenith of a configuration of gestation as deforming that is employed in more complex, less reductive ways by women writers of that time. It is especially important to turn to women writers for an examination of this theme because paradoxically, as Jacques Gélis writes, pregnancy "was 'women's business'—but it is men who talk about it and inform us about it" (45). The abject, dangerous deformity of the pregnant woman, whose body is a prolific ground for conceiving sexual differences, can be used both as a representational tool that fits into that abundant turn-of-the-century repertoire of woman's evils (catalogued and analyzed by Bram Dijkstra in *Idols of Perversity*) and as a literary strategy that ambivalently, at times self-destructively, attempts to deconstruct traditional notions of female roles. The latter mode, which is never ideologically disengaged from the former, is prevalent in the literature of Italian women writers from the late nineteenth and early twentieth century; some of their work even extends well into the era of fascism with its mystique of motherhood. This is a profoundly ambivalent strategy which in borrowing from the iconography of misogyny often has the effect of reinforcing it, so that its subversive potential is continuously tamed by a bowing gesture toward the status quo. And, as I have noted earlier, this double stance of late-nineteenth- and early-twentieth-century women writers is not limited to their representation of pregnancy and motherhood but rather informs their writings at large.

The looks of the pregnant woman are trapped in a cultural double-bind. If images of deformity and contamination are prevalent, so is idealization, rooted in both the bourgeois cult of the angel of the household and in the Catholic veneration of the Madonna as bearer of the Word. As Clarissa Atkinson notes, "interactions between the history of Christianity and the history of motherhood have been intense and complicated" (5). This is especially true in a culture such as the Italian one, so permeated with both Catholicism and that cult of mothers known as *mammismo.* In the germane words of Andrea Henderson,

> the simultaneous spiritualization and corporealization of the middle class woman during the [nineteenth] century reflect the pressure of the middle class to distance itself from its modes of production (which it does by making its ideal woman "aristocratically" spiritual, angelic) while restricting the power granted to women (through the common focus on the body in representations of women and members of the working class). (109)

Thus in the Italian popular imagination of the nineteenth century, bourgeois and Catholic, the pregnant woman presumably acquires a supernatural beauty arising from her (pro)creative role, and her implicit association with Mary of Nazareth—a figure impossibly both mother *and* virgin.

Ultimately gestation is an act of communication and of fissure, a relationship that is also in a sense a *mise-en-abîme* of motherhood: just as the objective of the pregnant body in the course of nine months is to enable the fetus to leave it, so the mother, or the parent, over a longer and more variable period, prepares her or his child for independence. One of the ironic goals of parenting, exemplified on a smaller and less complex scale in pregnancy, is to make oneself no longer necessary; it is an ethical process of letting grow, letting go. In *Maternal Thinking,* Sara Ruddick suggests that "neither pregnancy nor birth is much like mothering," a distinction rhetorically necessary to her project of separating mothering from gestating and giving birth (50). Yet in a later essay she makes an argument analogous to mine when she indicates instead that "the natal connection foreshadows the maternal relation: both aim for a differentiation that does not deny, but rather is sustained by caring, careful dependence" ("Thinking Mothers/Conceiving Birth," 43). And thus, as we read these polyvocal and formerly popular literary texts, we necessarily note the wide range of meanings assigned to as well as produced by the literary figurations of the reproductive body. Because pregnancy may be said to recapitulate motherhood in some ways, its literary and cultural reproduction can provide a concentrate, a preview, a symptom of the mother–child relation that is to grow out of it. In the context of this chapter, furthermore, the interpretation of the pregnant body foreshadows the cultural construction of the maternal body. The perceived deformity of the pregnant shape, for example, mirrors and even previews the progressive loss of beauty that women, and especially and more quickly, mothers, are seen as inevitably experiencing over the years. If, as I discussed in Chapter 1, through the theory of maternal impressions the mother's thoughts and behavior are held responsible for her child's deformity, the reverse is more commonly true. But in this case the pregnancy itself, hence the peculiar functioning of the female body rather than the child's desire is normally held responsible for the woman's deformity.

The ambivalent threat that childbearing poses to female beauty, even as it may temporarily exalt it, is outlined in Grazia Deledda's novel—and for some her first masterpiece—*Elias Portolu,* first published in installments in 1900 and then as a volume in 1903. As in Deledda's other works, the center of this novel is, in the words of Sharon Wood, "an investigation of the conflicts between different ethical orders. If transgression is the crossing of a boundary, it is the moment when the individual reaches that boundary that interests her. Transgression in her work is a moment of rupture, a nexus of psychological, social, and historical collision" (64). Sexual identity is in *Elias Portolu* one such point of transgression. Thus, femininity is in this novel the signifier of weakness and malady. The protagonist Elias is compared to a woman for his beauty and the whiteness of his hands and face (as was the case for Fortunio in Deledda's *Cosima,* discussed in Chapter 1), which set him apart from his brothers. But he is also an irresolute and fragile character in whom passion brings about pain and paralyzing illness. Thus when Elias falls in love with his brother Pietro's fiancée, Maddalena, he chooses the priesthood to flee his intolerable predicament. Elias and Maddalena nevertheless become lovers and have a child who is in everyone's eyes Pietro's, now Maddalena's husband. Yet even when Pietro dies Elias does not marry Maddalena, though he has not yet taken his vows. Maddalena then marries someone else. Elias desperately loves his young son, and it is only when the latter falls ill and dies that the protagonist feels liberated from human passions and able to achieve some peace.

The slovenly future of the eponymous protagonist's beautiful lover Maddalena (his brother's wife and thus, for a future priest, a doubly forbidden object of desire) is foreseen in ominous terms by Elias's old and wise uncle: "She'll have children, she'll lose her looks. . . . she'll become like so many other mothers of families in town—with dirty dresses, old, slovenly, ugly," to which Elias combatively replies, clearly if indirectly confirming the connection between childbearing and ugliness: "she'll never have children, she'll keep her beauty and freshness for a long time" (103). Maddalena's continued beauty and freshness, her sexual attraction, are predicated on her not becoming a mother, on not being impressed with the deforming mold of maternity. So what happens when she does?

Pregnancy at first brings about for Elias an increase of love and a decrease in guilt: when Maddalena tells him that she is pregnant with his child Elias feels "madly in love . . . finally . . . happier" (147), and it is only with this revelation that he overcomes his incipient "disgust and contempt" toward Maddalena as "the tempter" (146). Yet is the enforced abstinence of her pregnancy ("they parted, deciding to stay away from each other until the baby was born," 147) proleptically related to the perception of the pregnant woman as ugly and deformed, as no longer herself, and therefore as no longer lovable? Although this abstinence stems from both medical prescriptions and ancient taboos, Deledda's novel seems to imply such an aesthetic and existential connection. Once again, deformity is difference, embodied in an alteration of shape and of meaning. At first, Elias thinks of the pregnant Maddalena "differently . . . chastely" (148). Ultimately, however, her multiple changes (of role, of shape) diminish his love for her: "the rhythm of his heart slowed down day by day" (150), the narrator notes, and Elias himself muses: "Perhaps it's because she is in this condition, but after the baby's born I'll go back to loving her like I did" (132). Elias's diminished desire escalates into "an intense disgust" (150). So despite Elias's forceful statement in his earlier conversation with his uncle that his love was not contingent on the beauty of Maddalena's body—"I don't love her for her beauty! I love her because . . . *she's who she is*! . . . " (104, Deledda's emphasis)—the uncle's prophecy is fulfilled well before their child is born. Pregnancy changes Maddalena to the point that for Elias she is no longer herself. Elias thus implicitly answers in two apparently contradictory ways what philosopher Susan Dwyer calls the question of "whether having a certain body (1) *fully determines* one's subjectivity, or (2) inescapably *affects* one's subjectivity" (33). If before Maddalena's pregnancy Elias is able to disengage Maddalena's beauty from her essence, loving her for who she is rather than for how she looks, this separation does not survive Maddalena's physical alteration. The bodily changes brought about by motherhood fully determine for Elias who Maddalena becomes. And Elias cannot now love her.

From an anthropological perspective, Anthony Synnott confirms that "The identity of body and self is perhaps most clearly illustrated by body-change. Self-concepts change, often dramatically, at puberty, pregnancy, and menopause. Body changes change the self" (2). We have seen how this can be true in different ways for different women, how some grow (beautiful) through pregnancy while others are diminished or even deformed by it. Maddalena's body changes certainly transform her in her lover's eyes. As the narrator observes about Elias's feelings toward his pregnant lover, whose body is visibly different: "It seemed he no longer loved her, especially now that she had become nearly shapeless, her face yellow and swollen" (154). Maddalena, swollen and yellow-faced (and the face is a prime symbol of the self), is the site of a deforming otherness. Is she no longer herself, then—and therefore no longer lovable to Elias who would love her "because . . . *she is who she is*"? The deformity brought about by pregnancy is double. It is a bodily disfiguration and a change in meaning. Maddalena is no longer a beautiful lover but rather an ugly mother. And this double deformity is the first force capable of stopping, if only temporarily, the transgressive passion that alone animates the drama of this novel and that, as is characteristic of Deledda's work, neither sacraments nor vows had been able to halt.

As her depictions of the unattractive pregnant woman make clear, erotic appeal is for Deledda, as well as for other writers of her time, lined with disgust, the alteration of the body implies an alteration in meaning, the proliferation of the flesh precipitates the emptying out of desire. In her discussion of the significance of pregnancy for women in *The Second Sex*, for example, Simone de Beauvoir notes that "women who are primarily interested in pleasing men, who see themselves essentially as erotic objects, who are in love with their own bodily beauty, are distressed to see themselves deformed, disfigured, incapable of arousing desire. Pregnancy seems to them no holiday, no enrichment at all, but rather a diminution of the ego" (503). Through an ambiguous discourse, hovering between agreement and disagreement with the masculinist aesthetic judgment she ventriloquizes, Beauvoir reaffirms the same premise and double-bind that puzzled and profoundly disturbed me at the outset of this chapter: that the pregnant body, and also, more generally, the body of women who have borne children, should be viewed as "deformed, disfigured, incapable of arousing desire," in Beauvoir's language, when it is its desirability that has led to its current shape. In general, I agree with Mary O'Brien's criticism that "Gestation, for Beauvoir, is woman eternally in thrall to contingency. Her analysis suggests that the denial of this contention, the assertion by woman of creative pride and satisfaction in the birth of her child, or an understanding of nurture and child-rearing as authentic project, are simply evasions" (75). Yet in her oversimplification Beauvoir touches on what I see as the crux of the dilemma: that the disfigurement and deformity of pregnancy, its destruction of desire and desirability, are due to the view of women as men's erotic objects. The interplay of eroticism and abstinence, fullness and emptiness, presence and absence, played out on the pregnant and maternal woman's body, reveals disgust to be the other, complementary yet ever differing side of desire.

In contrast to (but at times also disturbingly in collusion with) the morbid, even abject reproduction of the maternal body in the writings of D'Annunzio, Mantegazza, and Lombroso, the often ambiguous figurations of Deledda, and of some of her contemporaries—such as Neera, Ada Negri, and Maria Messina—vacillate between sympathy for the condition of the pregnant woman and distaste for her altered looks, with a striking ambivalence that must constitute a symptomatic point of entry into the analysis of these women's texts. And if the bodily changes pregnancy brings about could conceivably be posited as "only" natural, biological events, as pure body, as Lacan's "real," still they cannot be known as such. Their effects and interpretations, their impressions and expressions, like the pregnant body itself, are practices swaddled within our cultural discourses, within the realms of the symbolic. The body at the threshold is a body made up of an interiority and an exteriority that are inseparable, so that the somatic, the psychic, and the sociopolitical are hinged together: *écriture féminine*, proprioception, the mucous, are some ways of figuring this hinge.

If Mantegazza and Lombroso do not find the pregnant shape attractive and refuse to give it a voice, one of the effects of their silencing of the female body is, as Mary Poovey has convincingly argued about British doctors, "an excess of meanings, and the contradictions that emerge within this excess undermine the authority that medical men both claim and need" (152). But for Deledda and some of her contemporaries, the literary reproduction of the pregnant shape is an occasion for staging the polyvocal imbrications of the female body—as sexual, as reproductive—within discourses that would flatten it into a socially expedient univocity. Hence the recurrence of paradox and contradiction in the texts I have been reflecting on: male voices of female experiences, gestating wombs as selves and as others, pregnant bodies as beautiful and ugly. Maternity as empowering and as self-destructive. This is an effective way for many writers, especially women authors, to escape nineteenth-century biological essentialism concerning the nature of woman, to indict the dichotomy that would forever and impossibly divide the female body into reproductive *or* sexual, maternal *or* hysterical, deformed *or* desirable. And it is a literary practice that as we read allows us, impels us, even, to imagine bodily changes and related linguistic alterations, as neither in need of discipline nor as deserving of destruction, but instead as demanding a dialogue through which, according to French mystic and philosopher Simone Weil (a figure central to much Italian feminist theory), we create ourselves even as we pay "attention" to others by letting them exist in their own right. *Attention* is the capacity enabling preservation and growth. From a phenomenological perspective, Drew Leder has noted that when our bodies are in a "*dys* state"—namely, bodily states of rapid change: pregnancy and childbirth as well as aging and puberty, for example, but also illness and pain—they demand attention. These states heighten our body-focus, place on us existential demands, throw into question our self-interpretation. Epistemologically, they offer a chance to rethink ourselves and perhaps to practice connection rather than separateness, empathy rather than impersonal judgment. This, I believe, is the ethical challenge of many pregnancy texts on and by women. From Weil's spiritual perspective informed by political and philosophical discourse, we become fully human by realizing the others' full humanity and attentively reading and discerning them as such, for, in Weil's words, "The spirit of justice and the spirit of truth is nothing else but a certain kind of attention" (333). It is in the hope of understanding better the possible connections between maternity and ethics that I turn in the next section to the work of Julia Kristeva.

Maternal Deformity and Feminist Theory

In a lecture on women and religion given in Italy in 1984, entitled "Divine Women" and included in the volume *Sexes and Genealogies,* Luce Irigaray discusses women's beauty as external, as a "garment" whose purpose is to attract men and please others rather than to lead to self-fulfillment and self-love. In passing, Irigaray also points out, in a contradiction lodged within the same paragraph, both that "maternal beauty has been glorified in our religious and social traditions," and that "motherhood, with its associations to bodily deformity and the link often made between it and chastity," has been "passively abject, reduced" (64–65). The contradiction in Irigaray's argument corresponds to the aesthetic and ethical contradiction of the maternal body, the very paradox that animates maternity texts past and present, the insoluble dilemma about the (lack of) desirability of a body that cannot be understood outside the framework of desire. But rather than focus on what a contemporary aesthetics of the pregnant and maternal body might look like, so to speak, I dwell at this point on one of those junctures in contemporary theory where the body, like the pregnant and maternal body in turn-of-the-century discourses, crosses and is crossed by difference as well as alteration. Can identity be sustained in a subject traversed by difference? Feminist thought, especially in its French and Italian incarnations, springs to mind, with its ruminations, for example, on *écriture féminine* and *pensiero della differenza sessuale.* But while fear of essentialism has for years prevented many Anglo-American theorists from recognizing, much less accepting, the emphasis on the maternal body that recurs in the writings of those French feminists most translated and best-known this side of the Atlantic, essentialism per se does not frighten to the same extent the European theorists themselves. As Paola Bono and Sandra Kemp perceptively write in their introduction to the anthology *Italian Feminist Thought,* "Much Italian feminist theory is running the risk of essentialism as it has been hitherto perceived. By taking that risk 'seriously,' it may seem to speak essentialism, but enacts a new kind of empiricism" (17). In this spirit, a reflection on French and Italian feminist theory may help us unravel some aspects of the essentialist debate.

Julia Kristeva's writings—although not focused on sexual difference as is the case in Luce Irigaray's work—are concerned with the relationship between identity and difference, with the construction and the maintenance of alterity and the stranger. Kristeva returns time and again to what exists at and beyond the boundaries of human experience by analyzing how boundaries are shattered and sustained. There is a contradictory play, within her writings, of symbolic and semiotic modalities. While language corresponds to Lacan's symbolic, the semiotic is that bodily, pre-Oedipal drive in opposition to meaning proper; it is one of Kristeva's best-known theoretical elaborations and, like the chora and the abject, it is identified in her work as feminine and repressed. It is not surprising, then, that her writings themselves should have been the object of many contradictory readings: Kristeva has alternately been described as essentialist and antiessentialist, anarchist and conservative, feminist and antifeminist, post-Marxist and anti-Marxist. Although this is not the place to engage in a comprehensive study of the French-Bulgarian theorist, a linguist and psychoanalyst by training and trade, it should be noted that Kristeva's theories of motherhood are also fraught with contradictory interpretations: Is her conception of maternity as essentialist as her critics claim, and even if it is, does it ultimately silence women? Or is maternity for Kristeva subversive, double and even indeterminate? What is the relationship between her materialism and her maternalism? Does the mother belong to the imaginary or to the symbolic realm? Is she fixed in one or the other? Does Kristeva follow or break with Lacan's theories? Is her concept of the semiotic a maternal alternative to the symbolic order, a repressed feminine discourse, or does it imply that rational subjectivity can only be achieved by renouncing the (m)other?

In these symptomatic splits, Kristeva's work is analogous to that of some turn-of-the-century women writers, Neera and Matilde Serao for example, alternately accused or glorified by some for being feminist and by others for not being so: Julia Kristeva is radical for some, neoconservative for others; a member, with Irigaray and Cixous, of the "new holy trinity of French feminism" for some, not a feminist at all for others. And as it is true for turn-of-the-century Italian authors such as Deledda, Neera, Negri, Serao, so perhaps in the case of Kristeva as well there is more to learn from contradiction than from the relatively more comfortable reduction of her work to a body of nonconflictual statements. I find meaning in these authors' symptomatic oppositional receptions more than in a reductive, though perhaps more ideologically neat feat of taking sides. Kelly Oliver even claims that Kristeva's "writing is full of contradictions. But hers is not a discourse that strictly adheres to the logic of noncontradiction. Rather, hers is a discourse that breaks the law of noncontradiction upon which notions of identity are built. Kristeva's writing challenges traditional notions of identity" (*Reading Kristeva,* 1). It challenges the same notions, that is, that maternity texts in general, old and new, refuse to rely on for their elaborations of the female subject: "By simultaneously advocating maternal dissidence and criticizing female romanticism [Kristeva] challenges us to shake the bonds of rigid, conformist thought. She refuses the self-evidence of woman's identity," Walker perceptively writes (124). Thus, although her writings often accept a duality of semiotic and symbolic, father and mother, Kristeva's work overall exposes and disrupts dichotomies such as nature and culture, body and language, self and other, fusion and mediation.

I am most interested, in an obviously and I hope forgivably self-serving way, in reading Kristeva's writings as a corpus that allows us, by reflection and refraction, to better understand other maternity texts—which in turn may help us decode Kristeva's own stand in maternity matters. Like many of the pregnancy texts analyzed thus far, Kristeva's writings on maternity focus on the mother–child rather than the man–woman dyad, and she engages the maternal emblem in a number of ways. Her efforts, more than Irigaray's for example, continue to operate, although uncomfortably at times, within the institution of psychoanalysis. This is most obvious in her treatment of the Oedipal and pre-Oedipal, which at least on the surface maintains the phallus as third term and asserts the need for the violent separation and loss the phallus brings about: the thetic cut. But for all its collusions and shortcomings, I nevertheless believe that we owe to Kristeva a complex, fertile, and disruptive development of the maternal function as it predates and prefigures the paternal law. Largely ignored, or perhaps repressed, even foreclosed, in Freud's work, this development is unrepresentable as a specific textual practice. It nevertheless allows us to rethink the maternal as the trace, the site, even, not only of a renewed epistemology, as discussed in the preceding chapter, and of another aesthetics (one in which motherhood does not coincide with deformity), but also and perhaps especially as the birthplace of an ethical dimension.

The bodily and linguistic alteration of the pregnant shape that recurs in the maternity texts encountered thus far—an alteration both aesthetic and existential, as Deledda's *Elias Portolu* illustrates—finds a parallel in Kristeva's psychoanalytic elaboration of abjection and the abject, horror and disgust, at the center of her influential book *Powers of Horror* (1980). Like the pregnant body, the pre-Oedipal abject, as that which threatens identity, hovers at the limits between self and other, inside and outside; both are menacing liminal figures that blur identities even as they produce them. Indeed, the abject, at once somatic and symbolic, is associated with the repressed body of the mother: the child, that is, must abject the mother as container, the maternal envelope, to gain independence from her, to break the instinctual dyad and become something other, autonomous, a being capable of language—in short, a subject. For Kristeva the symbolic order is not strong enough to provoke separation from the mother on its own; rather, the mother needs to become abjected in order for separation to result and language acquisition to begin. Thus abjection, founded in the violent but necessary, and precarious, separation of birth, expresses both a division and a merging: *division* between the subject (who is not yet a subject) and the mother (who is not yet an object); *merging* between the future subject and the social sphere, the ethical dimension—even as the threat of a suffocating, annihilating return to the archaic maternal body, kept at bay, prevented by language (the symbolic/paternal), never completely disappears. The abject is unstable, ambivalent. Behind it, in its past, lies the mother's body; beyond it, in its future, language, the symbolic order. Yet the borders between all these elements are forever fragile, while the ability to signify horror, as the abject, can allow for a reconciliation with the mother's body—with the grotesque pregnant body too, then, splitting and divided like abjection itself. The grotesque pregnant woman, Deledda's swollen and yellow-faced Maddalena, for example, destabilizes her own former beauty and thus her lover's desire by splitting itself into an other, a self fractured from her formerly beautiful, desirable incarnation and never again made one, whole, same.

Hovering at the seams of abjection, the maternal body is instead the explicit protagonist of Kristeva's celebrated essays "Motherhood According to Giovanni Bellini" (1975) and "Stabat Mater" (1977). The latter was inspired by Kristeva's personal experience of giving birth to her son; it was titled "Héréthique de l'amour" (Herethics of Love) when it first appeared in the journal *Tel Quel*, then it was renamed for its inclusion in *Histoires d'amour* (*Tales of Love*), in 1983. The maternal body is also an important subject in "Women's Time" (1979), and it recurs, less centrally, throughout Kristeva's work. In these texts, as in the turn-of-the-century texts encountered thus far, the pregnant body is a signifier that is split, contradictory, disruptive of paternal/Oedipal logic. Pregnancy—a heterogeneous, polyvocal discourse in Italian women's fiction, where it is a topos that figures the breakdown of identity and a crisis of the female subject(s)—is comparably described in "Women's Time" as "the radical ordeal of the splitting of the subject" and a "fundamental challenge to identity" (206). It is a time when the body is redoubled up, alienated from itself, when the self and the other, as well as nature and consciousness, physiology and speech, separate even as they coexist (206). The maternal is the site of the *chora*, the preconscious womb figured with a term borrowed from Plato.

The chora is a matrix that defies metaphysics because it is unnamable and anterior to the One, to God; yet the chora is also the way through which all forms become representable, the receptacle that forms must enter to acquire a shape, an impression we might say, and thus existence itself. Through the chora drives enter language. A figure of pregnancy, the chora is heterogeneous and prelinguistic, challenging the linearity of time, identity, and language. The chora is always other to the symbolic order, fundamentally asymmetrical to it. Once it acquires a shape, it ceases being the chora and becomes instead one of the shapes that come into being through the chora. Echoing Cixous' emphasis on the connection between *écriture féminine* and the mother's voice, Kristeva also notes an analogy between the chora and the human voice (*La Révolution du langage poétique,* 25–26). "Like Plato's *chora,*" maintains philosopher Philippa Berry, "Kristeva's maternal origin occupies a liminal position. It is on the borderline between all polarities: between being and nothing, idealism and materialism, sacred and profane, silence and language" (256). The chora then, rather than positing maternal fullness, points toward maternity as the experience of negativity.

Negativity is another fundamental concept in Kristeva's theoretical elaboration. As Walker asserts, "Kristeva is clear, though, that in pregnancy women experience negativity" (123). It is the effect of this negativity that remains uncertain for some critics. For Judith Butler, for instance, rather than leading to "the possibility of subversion as an effective or realizable cultural practice," in Kristeva's construction "poetic language and the pleasures of maternity constitute local displacements of the paternal law, temporary subversions which finally submit to that against which they initially rebel" (*Gender Trouble,* 88). If the semiotic is ultimately recuperated by the symbolic, remaining beneath the territory of its law, then there can be no pleasure beyond the paternal, and the subversive potential of maternity postulated by Kristeva is in Butler's view an illusion that confirms an invisible, and inevitable, "biologically necessitated maternity" (93). For Butler, Kristeva only claims maternity to be disruptive, heterogeneous, multiple, escaping the charge of self-identity and noncontradiction, while in reality her principle of maternal heterogeneity "proves to be a closed concept, indeed, a heterogeneity confined by a teleology both unilinear and univocal" (90). But, as Tina Chanter more productively argues from a perspective aimed at understanding the essentialism debate and the popular feminist dualism between sex and gender,

> Against the background of the need to rethink the sex/gender distinction as no longer a hierarchical and rigid dichotomy, but rather as a less stable,

> more fluid, and amorphous difference, Kristeva's distinction between the semiotic and the symbolic cannot be held up as a travesty of feminism. Instead we might see it as having anticipated some of the complications that feminist theorists of science are now confronting in their recognition of the need to revise the sex/gender distinction. (186)

For if Butler's critique is not altogether unfounded, still I wonder if her critical conceptions are not too harsh, her critique too pregnant, and thus expecting too much: Does Kristeva's inability to speak beyond the symbolic not always implicate all of us who speak and write in the Law of the Father? Are we not better off claiming, with Muraro, that our symbolic order is also necessarily the mother's symbolic order? Otherwise, who can speak legitimately of maternity, without recourse to the symbolic? I must say that I get discouraged when I read so many contemporary feminist critiques of, for example, French feminists' (whatever that description means anymore) work on motherhood as yet another silencing of the mother. I am disturbed by their/our expectations, their/our harshness, their/our destructiveness. Yes, maternity is always-already embroiled in heterosexist institutions, but so are we as feminists, as women, as scholars, as mothers. And throwing out the baby, or the mother, with the bathwater, to modulate on a particularly poignant expression, is unlikely to be a more life-sustaining approach than the frank admission that a pure maternal discourse is impossible, maybe even undesirable, and that building a multidimensional and not necessarily non–self-contradictory mosaic of maternity is a more realistic approach to understanding the many paradoxical layers of this experience. It is also helpful in this context to remember, with Alison Weir, that "Resistance to the given symbolic order requires that we identify with that order, learn its language. It requires, moreover, that we recognize and insist that the symbolic order is not purely 'phallic,' that it is not an unassailable monolith, but that it is a product of, and constantly changed by, conflicting, heterogeneous processes" (80).

In hopes of effecting a more constructive critique, then, let me now turn to those texts in which Kristeva makes her case for the heterogeneity of maternity. In her essay "Motherhood According to Giovanni Bellini" the maternal body is "the place of a splitting," as well as "a threshold where 'nature' confronts 'culture' " (238). As such, the maternal body cannot be wholly assimilated into the symbolic order. The essay begins with the physiological image of cells and tissues accumulating, dividing, multiplying, proliferating into otherness, with the depiction of a body growing and impressing another body within it, and in this process transforming and impressing itself into a maternal body. Humans belong to "the species that either binds together or splits apart to perpetuate itself" (239). Splitting, therefore, lies at the origin of our very existence. And this splitting implies a more vertical connection as well, a connection, more specifically, between the new mother and her own mother—what Muraro and Irigaray posit as the all-important concept of female genealogies: "By giving birth, the woman enters into contact with her mother; she becomes, she is her own mother; they are the same continuity differentiating itself" (239). Birth is for Kristeva the privileged instance of that mother–daughter bond so central to contemporary feminist theory; birth exemplifies the way in which a woman's access to subjectivity rests on a discourse of motherhood involving a reformulation, and not the repudiation, of the relation to the other woman.

In this collapsing of identities, however, Kristeva's mother hovers perilously close to psychosis, defined as the inability to separate the other from the self. Indeed, this proximity between motherhood and madness in Kristeva's work can and has been criticized as establishing a natural affinity between women and psychosis, with pregnancy as a socially acceptable version of psychosis: Can the mother maintain her identity if the other resides within her? But it must also be remembered that this is also the very proximity that art entertains with madness, with that which exceeds language (as in Schreber's psychosis): "The maternal body slips away from the discursive hold and immediately conceals a cipher that must be taken into account biologically and socially" (241). This is because motherhood is dangerous for the woman's identity, yet it also brings with it the power of symbolic instance through its subject's ability to reside within the most archaic differences. The act of giving birth is just this "strange form of split symbolization (threshold of language and instinctual drive, of the 'symbolic' and the 'semiotic')" that impels the childbearing woman "to cathect, immediately and unwittingly, the physiological operations and instinctual drives dividing and multiplying her" (240–41). The division and multiplication of the maternal body lead to its division as artistic subject, which is the core of Kristeva's artistic discussion in this essay. If for Leonardo da Vinci the maternal body is representable, figured as fetish, focused on the child, for Giovanni Bellini the maternal body is instead a play of chromatic differences, serenely beyond physical representation, on the other side of figuration. The mother is inaccessible because every univocal identity has been shattered, lost, and thus her ravishing maternal *jouissance,* that pleasure that is physical and spiritual at once, cannot be attained, touched, made visible. Bellini's paintings of Madonna and child embody and accentuate the split between mother and child and (thus) within the mother herself.

Likewise, in "Stabat Mater" the mother is "a continuous separation, a division of the very flesh. And consequently a division of language—and it has always been so" (254). Body and word are permanently divided, recognizing the otherness that unsettles and dismantles the phallogocentric order more than blindly relying on it. In this essay, furthermore, language and childbirth are seen as originating from the site of a primary wound. The experience of reading is analogous to the experience of pregnancy. "Stabat Mater," by the way, indirectly acknowledges the centrality of maternity to Schreber's psychosis by quoting Sollers' definition of the mystics as those "happy Schrebers" (Lacan himself, in his seminar on Schreber, noted the obvious differences between accounts of authentic religious experiences, such as Saint John of the Cross's, and Schreber's own), and then by Kristeva's own definition of the mystics as those who assume themselves as "maternal" (235). Far from essentializing her, then, Kristeva here points the mother as a negative and liminal place, "as empty, as a 'non-subject' whose precise place can be taken by countless others: it is a love which is produced via that dissolution of subjectivity, of the boundaries between self and other, which the semiotic *chora* promotes" (Berry, 258). This empty place is figured in the doctrine of the Virgin Mary's bodily assumption into heaven, a mysteriously empty divine mode of being that is neither substantial nor essential, and that figures instead negativity and apophasis.

Kristeva is after all also talking about the mystics, those lovers of the negative and of transgression and thus of the chora as a place without a place that is ever displacing itself in order to make more space; but the chora is also a (dis)place(ment), which, in its negativity, threatens the very possibility of being. The initial subject of "Stabat Mater," its impetus for the discussion of maternity, is the Virgin Mary: an enigmatic figure and the most privileged Western representation of maternity and perhaps of the feminine itself. Across this subject intersect the discourses of motherhood, religion, love, the avant-garde, feminism. And on this subject depends the very possibility of a discourse of motherhood, of a clear symbolic place for the maternal body. In our society motherhood is the only available representation of femininity as sacred, as consecrated. Yet, if this representation of ideal motherhood has been satisfactory to women for hundreds of years—because it denied men's role in procreation, fulfilled women's lust for power, valorized breast and pain, flattered women with the promise of immortality, and repudiated the possibility of the other woman, though all this is obtained at the price of subjection to the Son—that is no longer the case, Kristeva notes. The myth of the Virgin Mary no longer provides solutions, it is felt as coercive, it leaves too many things unsaid; above all, it fails to address the experience of childbirth and the mother–daughter bond. Hence contemporary women's discontent, annoyance, even, with matters of conception and motherhood.

This indissoluble connection between motherhood and pain—which returns even where it is not meant to be, which contradicts the logic of nature and the nature of woman as described by Mantegazza, which is confused with pleasure and which questions any neat division of gender and proclamation of difference—is echoed in Kristeva's "Stabat Mater," where the author claims that "One does not give birth in pain, one gives birth to pain: the child represents it and henceforth it settles in, it is continuous. . . . a mother is always branded by pain, she yields to it" (241). Kristeva writes this reflection in the bold-faced section of the essay, the autobiographical, lyrical (semiotic) meditation accompanying and interrupting, with its irregular appearances, our reading of the more traditional expository (symbolic) form of the piece. She thus speaks of her own pain in childbirth, in motherhood, paradoxically, breaking its symbolic silence in the Law of the Father, complicating the claims of her own cultural and psychoanalytic theory. For in the (symbolic) body of the essay, more than once at odds with its bold-faced counterpart, Kristeva later indicts the heavy silence weighing on the suffering of childbirth, both corporeal and psychological. Indeed Kristeva begins to elaborate in this section the possibility, tacitly contemplated by Mantegazza and not so tacitly by Lombroso, that motherhood might be woman's paradigmatic perversion, the perversion of a being who, according to psychoanalytic theory, is refractory to perversion itself. For motherhood is ambivalent; it verges on masochism because the suffering of motherhood is lined with jubilation, *jouissance*. The law of reproduction, Lacan's Law of the Father, promotes this female masochism, which ensures the continuity of social norms and biological species and legalizes this perverse behavior that is after all the ultimate guarantee of civilization. As for Mantegazza and Lombroso, motherhood is in "Stabat Mater" risk and self-sacrifice.

But a mother, although divided, because divided, is not alone. A mother exemplifies the subject's position at the crossroads, at the junction of pain and pleasure, absence and presence, identity and difference. There is no such thing as "the mother," for Kristeva, because the maternal is an empty space and because, as a figuration, the maternal develops in at least two forms: the archaic mother (before the awareness of sexual difference, and thus a retroactive fantasy on the adult's part), and the mother as sexually marked, as symbolic. Nor can woman, for Kristeva, be reduced to the mother. Femininity is absorbed by motherhood, Kristeva claims, but this must also mean that we need to disengage the two, however difficult a task that might be. We must, again, split the terms of illusory identifications: of woman and mother, of the maternal and the semiotic/imaginary (not to be collapsed together), of the paternal and the symbolic, of mothering and giving birth. Indeed, paradox and contradiction may line the only understandable and understanding path to the description of an experience that is not only other but that incarnates the very experience of otherness through the dissolution of the unity of self. In psychoanalytic terms, the subject is split, divided, separated, and this experience goes hand in hand with the dissolution of language. As Carolyn Burke puts it, in "Stabat Mater" Kristeva "attempts a reconsideration of the problematics of maternal love that allows her to think beyond the conceptual limits of unified discourse" (Burke and Gallop, 112). Motherhood functions, among other things, as a model, a metaphor, or perhaps even a symbol, for this radical splitting—itself a metonymic *différance.* All subjects exist at the junction of pain and pleasure, lack and plenitude, identity and difference. Motherhood undermines conventional discourse, threatens its collapse. The maternal body is an empty emblem of the subject's ambivalent, ambiguous position between the sensuous pre-Oedipal attachment and the disciplined detachment that constitutes the Oedipal. It is the source of disruption—the terrain of the semiotic, of primary processes—and the precondition for the production of the symbolic, the secondary processes of signification. "Any attempt to transform the maternal body into a coherent signifying position is a fraud, precisely because it is a heterogeneous site, constantly doubling itself and separating itself from itself," writes Ewa Ziarek (334). Thus the mother's division, for example, allows her to engage in a complex identification with and participation in a symbolic order that, in any event and as I pointed out above, is not monolithic, but rather multiple, made up of heterogeneous practices and alternative discourses.

Allegorized in turn-of-the-century pregnancy texts as bodily deformity, and perceived by the same texts as the abjected maternal body, the dissolution of the self is represented as an alteration, as an experience of otherness and therefore of the difference that traverses the subject, the difference that is intrinsic to identity itself. Identity is nothing short of a bodily struggle, a *corps à corps* to quote Irigaray, with or against the mother. Within the phallogocentric economy pregnancy marks the female body as morphologically dubious, as troublesome because it defeats the notion of fixed bodily form based on a masculine paradigm; its change of shape is a deformity, it is monstrous—and as such it elicits both fascination and horror. But this morphological malleability, this difference, can also be interpreted "differently." Like pregnancy in the literary texts analyzed earlier, maternity is a liminal figure that functions, in Kristeva's discourse, for example, to point to the alterity that, by residing so conspicuously within the self, threatens (productively) the very notion of a unified subject. To cite Lynne Huffer, "one could say that [Kristeva's] entire project has an aim to undermine the philosophy of being that constitutes the construction of the unified subject" (*Maternal Pasts,* 87). Signification, or the play between semiotic and symbolic, dissolves the subject's cohesion—much like pregnancy, I might add. For the subject, in Kristeva's elaboration, is not simply split into conscious and unconscious by its initiation into the Name of the Father with its paternal function of Law. Rather, it is in its relationship with the mother's body, with the maternal function, that the unity of the subject is called into question and the precarious borders of subjectivity are initially ruptured.

Indeed the semiotic does not disappear with the child's entry into and acquisition of language, of the symbolic, the paternal law. Rather, it continues to operate within signification. If for Lacan the unconscious is structured like a language, for Kristeva, in a sense, the unconscious is heterogeneous to language. Therefore the subject, more than simply divided, is the subject of scission, always threatened by the semiotic as the pre-Oedipal, the prelinguistic, which is heterogeneous to rational logic and to meaning itself, and which enjoys a privileged relation to the maternal body. Absolute refusal of the symbolic entails psychosis. Yet the semiotic, as the maternal and the poetic, erupts, transgresses, and thus expands on the limits of the symbolic. One of its privileged sites is thus the poetic text. Another, the maternal.

The articulation of semiotic and symbolic can help us make sense of the body as well as of the making of the subject. The subject-in-process is, I would claim, exemplified by the pregnant body in texts such as Neera's and Deledda's. In these texts, the configuration of the mother as "threshold of nature and culture" ("Stabat Mater," "Women's Time"), as the bridge between drives and the symbolic, points to multiple contradictions—between, for example, transgressive pleasure and social conservatism, difference and identity, semiotic and symbolic. These apparent contradictions or dichotomies are deconstructed by the mother's position at the threshold. Like the maternal body in "Motherhood According to Giovanni Bellini," these maternity narratives are "the place of a splitting" in terms of character, story, reader, and ideology. The mother, the pregnant woman, is always positioned at a crossroads, her body is the fold between nature and culture, its expression and its impression, as it is stretched between, traversed by the semiotic and the symbolic, identity and its erasure. And yet she is silenced, mute in Western art, spoken for, even in Kristeva's essay, only by the male artist/son. A pregnant woman, in particular, visibly embodies a split identity: She is one and more-than-one; she supports and at the same time dissolves the symbolic order; she experiences, displays, performs negativity. Can ethics find a place, then, in this elaboration? Or, to go one step further along with Kristeva, can this elaboration constitute the model for an ethics of practice, what in "Stabat Mater" Kristeva calls a "herethics"?

In her book *Maternal Pasts, Feminist Futures* Huffer argues that "Kristeva's theory of liberation through language is therefore ultimately inimical to what Irigaray, and many others, would call a liberatory politics: a politics based in the primacy of sociality and the ethical relation" (76). For Huffer, ethics is more than absent from Kristeva's theoretical edifice: It is fundamentally extraneous to it. Kristeva's theory lacks for Huffer "the conceptual vocabulary to talk about justice, work, and social responsibility" (93), in contrast to Emmanuel Levinas's statement concerning the ethical self's responsibility for the other: "Responsibility for the other, this way of answering without a prior commitment, is human fraternity itself, and it is prior to freedom" (in Huffer, *Maternal Pasts,* 94). It is not a traditional ethics that we find in Kristeva's work, to be sure, but rather an ethics of practice and process in which alterity takes precedence over identity, in which, in fact, identity is impossible without alterity. Ontology is subsequent to ethics, for only in recognition of the other do we access our self. To some extent, perhaps, Huffer's elision of the ethical from Kristeva may be related to what Alice Jardine describes as "the sensitive point of contact between American feminist thought—a primarily *ethical* discourse *as prescription for action* and a certain French emphasis on the *human subject's inscription in culture through language*" ("Prelude," xxvi). Or one could even say, with Oliver, that "neither traditional phenomenology nor traditional psychoanalysis is ethical, nor can they set up the possibility of ethics," because their theories of the subject are based on the exclusion of the other, and are therefore unable to discuss and describe "reciprocal and nonsacrificial relationships" (*Family Values,* xviii). The question, then, is to ascertain whether Kristeva's work ought to be regarded as traditional psychoanalysis or not. Overall, though, it might be more pertinent in this context to acknowledge that what many critics seek in Kristeva's thought is a straightforward, logical, abstract epistemology that discourses of maternity are, in my readings and experience, unable, or, maybe, unwilling to convey.

The original title and thrust of "Stabat Mater" was "Héréthique de l'amour," or "Herethics of love," highlighting the essay's reinscription of a maternal ethics based on the mother–child relationship in pregnancy and birth, and thus an ethics founded on otherness—emphasizing, in Mary Jacobus's words, "the difficult access to a radical Other demanded by maternity" (169). Kristeva's definition of the ethical is indeed a "reaching out to the other ("Stabat Mater," 259–60), "that which in life makes bonds, thoughts, and therefore the thought of death, bearable" (263), a relational practice rather than an abstract set of principles, a recognition of otherness in both the other and the self—of which motherhood as the child's arrival gives women the possibility, though not the certainty. In motherhood, the encounter with the other is inevitable, implacable, goes without saying—literally as well as metaphorically. The mother's other, however, is multiple, not one. It is herself grown different, and it is the child, certainly (and more specifically a son in "Stabat Mater"), but it is also the mother's own mother. At this point, Kristeva's "herethics," a herethical ethics (going beyond, that is, the paradigm of the Virgin Mary, but also beyond the psychoanalytic account that Kristeva at one level endorses and elaborates) is reminiscent of Irigaray's and Muraro's emphasis on female genealogies: "at night, opaque joy that roots me in her bed, my mother's, and projects him, a son, a butterfly soaking up dew from her hand, there, nearby, in the night. Alone: she, I, and he" ("Stabat Mater," 247). Thus, as Oliver notes, "the love that founds 'herethics' is a daughter's love through identification with her mother" (*Subjectivity without Subjects,* 73). For a mother, love for the other is love for the mother, for the mother as other and for the mother as self—hence the reference to narcissism in the first of the essay's subtitles: "The paradox: mother or primary narcissism." One might agree, optimistically, with Alison Ainley's conclusion to her essay on Kristeva, namely that "the possibility of formulating conceptions of maternity which are not definitional of women may indicate ways of informing and perhaps transforming ethical relations. But this possibility is not divorced from both informing and transforming understandings of maternity" (61). Our understanding of maternity, then, can be transformed by first informing ourselves of its cultural-historical specificities and, above all, of its intrinsic difference. Only as *pure* difference, however, as it is in *pensiero della differenza sessuale,* and not as difference *from* a male norm, can maternal discourse, despite and through all its contradictions, flourish and begin to be understood. Only then might we be able to formulate notions of maternity as conducive to, indicative of ethical transformations: an ethics of otherness and love, an ethics based on the access to and care of the Other by means that are both bodily and linguistic.

In her book *Mothering,* Silvia Vegetti Finzi also posits motherhood as an ethical paradigm, for in this relationship that is so asymmetrical as to appear as the most violent form of domination, the mother's ability to split (part of her contains the child, part of her aids the child's separation and individuation) allows her to be "the only absolute master who limits herself, the only tyrant who loosens the hold that she maintains over her subject" (175). Philosopher Sara Ruddick developed the concept of "maternal thinking" as the philosophical elaboration of motherhood as ethical practice. The practice of mothering is for Ruddick cognitive and intellectual as well as bodily; it includes complex modes of thought and action that indicate particular ways of conceptualizing, ordering, valuing—in turn implying philosophical and political ramifications. Ruddick's words resonate with Finzi's and, in more complex ways, with Kristeva's, when she asserts that "Love, the love of children at any rate, is not only the most intense of attachments; it is also a detachment, a giving up, a letting grow. To love a child without seizing or using it, to see *the child's* reality with the patient, loving eyes of attention [in Weil's sense]—such loving and attending might well describe the separation of mother and child from the mother's point of view" ("Maternal Thinking," 358). This emphasis on ethics is reminiscent both of Irigaray's *Ethics of Sexual Difference* and of Spivak's reading of Hélène Cixous that I discussed in Chapter 2. The ethics of maternity is an ethics of the threshold, the border; it is grounded in sexual difference; it compels an effortful and responsible practice; it invites us to the ethical project of self-understanding and self-definition through the risky play of separation and identification, difference and communion.

The reformulation of ethics as maternal ethics demands, in Kristeva's view as well as in Finzi's and Ruddick's, the contribution of women, of mothers; and yet maternal ethics, maternal love, maternal thinking is at least partly elicited by the child—rather than spontaneously arising from a romanticized, idealized womanly essence. Maternal thinking is not one, to echo Irigaray, for it is steeped in mutuality and reciprocity as well as in difference. Maternal ethics transforms the subjects through mutual self-constitution. In this renewed ethical framework, splitting lies at the basis of healing, for without splitting there is no otherness, and no possibility for either language or love; yet at the same time a purpose of ethics is to make and maintain bonds. Thus Chodorow can claim that "Differentiation is not distinctness and separateness, but a particular way of being connected to others" ("Gender Relation," 11). Furthermore, "we can only think of differentiation and the emergence of the self relationally. Differentiation occurs, and separation emerges, in relationship; they are not givens" (11). The division of the flesh that is also a division of language establishes both the *jouissance* of difference and its maternal, ethical imperative to and of love. Difference, and specifically sexual difference, can become a paradigm for social and political theories that resist the unified and stable subject of individualism—and thus, implicitly, the reductive view of woman as mother that is otherwise risked throughout Kristeva's works. Mothers embody differentiation in sameness, as is most obvious in the mother–daughter bond—a relationship grounded in the need to recognize difference without denying sameness (and vice versa); a relationship in which maternal impressions need not obfuscate the daughter's expressions. By establishing a link between woman and the world—the child—maternity is one privileged means of entry into society, culture, the symbolic—rather than the exclusion of and from all this. Connection, rather than separation, can mediate the way to the Other. Let me then end this chapter with Kristeva's own plain and explicit words from her essay "Women's Time":

> The arrival of the child . . . leads the mother into the labyrinths of an experience that, without the child, she would only rarely encounter: love for an other. Not for herself, not for an identical being, and still less for another person with whom "I" fuse (love or sexual passion). But the slow, difficult and delightful apprenticeship in attentiveness, gentleness, forgetting oneself. The ability to succeed in this path without masochism and without annihilating one's affective, intellectual and professional personality—such would seem to be the stakes to be won through guiltless maternity. It then becomes a creation in the strong sense of the term. For this moment, utopian? (206)

FOUR

Childbirth, or the Paradoxical Body

Impressions of Parturition

Parting and Parturition in Advice Manuals and *Midwives*

The advice manual that my husband and I were assigned to read during our childbirth preparation class, in 1994, begins its preface with what struck me as a shocking proposition: "Birth never changes. Society and culture change. Maternity care changes. Women, men, and families change. But birth never changes" (Simkin, Whalley, and Keppler, 5). This is a book I cherished for many months, my favorite among the plethora I purchased, borrowed, read, or skimmed during my pregnancies. Yet this opening statement made little sense to me then, and it makes no sense now. What is birth aside from society and culture, aside from maternity care, aside from, especially, women, men, and families? Does maternity not matter for birth and delivery? Can we really advocate the existence of a biological birth as a bodily process independent of its environment—including, first and foremost, its maternal environment, the woman? Can we say the same about other bodily processes—say, digestion? Or are the movements of our gastrointestinal tract so determined by our cultural rhythms (what foods we eat, when we eat them, how we eat them, what we do before, during, and after we eat them, for instance) that they cannot be understood apart from them? How much truer that must be, then, for a bodily process that involves the transformation of one subject and the coming into being of another.

Because it is such a radical process—a process of splitting and separation, of loss and transformation—the act of delivery and childbirth evokes fear; the taboos and curses of old survive into, for example, our present phobic aversion to pain and suffering. In this framework, maternity manuals mention, usually at the beginning of their discussion of birth, several delivery choices for today's pregnant women. Hospital birth is the most common, though even within that type there are many possibilities according to variables such as geography, economics (can the local hospital afford special birthing suites?), ideology of the practitioners, attitudes toward the particular woman (influenced by factors such as age, class, race, education), and so on. But there are also, in some places, free-standing birthing centers, and an increasing number of women opt for home births, coached by a lay midwife in addition to their partner. The trend seems to be, at least in theory, toward a de-medicalization of childbirth; this is certainly true of the ideology of childbirth advice manuals, bent on extolling the naturalness of the childbirth process—although this trend is in practice counteracted by the increasing percentage of births through cesarean section. Many at our turn of the century, then, seek to undo, through the alternative birth movement, what the last turn of the century so pervasively accomplished: to reverse the transformation of childbirth into a depersonalized medical procedure in which women have no voice and return it back to where it belongs, to the practice of daily life. While for some women this means avoiding drugs or a C-section, for others it means birth at home with a lay midwife.

Now I do not speak in the name of the good old days, I am not a *laudatrix temporis acti* where pregnancy, labor, and delivery are concerned: I do not yearn for the idyllic past of maternity because I have no reason to believe that there ever was one. The biblical curse, "In sorrow thou shalt bear children," is not meaningless. In fact, I get irritated when I hear or read references to how wonderful and easy it used to be to have children the natural way, just squatting in the fields and going right back to work, without doctors or drugs to turn this joyfully simple event into a nightmare of complications. Women used to die quite frequently of childbirth, and childbirth, from what I have read about it, was not as a rule eagerly anticipated by pregnant women as an enlightening experience—on the contrary.

In this respect, I find exemplary the behavior of Antonietta in Maria Messina's novel *A House in the Shadows*. As Antonietta approaches childbirth for the third time, the narrator relays that each time she cleans and orders her house and goes to confession, acutely aware of the possibility that she may well die in the upcoming event of labor and delivery: "She was pregnant again. Each time it happened, she would go over the whole house, from top to bottom, with her own hands, and go to confession in the nearby church, as though about to leave for a long journey. 'Well, isn't it as if I was going away?' she said softly. 'I have to say goodbye to things, and to all of you. How can I be sure I'll ever open these chests again, or touch any of these things with my own hands?' " (38–39). Childbirth was a journey from which one did not necessarily return alive, so Antonietta prepares for it as she would prepare for death. She cleans her house from top to bottom so that, if she should die, people would not say that she was "a bad, untidy housewife" (39). On top of that, she goes to confession. As it turns out, Antonietta barely survives the delivery of this child, a daughter, and has to convalesce in bed for over two months—during which time her husband repeatedly rapes Antonietta's sister, who lives with them. Death, then, is not an inappropriate expression for the impressive transformation about to take place in this woman's life.

Women in our own, late-twentieth- and early-twenty-first-century Western society rarely approach childbirth with Antonietta's level of apprehension, especially if all has gone well during their pregnancy. Yes, pregnancy is a time of worries: that is after all the motivation behind the composition of the popular manual *What to Expect When You're Expecting*, "written with the hope," explain the authors in the preface, "that it will help fathers- and mothers-to-be worry less and enjoy their pregnancies more" (Eisenberg, Murkoff, and Hathaway, xxiii). *Worry* in this context is the opposite of enjoyment and "one of the most common complaints of pregnancy" (xxiii), and not, as a century ago, the fear of death—the opposite of which would be survival. The mother's fear of dying is expressly addressed in this manual in the section on the eighth month, where it is dismissed because founded on a risk that is virtually nonexistent. Fewer than one in ten thousand women die in childbirth in the United States today, an inclusive figure that counts even those who deliver without any professional assistance. In short, "you stand a lot better chance of surviving labor and delivery than you do a trip to the supermarket in your car, or a stroll across a busy street" (Eisenberg, Murkoff, and Hathaway, 240). Childbirth is no longer the equivalent of a perilous and life-threatening journey, though the "nesting instinct" may lead many of us, like Antonietta, to scour and straighten our house in preparation for the new arrival—and not, as for Antonietta, in fear of a postmortem verdict on our housekeeping skills.

But to what extent is this disconnection between birth and death the result of our society's general repression of death—its experience, its anticipation, its fear? Will we, should we start fearing giving birth in a hospital the way we generally fear dying in a hospital? For although it is certainly true that women in our society rarely die from childbirth or its complications, it is also true that, at an existential level, thinking of birth is linked to thinking of death, for generativity points to finitude. I am laboring so hard to bring my child into the world, yet this child is condemned to die: whether in days or in years, it *will* happen. "Preoccupation with death is not an irrational response to the anticipation or to the experience of birth. Birth and death are close together, and in giving birth a woman may learn more about death than in any other experience," writes Penelope Washbourn (98). At the same time, as I give birth I experience a crisis little recognized and acknowledged by society and the medical profession. My own self, the not-mother self that took my whole life to develop, is shattering into a new being—a mother. My self-identity is challenged and often destroyed and re-created in vital ways, different for each woman, in the course of pregnancy. And the identity forged in the course of those momentous nine months is in turn short-lived, for at birth a new relationship begins between woman and infant, and a new role faces the mother.

In spite of all my reading and many medical appointments, I was little prepared for the radical upheaval that having my first child was to entail. This may be one of life's best-kept secrets (if I may resort to a cliché)—a maze through which you have to find your own way because no one can adequately prepare you for it. But no one even tried, it seemed to me, certainly not any of the six doctors in the practice that assisted me in the birth of my first two children. Their job was to take care of my body, to read it for signs of pathology, for symptoms of dangerous motherhood, and not to soften the impact of its wild storms of passions, hurricanes of love, pleasure, desire. Pregnancy and childbirth, as maternal impressions, are indeed singularly unspoken.

If turn-of-the-century texts depict survival of mother and child as the most desirable outcome of childbirth, as indeed all that one could possibly want or hope for, the relative safety of childbirth today has left a gap of meaning that insistently demands to be filled by a different set of hopes and expectations. Educated women especially tend to imagine childbirth as a transformative process to be lived at its fullest and its most "natural," even as we remain aware of the dangers lurking behind the notion of nature. Although it is constructed as liberating, the rhetoric of the natural can subtly and not so subtly constrain, shape, and even reduce the experience of maternity. Helena Michie and Naomi Cahn succeed in crystallizing the rhetoric of the natural childbirth movement and its dangers for women's self-understanding around the two burning issues of pain management and the cesarean section; the latter is viewed as the epitome of the technologization of the birthing body and thus as the ultimate failure in natural childbirth. As these authors conclude, "women have a natural relation to their bodies; the intimate connection of the body to nature is a sign of appropriate femininity . . . a cesarean interrupts the relation of the body to nature at the cost of the feminine" (61). Childbirth as the test of true womanhood is analogous to war for males, for once on the battlefield, the soldier does not have the choice to leave, just as a woman in labor cannot stop what she is doing. But this battle is no longer won by physical survival alone. Rather, victory consists of the ability to withstand pain and avoid drugs, to avert any other possible medical intervention—above all, the dreaded cesarean section, on the increase in the United States—and to be psychologically enlightened, spiritually enriched, personally fulfilled by this climactic event. The authors of the preface from which I quoted at the beginning of this chapter, for example, state: "We want childbirth to be a marvelous memory. We hope that this book, along with the essentials . . . will contribute to a safe birth, a healthy baby, and an experience that will always evoke feelings of fulfillment, satisfaction, and accomplishment" (Simkin, Whalley, and Keppler, vi).

Alas, along with many women I have failed on many of these counts each time I have given birth. The delivery of my first child, my son Paul, was induced after a week-long amniotic leak; I had an IV and an external fetal monitor around my belly for the entire eighteen hours it took to give birth to him, after about twelve of which I begged for epidural anesthesia, and I pushed for no less than four hours. An episiotomy was also recommended, and who was I to say no? The attending medical student was a surgeon-to-be who had no interest in what I was experiencing and whose perfunctory questions made him an irritating sight; it was he who stitched me up in unspeakable places despite my clearly stated request that he be only an observer. I did not get to hold my son right after birth because I had been running a fever during labor and he had to be examined by a pediatrician—so much for immediate bonding. In fact, Paul had no interest in breastfeeding when he finally was handed to me, an attitude generally interpreted as a bad omen; and sure enough I did have problems breastfeeding him for the first few weeks. Were it not for the help of several nurses, doctors, and lactation consultants, and my own stubbornness, I would have been unable to nurse him.

I had great hopes for Gemma, my second child. Having begun my study of the history of childbirth during my pregnancy with her, I was eager to experience this birth 100 percent, without drugs or medical interventions. The second one is much easier to deliver, everyone said, experts included: "Second and subsequent labors are usually easier and shorter than first ones—often dramatically so" (Eisenberg, Murkoff, and Hathaway, 259). My doctors recommended against a doula, or female birth attendant, as an unnecessary encumbrance. Well, labor started naturally, though almost two weeks after my due date, and it was shorter. My waters gushed and labor started soon thereafter. Eleven hours are fewer than eighteen, are they not? They were all night hours, 8 P.M. to 7 A.M.; my husband and I were exhausted and left to our own poor devices much of the time (there had been budget staff cuts at the hospital). I begged for an epidural even more desperately than in my first labor, and cursed the fact that the anesthesiologist could not come immediately to my assistance. I pushed for "only" two hours. Gemma was fine despite her ice-cream cone–shaped head due to the doctor's use of a vacuum extractor to help ease her out: I was too tired to push effectively. I did, however, get away without an episiotomy. Small consolation. I got to hold her right away, but all I could think was that I wished they had cleaned her up first. I was too tired to see much beyond the blood and mucus. She suckled so eagerly that, after an hour sucking at the breast and another hour at my husband's little finger, I begged the nurses for a pacifier; they did not want to give it to her for fear of nipple confusion: that baby was not at all confused, could they not see? In the end, I was stuck in a hospital bed for five days because in the course of labor and delivery I injured my neck though no one noticed. Doctors and nurses paid no attention to me when I asked for someone else to hold the baby out of the delivery room—I was terrified that I would drop her, and it was not an irrational fear: my arms were giving out with exhaustion. But I was told that hospital regulations demand that the mother carry the baby out. The next few hours were characterized by nurses pushing me to do what I was physically unable to do, to which my body reacted with vomiting, fainting, and passing blood clots.

I took all these signs to mean that I needed a more mother-centered and less doctor-oriented delivery for my third child, though I never seriously considered the possibility of home birth. So I chose the only local midwife group that works in and with the hospital to take care of Sophia and me. Ironically, however, as I recounted in Chapter 2, I ended up needing an emergency cesarean section, so that although my midwife was there holding my hand while my husband held the other, it was the doctor on call who delivered my daughter. All's well that ends well, we both survived and recovered faster than Messina's Antonietta, and soon thrived. That is certainly more than would have happened at the turn of the century. I had no complaints about the C-section because I appreciated not having to go through labor; the doctors who performed it, although I had never met them before, were the most empathetic I had encountered; and recovery was easier than it had been with my second child. I cannot identify therefore with the women interviewed by Emily Martin for whom cesarean section was analogous to crucifixion, rape, and evisceration (*The Woman in the Body*, 84). To have enjoyed one's C-section is another unspoken paradox of the birth experience. And although none of my deliveries was the exhilarating ecstasy that I was led to believe I would have, or was supposed to have, still I would place myself among those many mothers who, when interviewed for the book *Women's Ways of Knowing*, selected childbirth as "the most important learning experience [we] have ever had," because "it is as if this act of creation ushers in a whole new view of one's creative capacities" (Belenky et al., 35).

Even when they pose as coolly open to all options, maternity manuals tend to reinforce this expectation of exhilarating, transforming power. *What to Expect When You're Expecting*, for instance, states that "the only goal—which all parents share—is a healthy mother and a healthy baby" (Eisenberg, Murkoff, and Hathaway, 208). It sounds nice, if a bit optimistic. One of Carolina Invernizio's shady characters, for example, hopes not for health but for his wife to die in childbirth so that he may inherit her fortune (*Cuore di madre*, A mother's heart, 73, 105, 231). But what does "healthy" really mean? Was I healthy when confined to a hospital bed for five days following the healthy delivery of my healthy second child? Is the safety of childbirth only a matter of life and death? And surprisingly, in spite of the authors' recognition of the "miraculous medical advancements" in the field of childbirth, they too resort to the myth of natural childbirth when they urge the reader "not to become so obsessed that you forget that childbirth is a natural process—one that women managed to stumble through successfully for thousands of years" (Eisenberg, Murkoff, and Hathaway, 208). Do they really mean it? What is the use, then, of what they term "miraculous medical advancements"? If childbirth is so natural, why read and study their detailed book? Why mess with Mother Nature if she is so successful, as this book repeatedly notes (e.g., 240, 273)?

Why is this invocation of the natural process of childbirth problematic? The creation of an ideal perfect birth makes all others (my children's included) at best pale and at worst failures in comparison. Which of course leads us to the subject, or perhaps I should say the question, of *natural childbirth*. What does it consist of? After the medicalization of pregnancy and childbirth, the discourse of natural childbirth struggled for a "return," real or imagined, to a premedical time, a time of woman-centered support and holistic care. On the other hand, medical discourse itself appropriated the term "natural," applying it in places that its original proponents certainly would not have approved; thus, for some, "natural childbirth" means that the woman is conscious when she delivers. That feminists should be skeptical of the concept of nature comes as no surprise. It is in the name of nature, and particularly the nature of reproduction, that women have traditionally been subjected. Nature has been coded as prescriptive and proscriptive. In the area of pregnancy and childbirth, nonetheless, medicalization has likely gone too far, as the medical establishment itself has repeatedly recognized: total anesthesia and routine induction of labor, for example, used for the convenience of the doctor, who could thus schedule the deliveries of his or her patients around other engagements, are no longer recommended as they used to be just a generation ago. At the same time, it seems clear from anthropological as well as literary and historical evidence that childbirth is never purely physiological or natural, but rather embedded in a cultural context that defines and enacts it. And, as Rosalyn Diprose suggests, "the maternal body is a privileged target of medical and moral attention because it is the site of the reproduction of the social body. Through this attention, caught as it is within the political investment of 'healthy' productive bodies suitable for exchange in a labor market, the maternal body is constituted as other to the 'normal' body" (125).

Whereas a century ago, for pregnant women such as those figured in Messina's Antonietta, the test of childbirth as proof of womanhood was passed by sheer survival, ideally of both mother and child, the mother's sexual identification in today's birthing experience in the West is both more superficial—inasmuch as it does not usually involve an actual confrontation with death—and more complex: cultural dictates on the subject, whether they assume a descriptive or a prescriptive guise, are polyvocal and often contradictory. Our culture's ambiguous stance toward the ideal outcome of childbirth is reflected in the success of Chris Bohjalian's 1997 novel *Midwives,* selected for Oprah Winfrey's influential Book Club and a best-seller for a number of weeks. The protagonist, Sibyl Danforth, is a respected lay midwife who has been assisting at home births for fifteen years. When one of her patients, Charlotte Fugett Bedford, dies after a long and complicated labor, Sibyl performs a cesarean section on her and saves Charlotte's child. But the prosecutors claim that the patient was not dead and that Sibyl's illegally performed C-section is what killed her, since midwives are not trained or allowed to operate. On trial through the book, then, is not only Sibyl Danforth as an individual midwife but rather, more generally, the safety of home births. For example, the extraordinary circumstances that prevented Charlotte from being transferred to a hospital—a snow and ice storm that downed telephone lines and made roads impassable—are not all that extraordinary if we remember that the story is set in northeastern Vermont, where such weather vagaries in winter are to be expected. And from a historical perspective, it is significant that

Sibyl should have been damned by an illegally performed cesarean section because the exclusion of midwives from this obstetrical procedure starting in the fifteenth century was the first step in the marginalization of women from the scene of childbirth and from the healing professions more generally (Blumenfeld-Kosinski, chap. 3).

Bohjalian's novel struck me in many ways. Unlike the other fiction I discuss in this book, *Midwives* displayed a contemporary setting that made it quite vivid for me; it was set in Vermont, where I live, and some of the consultants acknowledged by the author at the end of the book had been my own caregivers. More important, several of my family members, friends, and acquaintances had read *Midwives* and had strong opinions about it, which were fascinating and instructive for me to hear. Women who themselves had home births, for example, harshly criticized the novel for not doing justice to the good sense of midwives—who would not attempt a delivery in the middle of an ice storm—and for being unfairly detrimental to the perception of home births and especially of their safety. For although the novel is very sympathetic to Sibyl and richly develops the physical and spiritual advantages of giving birth at home, making the process sound desirable indeed, it also implies that this fabulous experience carries definite risks, that one may have to pay dearly for its pleasures. The negative viewpoint expressed by the medical community throughout the book is confirmed by Charlotte's death. Whether Sibyl did kill Charlotte by cutting into her belly with a kitchen knife is left only mildly uncertain. In the two pages of her notebooks that are not revealed to the reader until the end, Sibyl admits to having seen Charlotte's body flinch when she cut into her, though it is also reasonable to doubt, as Sibyl herself does, the accuracy of the perception of such a small movement on the part of an exhausted and distraught midwife. Was it a maternal expression, or just the midwife's wrong impression?

Despite its contemporary American setting, Bohjalian's *Midwives* shares with turn-of-the-century women writers many important elements. The mother–daughter bond is central to the thematic and narrative development of the novel, which is told in the first person by Sibyl's own daughter, Connie. At thirty years of age, Connie recounts in incredible detail the events that forever changed the life of her family sixteen years earlier, when she was fourteen years old. It is Connie who saves her mother from conviction by hiding those self-indicting pages from the notebook, the very pages that conclude the novel. But those pages do change Connie, whose career choice clearly questions the safety of her mother's practice: Connie becomes an ob-gyn. She insists that she continues what her mother did, deliver babies, and yet at the same time she radically changes it. She delivers babies in a hospital, not in homes; she is an M.D., not a midwife. This choice fundamentally separates her from her mother's vocation and severs their professional genealogy, even though Connie takes great pains to distinguish herself from "bad ob-gyns"—the ones, that is, who don't give their patients enough time (143–44). The management of time is indeed one of the great differences between woman-centered and doctor-centered births, the time needed to develop empathy and thus the ability to understand and truly assist, help, the parturient woman, the time needed in order to give her what Simone Weil defines as "attention."

Of great importance for the genealogical connection between *Midwives* and its turn-of-the-century Italian predecessors is also the discussion of quickening and of the feeling of fetal movement in general. Presented in one of the epigraphs that introduce almost every chapter, all taken from Sibyl Danforth's notebooks, quickening is included among the "little miracles" (along with conception, hardening of bones, presence of fingerprints, turning, descent, and so on) that foreshadow birth, the big miracle. Quickening is later described as Sibyl's personal favorite among these little miracles (148–49). The book abounds in vague spiritual imagery, especially in the pages from Sibyl's notebooks—where the whole community of midwives, actively involved in Sibyl's professional, personal, and legal ordeal, is described as deeply spiritual. Charlotte herself is the wife of a minister. This spiritual dimension of midwifery contrasts with the scientific detachment of the medical approach to pregnancy and childbirth depicted in the novel and recapitulates the medicalization of birth as the victory of a secular science over an approach deeply connected to tradition and theology. While for the medical experts called on the stand at Sibyl's trial the body is a machine grounded in and limited by biological factors, with the doctor implicitly positioned as the mechanic who alone is able and should be entitled to fix it, for midwives such as Sibyl there is an unbreakable continuity between pregnancy, childbirth, and a woman's spirit.

Nowhere is this continuity clearer, in pregnancy, than in quickening. Thus, quickening demands metaphor as the trope enacting connection, with the background of a metonymic movement: Sibyl feels "this tiny flutter," "a tadpole flicking its tail," "a ripple, a wave," "a psychedelic little person doing the breaststroke in a lava lamp," "a bubble bouncing euphorically, but in slow motion" (149). Quickening is for Sibyl, as for writers before her, "knowledge": "You want to feel your friend, you want to know he or she's there" (149). Quickening in *Midwives,* as for Bohjalian's predecessors in maternity narratives, is bound through metaphor and metonymy to the movements of the heart as the organ of sexual difference and sexual communion, as physically and functionally contiguous with the uterus, as well as morphologically and semiotically similar to it: "*quickening* is the perfect word to describe it, because your heart races, and the pace of pregnancy just takes off" (149). Quickening signifies for the pregnant woman an awareness of the other, of the ethical dimension of her body in relation: "I just sat on that rock grooving on the little person—my little person—inside me" (149). Ultimately, quickening implies change, the radical transformation brought about by metaphoric knowledge on the metonymic path to love of and for the other. It may be a joyful metamorphosis, as it is for Sibyl when she first feels Connie move, but it may also be used, doubling the metaphor, to refer to painful knowledge changes; for example, when, in the courtroom, Sibyl makes eye contact with Charlotte's sister and mother, she feels "absolutely pregnant with guilt. I feel it growing inside me, I half-expect to touch my tummy with my left hand and feel something move. A little kick. One of those hiccups" (220). As in Oriana Fallaci's *Letter to a Child Never Born,* the pleasurable, empowering, enlightening value of quickening can be easily turned upside down, troped into a metaphor of pain and loss, and of untrustworthy signs that deceptively figure semiotic fullness in the place of corporeal emptiness.

Childbirth is presented in *Midwives* with a scientifically accurate yet also a poetic vocabulary, mediated by a narrator who witnessed the events, including several births in her mother's tow, as a child—with an immature outlook, then—and who is now a physician, an ob-gyn, no less, equipped with all the right words: with those technical, impersonal words that allow a distance between the speaker/caregiver and the pregnant/birthing woman; those powerful, empowering words that protect us from the uncomfortable functions of the messy, grotesque, leaky reproductive body, the obscene body with the disturbing power to produce life through, across the sexual act. The sexual body, embraced by the midwife's discourse, becomes for the ob-gyn—and thus for Connie, as well—a medicalized, mechanistic body. This is a body defined by science and reason, a functional body controlled by objective technology. It is a pathological body, therefore, for if it were otherwise that body would be incomprehensible, beyond medicine's grasp. Its changes are dangerous and impel the doctor's crisis-oriented, preemptive, proactive approach—the only modus operandi equipped to deal with the range and rapidity of the birthing body's potential problems. But Bohjalian's novel revels in the changes of pregnancy and childbirth as a desirable outcome rather than a pathological perversion of healthy adulthood: "in the first stage of labor . . . each surge has the potential to change the mother, and eventually one will" (190). Change, exemplified by quickening, subtends the continuity of the maternal experience. And, like the laboring women it repeatedly evokes, this novel emits a scream, a lacerating scream, as well as a silence. Its pleas for home birth and especially for the de-medicalization of the reproductive body are strong and fair.

Yet the protagonist's legal acquittal is based on the illegal removal of evidence: Connie hides her mother's self-incriminating notebook pages. And after the trial, Sibyl, although legally allowed to deliver babies once again, promptly finds herself unable to do so. Her life's passion and the voice of home births is silenced by this abdication as much as by Charlotte's death and by Connie's career choice as member of the very profession bent on silencing her mother's work, and, more important, by Connie's ideological allegiance to a secular, disempowering conception of the maternal function. The intimate link between the biological fullness of the pregnant uterus and the social, if not spiritual character of its product, its creation, its impression—the child—marks the impossibility to disengage the body from the spirit, nature from culture, maternity from society. Or, in Bohjalian's book, mother and daughter and/as narrator and protagonist. Their inescapable connection, beautifully represented in Sibyl's description of Connie's quickening in her pregnant uterus many years before, and problematically antagonized by Connie's career choice as good doctor, yet a doctor nevertheless, imbues the narration with a continuous double-bind, an inevitable impossibility. There is no junction, and yet there can be no disjunction, between two bodies one of which has spent nine months inside the other, as there is no junction, and yet no disjunction, either, between body and mind, nature and culture, psychology and physiology, active and passive, male and female, private and political, and all those impossible oppositions that are endlessly invoked in feminist and cultural theory. The impossibility of motherhood is, also, the paradox of the parturient body, of the parting of one subject from another with whom it was never one, anyway.

Parting and Parturition in Turn-of-the-Century Science

In her study of the construction of the female body in the scientific discourse of reproduction, Emily Martin has accurately portrayed the contradictions inherent in the medical descriptions of labor and delivery through mechanical metaphors: "In sum, medical imagery juxtaposes two pictures: the uterus as a machine that produces the baby and the woman as laborer who produces the baby" (*The Woman in the Body*, 63). Contradiction and paradox also characterize the representation and construction of pregnancy, labor, and delivery in turn-of-the-century scientific accounts. "Childbirth is the capital event in a woman's life," states

Mantegazza in *Fisiologia della donna* (2:63). "Capital" because most important, but "capital" also because not unlikely to turn into a deathly punishment, proceeding from Eve's infraction and the consequent biblical injunction, in Genesis 3:16: "In sorrow thou shalt bring forth children." With his pithy phrase, Mantegazza articulates the biologistic sentiment of the scientific community of his age regarding women. Perhaps because of this dual link to both life and death, childbirth, a subject largely absent from the texts of high literature, is repeatedly evoked in the analyses of women carried out in turn-of-the-century scientific treatises in Italy. The best-known and most influential among these, Mantegazza's *Fisiologia della donna* and Lombroso's *La donna delinquente, la prostituta e la donna normale*, peremptorily define childbirth, on the basis of medical and anthropological evidence, as the culminating event in every woman's life, its ultimate and impressive expression. Childbirth is inherently telling of woman's condition, the ultimate and hegemonic metonymy of her state: "every human female must necessarily give birth," Mantegazza firmly declares (*Fisiologia*, 2:224). And Lombroso, faithful to his anthropometrical method that posits the somatic as inherently semantic, even goes so far as to claim that "motherhood is an eminently physiological phenomenon" (*La donna*, 499), thus making the birthing body the proleptic emblem of the maternal function—a physiologically dictated destiny.

Many complex social and cultural motivations underpin the turn-of-the-century scientific ideology of maternity. As Valeria Babini puts it, "the emphasis on the value of motherhood and on the sacrality of the female role appear to be explicitly instrumental to the defense of the bourgeois family, a relatively new value that was already being undermined by the same economic transformation which had brought it about" (64). Yet a comparative analysis makes it possible to relate Mantegazza's reductive and essentializing statements concerning women as mothers to contemporary reevaluations of childbirth, on the part of feminist voices, as an empowering, or, alternately, a disenfranchising activity for women. Judith Walzer Leavitt begins her history of childbirth in America with the sentences, "Childbirth is more than a biological event in women's lives. It is a vital component in the social definition of womanhood" (3). Whether this "vital" component contributes to or detracts from women's own vitality, whether the capital event turns into a capital punishment depends on multiple factors that are increasingly controversial now that doubts are arising concerning the actual safety for most women of childbirth in the hospital.

In her polemical study *Safer Childbirth?* for example, Marjorie Tew effectively argues that the increased safety of childbirth depends not on obstetrical interventions, which are in her view prejudicial to it, but rather on the good health of the mother. So according to Tew "the great decline in mortality was brought about, not by life-saving medical treatments, but by the life-saving consequences of non-medical treatments"—such as, above all, improved nutrition. This caused the greater health and fitness of female, but also male bodies over the course of several generations (3). Malformed pelvises, for instance, were prevalent among nineteenth-century childbearing women, and the cause of much maternal mortality and morbidity. The biological as well as emotional importance of the mother–daughter bond is apparent in this argument, for to bear children successfully a woman needs proper nutrition from the time of her own conception, which links her health and physique to the health and physique of her own mother, and thus of her grandmother, and so on, in a vertical and cumulative process over generations of women. Furthermore, if we take *safety* to mean more than the relatively simple matter of life and death (since death during childbirth is, after all, extremely rare nowadays in the West) to include what happens in the postpartum period as a consequence of labor and delivery in an interventionist environment such as a hospital (e.g., pelvic infections, incontinence, depression, inability to breastfeed), then it seems that it is safer for low-risk women—though Tew would also include most high-risk women—to give birth at home. The transition from home to hospital, from midwife to physician, was due, according to Tew's combative but persuasive argument, to the following factors: the desire to reduce the casualties of reproduction; women's indoctrination into the perception that "doctor knows best"; the contemporary cultural and social preeminence of academically trained doctors in matters of life and death; the monetary and power rewards obstetricians reaped in their takeover of the reproductive realm; the inability of midwives to unite to adequately protect their professional interests against discreditations by the medical profession; the deceptive temporal coincidence between the transition from home to hospital and the improvement in maternal health and physique. This coincidence made it appear that the improvement in maternal mortality was due to the new medical treatments, but only a few, such as the use of antibiotics, had a verifiably positive impact.

For all his reiterations of women's intellectual inferiority, Mantegazza was ahead of his time in his sympathetic stance toward the needed social and legal reforms regarding maternity. He strongly advocated greater social protection for women and, especially, for pregnant, birthing, and breastfeeding women, who experienced conditions making them "more fragile than ever" (*Fisiologia*, 1:60). He also lamented the moral inequality between the sexes; for example, unwed mothers who alone had to bear the burden of an illegitimate pregnancy, an inequity seen by Mantegazza as the cause of the higher rate of infanticides among women than among men. Infanticide is consequently described as "the fruit of our prohibitions and cruel prejudices, which throw in woman's face alone the ignominy of love outside of marriage" (*Fisiologia*, 2:166).

On the one hand, childbirth constitutes for Mantegazza the ultimate proof of women's heroism in carrying out their life's mission and of their extraordinary ability to withstand pain: "Woe if man had to give birth!" (*Fisiologia*, 1:277), Mantegazza warns, connecting like Neera's *L'indomani* the experience of sex with that of maternity in terms of pleasure and pain. It is significant for Mantegazza that woman's sexual experience, vowed to pleasure, is linked in its inception by nature with the experience of the pain of defloration. So also motherhood, woman's "sovereign passion," ironically and perhaps even deceptively begins with the horrible suffering of parturition. Despite her greater resistance to pain, however, woman's intellectual inferiority, Mantegazza claims, condemns her to experience both pain and pleasure more acutely. Mantegazza expands on this in his famed *Fisiologia del piacere* (The physiology of pleasure, written in the 1850s and published in 1880), where he notes that, in woman, the surface of the "apparatus" destined to the pleasure of sex covers a much bigger area than in man, thus woman is capable of more intense and more frequent sexual pleasure than man. Her desire, too, is more intense and more frequent, although more easily concealed (48–49). This is at least in part because nature owed woman some "compensation" for the pains and dangers she faced as a consequence of sex—the pains and dangers of maternity. But lest we might give the parturient woman too much sympathy, the author is quick to remind us that man, because of his greater physical and intellectual struggles, "has new and fertile sources of pains that our companion ignores" (*Fisiologia*, 1:283). Indeed, Mantegazza writes that there are peoples, such as the Samoyeds, whose women give birth easily and without pain (unwittingly confirming Tew's arguments)—"so that, if by exception the birth should turn out to be difficult and laborious, it is assumed that the father is from another race and the poor parturient woman is beaten and abused, in order to make her confess a sin that is often imaginary" (*Fisiologia*, 1:170).

Still, the pains of childbirth seem to remain a mystery for Mantegazza, who even uses them to boldly object to Darwin's theories: Why does the pelvis not evolve into a wider opening, or why does pregnancy not end a month earlier, since both of these evolutionary changes would facilitate the propagation of the species by diminishing the dangers of childbirth (*Fisiologia*, 2:63)? For no other animal suffers like woman in giving birth, to the point that the association of one of life's happiest events with such great suffering seems to most humans an incomprehensibly "great crime of nature" (*Fisiologia*, 2:61), explained by all peoples with myths and theories that Mantegazza goes on to enumerate for several pages. Yet the connection he firmly establishes between the pain of sex and the pain of motherhood is a telling one, first of all because Mantegazza himself does not seem in the least disturbed by it; he leaves the rationalizing and mythmaking to peoples of antiquity, whom he calls "savages." Mantegazza biologizes this connection between woman, sex, and motherhood by seeing it as the will of "nature," which in Mantegazza's work replaces God. Nature provides for Mantegazza the myth that explicates the inexplicable. But nature has traditionally been conflated with the feminine, as opposed to masculine culture; *natura* in Italian is a euphemism for the female genitalia; indeed the word *nature* shares the same etymology as *birth* (from the Latin "nasci, natus" [to be born]). These discursive encounters heighten both the tautology of Mantegazza's arguments and the destabilization, on the part of his text (and of others, such as Lombroso's), of the artificial separation in contemporary academia between the history of science as a humanistic discipline, or a social science at best, and the construction of science proper. Biology, psychology, and anthropology blend in these turn-of-the-century texts to refute for the contemporary reader at least the legitimacy of the distinction between science as an objective discovery of knowledge and the interpretive enterprise of, for example, cultural criticism.

For Mantegazza, the physical pain associated with woman's bodiliness, be it in the first sexual contact or in parturition, is the natural outcome of an unstable constitution. Together with pregnancy and breastfeeding, for example, the postpartum period is described by Mantegazza as one of the "perturbing causes of the nervous system" (*Fisiologia*, 2:175), so that once again woman is destroyed even as she is biologically and socially fulfilled. There is something inherently sick in woman's nature if, as Mantegazza maintains in his *Fisiologia dell'amore*, "the woman giving birth is a wounded creature" (304)—a wound that he implies occurs also at defloration. But this wound is social as well as biological because procreative adultery (women who give birth, that is, to children not their husbands') is for Mantegazza "the most sordid and cancerous wound of our modern marriage" (*L'arte di prender moglie*, 24). In a sort of contagion, this wound is related to the wound of woman's nature. If newborns could proclaim the name of their true father, then we could see that "the belly of women" is "only a mint of false coins." But "the bellies of women are silent, proceeding with their work of counterfeiters" (*L'arte di prender moglie*, 25).

In their silence, Mantegazza identifies women's birthing bodies as deceptive rather than pained, as crossed by illicit pleasure rather than inexorable contradiction. And yet it is childbearing that ensures women's conformity to social values. In a detailed study of the sense and physical anomalies of normal women and prostitutes, published in the same year as Mantegazza's *Fisiologia della donna* and Lombroso's *La donna delinquente, la prostituta e la donna normale*, 1893, and entitled *I sensi e le anomalie somatiche nella donna normale e nella prostituta*, Raffaele Gurrieri and Ernesto Fornasari repeatedly note that prostitutes who have borne children are both more sensitive than childless prostitutes (although morally upright women, as expected, are more sensitive than any prostitute) and, more generally, less likely to exhibit degenerative traits such as precocious wrinkles, facial asymmetry, flattened nose, facial hair, and so on (14–17, and throughout the book). Following to the letter Lombroso's method of physical anthropometry, Gurrieri and Fornasari compile a catalogue of measurements of pain and pleasure, of heads and bodies, whose utter madness is matched only by the degree to which it takes itself seriously. Of relevance here is perhaps Mantegazza's criticism of Lombroso, his former friend, and his school: "as genial as he is rash, as impatient as he is inexact, he adds up crimes like eggs in a basket, like coins in a purse, and he then plays with the false sums like an artist of science" (*Fisiologia della donna*, 2:168).

Through this rash and genial mathematical inexactitude, Lombroso repeatedly produces and reproduces conceptions of childbirth and maternity. First of all, as a group, women can easily be generalized into the category "woman" because normal women are "monotonous," tediously resembling one another (*La donna*, 480); this is an effect of women's lower development in all of life's aspects. Furthermore, motherhood is for Lombroso what tempers woman's innate cruelty, a mediator between cruelty and piety (*La donna*, vii, 99). Motherhood curbs woman's propensity for crime: Lombroso speaks of maternity as exerting on woman a "beneficial anticriminal influence" (*La donna*, 438), and describes maternity as "a moral vaccine against crime and evil" (499). But Lombroso also claims woman's inferior sensitivity to both pain and pleasure, a "fact" he measures scientifically and with respect to all five senses. Lombroso concludes with his curious assertion that woman is "naturally and organically monogamous and frigid" (*La donna*, 57). Unlike Mantegazza, who dwells on woman's great pain in childbirth as indicative of her natural pathology, Lombroso minimizes the pains of childbirth. Lombroso resorts to the testimony of the principal surgeons of Europe to claim that women display a great facility to undergo operations, especially in the abdomen, and that despite their initial apprehension they are surprised to feel so little pain during parturition. (One of the frightening consequences of this theory is

Lombroso's proposal that new operations should be performed experimentally on women—"like savages, woman is an inferior being who displays therefore greater resistance to wounds," *La donna*, 59.)

Lombroso's conclusion is that, although women experience less intense pain than men, they are more "irritable" and "expansive"—in a word, they are louder. They do not suffer more, they just complain about it more. While Mantegazza refutes Darwin through his discussion of the pain of childbirth, Lombroso invokes and supports Darwin in the same context. He concludes his chapter on pain with the assertion that woman's "insensitivity to pain is darwinian if not even teleological; it explains why she so easily falls back into pregnancy in spite of the pains of childbirth and even though she takes such little part in the pleasures of love.—Man would not do the same" (*La donna*, 66). Like Mantegazza, Lombroso compares woman's perception of pain with man's. But while Mantegazza's comparison is aimed at highlighting woman's greater ability to withstand pain, Lombroso focuses on man's greater sensitivity and intellectual superiority. Why would any intelligent being put up with the pain of childbirth, however small, if it is not at least preceded by the pleasure of sexual intercourse?

Like Mantegazza, Lombroso also posits a causal and epistemological connection between coitus and childbirth. Once again, though, where Mantegazza expresses sympathy for women's plight, however tempered by the knowledge of their inferiority, Lombroso displays a continued sense of puzzlement at what he perceives as the darwinian, natural, biological masochism of women: not only are the occasions for pain more frequent in the life of a woman, but "pain is indissolubly linked even to the physiological functions of her life" (*La donna*, 512). Lombroso also connects the frequent infanticides committed by women with the postpartum period, a crime he relates to "the homicidal tendencies observed in nymphomaniac cows and mares, not only when they are in heat, but even after" (*La donna*, 186). Animalization, or women as cows and mares, is combined in this passage with anthropomorphization, or animals as nymphomaniacs, in order to homogenize femaleness in the entire animal world. In a misogynous twist on sexual difference, before being human, women are female, and it is significant that throughout the book women are compared more eloquently and frequently to female animals than to male human beings. Their allegiance is to their sex more than to their species: about that, Lombroso has no doubts.

The human experience of pain can be understood as involving, ultimately, a problematic encounter with meaning. This meaning is historical because it is determined by sexual identity, time, place, and culture as much as by the nervous system and, of course, by psychological and emotional states. Meaning alters how we suffer; it is central to suffering and pain. The bond between pain and meaning is dramatized in the experience of childbirth. The meaning of pain points to the child and thus makes childbirth, for many women, tolerable, "sufferable," literally.

Mantegazza and Lombroso, on the other hand, seem to encounter, in women's experiences of pain, meaninglessness. The scientists' inability to read the inexpressibility of women's pain leads to isolation and alienation. Their attempts to avoid it lead to trivialization and even dehumanization. The splitting that engenders the birthing pain, the splitting that pain as well engenders, Mantegazza and Lombroso are unable to read, dismissing it as a hole, a gap. This void begs to be filled with interpretation, with words, with another meaning. Women must enjoy pain, then; they must be masochists. Or else women do not really feel the pain; they are simulators, liars. In any event, the pain, real or imagined, is meaningless, unrepresentable, mad. These writers never imagine that the pain of childbirth could mean an ethical connection with one's self, with one's child, with others and/or the Other. Nor can the positivist approach of Mantegazza and Lombroso conceive of a spiritual dimension to an experience alien to the pleasure principle. Rather, in their impressionable texts the fear of pain blends quite seamlessly with the misogyny of a discourse unable or unwilling to identify, in woman, its Other.

Parting and Parturition in Women's Literature

Despite the vociferous evocations of childbirth on the part of scientists such as Mantegazza and Lombroso, and some of their lesser-known contemporaries, a pregnant silence enshrouds the subjects of childbirth in literary texts. This silence is perhaps intrinsic to the discourse of childbirth in general, and of motherhood as well if, as Michelle Boulous Walker claims, "the maternal body occupies the site of a radical silence in the texts of Western philosophy, psychoanalytic theory and literature" (1). But it is a silence dialectically related to speaking and hearing, a silence that productively accompanies a bodily and spiritual crisis. As Franca Pizzini notes, "*Silence* is in fact another key word for childbirth because someone else, and not the women who are giving birth, has spoken of the event, both as manipulator of the body which produces it, and as defining agent of the psyche that experiences it" ("Introduzione," 12).

Critic and poet Adrienne Rich was perhaps the first to recognize the paucity of literary representations of birth (166), a paucity that has led

Carol Poston to wonder: "Given that birth is such an overwhelming experience, why do we find it so rarely described in literature?" (20). Poston begins to answer this question by noting the consistent "slighting in our literature" of female experiences and the "tyranny" of a masculine language that, even in the texts of women writers, presents the description of childbirth from a male, or at least an observer's, point of view, rather than from the birthing woman's (20). Cynthia Huff believes that the pervasive metaphorical uses of childbirth as textual production "attenuate our analysis of birth itself, thus subverting its autobiographical import and in effect silencing birth as a cultural expression of a woman's life" (108). Carol Mossman, who comparably claims that "patriarchal tradition . . . has labored hard to suppress birth in its literality," sees the reasons for this silence as being political and ideological, and, like Huff, as constituting "a silencing" rather than "a silence born of reverence" (5, 2, 96). It is "since the turn of our century, with its general relaxation of taboos," Barbara Korte argues, that "the process of childbirth has been treated with increasing openness in bestsellers and classics" (31), culminating in the works of modern women writers such as Margaret Atwood and Zoe Fairbairns. By positing an evocative connection between antisepsis, anesthetics, and aesthetics, Susan Gubar sees the new centrality of childbirth in twentieth-century women's writing as related to the increased safety of the childbearing experience: "Feminists could begin to valorize maternity, precisely because the promise of a declining infant- and maternity-mortality rate relaxed the biological imperative" (25). Yvonne Knibiehler and Catherine Fouquet point out that the child was not talked about for as long as it was the outcome of a biological destiny and not of a choice (9). Childbirth is largely absent not just in literature but in iconography as well, as Finzi notes: "In our iconography the representations of pregnancy and childbirth are almost nonexistent. . . . By 'maternity' we mean the already-accomplished mother-child dyad, closed in its perfection" ("L'altra scena del parto," 190).

This chorus of critics invokes the need to take birth out of repression, exploring its literality rather than its metaphorical potential. It is a chorus that asserts the need to develop a "poetics of childbirth," or, in Patricia Yaeger's words, "an investigation into the literary tropes and principles that preside over the presentation, deformation, or concealment of the story of reproduction in literary and cultural texts" (264). As scholars such as Oakley, Knibiehler, and Gélis have pointed out, it was during the late nineteenth century that fundamental changes in the practice as well as in the representation of childbirth took place, and it is therefore especially useful to investigate this period, since, as Gélis asserts, "the present rapid rate of progress in the life sciences and in obstetric technique tends to obscure the fact that for very many years the process of childbirth remained remarkably unchanged" (xi).

In the literature of the late nineteenth and early twentieth century, childbirth is at once central and, paradoxically, invisible. This literary silence on childbirth, or, perhaps more appropriately, this silencing of the birth experience, could be related to any of the arguments set forth by the critics I cited from earlier: slighting of the female experience, tyranny of a masculine language, taboos about the body and its functions. Yet to these I must add another hypothesis; namely, that there could be an incompatibility between language and parturition. For language is based on difference, as Ferdinand de Saussure, among others, has well taught us: we know that a cat is a cat because it is neither a rat nor a bat. Parturition, on the other hand, is like pregnancy a bodily experience in which difference itself is erased or, at the very least, made highly problematic. It is after all the problematic nature of the sameness and difference between pregnant woman and fetus, and of the claims to personhood of each, that guides the ethical issues of the abortion debate.

Pregnancy and childbirth bring both language and the body to their limits, where they paradoxically encounter one another at the same time as they face their ultimate incompatibility: for the unity of the speaking subject, essential to its ability to formulate a univocal "I," gets fractured in the mother–child merging and parting, the process expressively described as parturition. At the same time, this fracture also refers to the eruption of the semiotic—in Kristeva's sense, that which escapes, precedes language, offering resistance to symbolic expression—within the symbolic dimension of univocal meaning and signification. The poetic and the maternal body become in this way analogous insofar as they are constituted and/as split by the self-deconstructive dialectic between the semiotic and the symbolic dimensions: although the semiotic cannot be contained by the symbolic, it can only acquire meaning within the symbolic realm. Thus Pizzini, echoing Kristeva in her choice of binaries, notes that "*Threshold, bridge, hinge,* are key words when we speak of pregnancy, delivery, birth, maternity, and not only between nature and culture, between singularity and ethics, but also within scientific and cultural production itself" ("Introduzione," 9). Pizzini also brings up what she calls "the *ineffability* of childbirth," which emerges, in the course of this author's discussion groups, interviews, and seminars, out of "unsaid words, associations, barely put together thoughts, but also in the 'gossip' or in the censorship about an event which involves deep levels of experience" (13). In an analogous vein, Poston remarks:

> [T]here is a poverty of language for events which take place in isolation, and the language of birth has little currency. . . . Pain is difficult to talk about of itself, but childbirth pain is nearly impossible because of the emotional umbrella which sometimes seems to transmute pain into ecstasy or triumph. . . . The birthing woman is from a different country; her experiences don't make sense because the language she must use cannot adequately convey them. (28)

Ambivalence, paradox, hesitation, and even silence are some of the strategies with which literary texts attempt to overcome the incompatibility of language and childbirth. These strategies can be interpreted from two complementary and, in my reading, inseparable, symbiotic perspectives: first, from a psychoanalytic perspective, as the workings of the text's unconscious or perhaps as the emergence of the preverbal, semiotic dimension of its utterances; as the surfacing of the discourse of the other, of the heterogeneous. And, second, from a cultural perspective, as an expression of the contradictory situation of women in turn-of-the-century Italian society, of the impossibility of their motherhood. These perspectives can be investigated by performing a close reading of the ambivalences, paradoxes, hesitations, silences that permeate turn-of-the-century discourses of and on motherhood, literary as well as scientific—with literature impersonating the unconscious of science, maybe? Some of the questions I have found myself asking of turn-of-the-century texts of childbirth, then, are the ones articulated in different contexts by theorists such as Yaeger, Finzi, and Kristeva: How does each text represent childbirth—what is its "poetics of birth"? How does each text portray the relative autonomy, the parting of psyche and body in childbirth? And, more generally, how does each text express the divisions and irreconcilability of birthing body and language that culminate in the process of childbirth?

Several turn-of-the-century texts offer preliminary answers to these questions: for a misogynist spin, one can read D'Annunzio's *L'innocente;* more complicated responses can be found throughout Neera's works. In what follows I focus on Sibilla Aleramo's autobiographical novel *Una donna* (*A Woman*), published for the first time in 1906 and an immediate success. *A Woman* came out when its author was thirty years old, and it is generally considered the first Italian feminist novel. Unlike Deledda's *Cosima,* this story is narrated in the first person. Like Deledda, Aleramo recounts the author–protagonist's childhood and youth, her sense of alienation from society, her complicated relationship to motherhood (her own, her mother's, her mother-in-law's), her rebellion against accepted social norms, and her liberating contact with books and intellectual life.

Fiora Bassanese has compared *A Woman* to a *bildungsroman,* for its emphasis on the protagonist's moral and psychological growth and maturation, and to a novel of awakening, for its exposure of the limitations traditional society imposes on women and the protagonist's consequent need to struggle for autonomy. In the course of this struggle, the protagonist has to experience a complex, painful identification with her mother. At first she adores and identifies with her father, as was also the case in *Cosima,* but in the course of the novel she establishes an ethical relation with the woman who gave birth to her. What stands out in this story is the protagonist's mother's unhappiness, silence, sickness, and finally madness—conditions all aggravated, it is implied, by her husband's lack of love and choice of a mistress—and the protagonist's own unhappy marriage to the man who had seduced her when she was barely sixteen. As a result of this marriage, the protagonist gives birth to a son she adores and in marriage and maternity is forced to face the emotions of her relationship with her mother. However, she must abandon at the end both her husband and her young child because of her husband's physical and psychological abuse. The protagonist's fear was to repeat her mother's destiny of self-sacrifice to the point of self-destruction, and both mother and daughter attempt suicide in the course of the novel. (After leaving her family, Aleramo lived a long life full of political involvement and intense love affairs with famous and not-so-famous partners about whom she wrote in her poetry and diaries.)

The representation of childbirth in Aleramo's *A Woman* seems to fit what Poston describes as the "heroine" tradition, which "reaches its apogee in the view that birth is a woman's highest moment" (Poston, 21). The other, opposite tradition of representing childbirth, according to Poston, sees it instead as "savage, barbaric, primitive, or loathsome in some other way," as portrayed in D'Annunzio's *L'innocente.*

The heroine tradition belongs to that "socio-cultural model" according to which, in Finzi's words, "maternity is placed at the pinnacle of femininity and the maternal role is heroicized, compared to that of former fighter and veteran of a great patriotic war" ("L'altra scena del parto," 185). Also according to Oakley, "both birth and war are tests of genderhood" ("A Case of Maternity," 629). This identification is still at work in today's image of childbearing. The column "Girlfriend to girlfriend" in the popular American magazine *Child,* for example, asks us to consider the "valuable wisdom" that "the stretch marks and 'recontoured' flesh of a woman who has grown a human being in her belly are like medals of honor to a war veteran. With that insight (and several good support undergarments)," columnist Vicki Iovine encourages her saggy-breasted reader, "not only will you be as good as new, you'll be a hero" (131).

Against the grain of other turn-of-the-century women's texts on motherhood, Aleramo's *A Woman* chooses to focus on the narrator–protagonist's heightened postpartum beauty. After giving birth to her first and only child, the unnamed protagonist of this autobiographical novel sees in the mirror a "beautiful image of maternity" (62, translation modified). Significantly, beauty in this passage is noticed by the woman herself, narrator as well as protagonist, and is related to the self-awareness of her creative force. Earlier in the novel, however, parturition was depicted, as in other turn-of-the-century texts, as a process of undoing: The narrator refers to "my lacerated flesh, my guts which were being devoured" (63). Still, the woman who emerges from this double division and parting is creatively active rather than passively sick, and it should be remembered in this context that, as Bassanese has written, "In recreating the significant moment in her own life, Aleramo seeks to associate *a* woman with Everywoman; the autobiographical tale becomes the story of woman-kind" (133). From this perspective, the descriptions of childbirth and its aftermath acquire heightened importance for the feminist framework within which the novel places itself.

Let us therefore turn to the account of the protagonist's labor and delivery. There are actually two such accounts in *A Woman*, in a poetic division significantly involving a linguistic contradiction. The doctor's chronicle is the voice of an observer who is distant in multiple ways. He is male, a member of an increasingly powerful scientific profession, and incapable of experiencing birth himself. His medical perspective is ordered by an abstract linear temporality that is alien to the woman's physical recollection: "the doctor recounted . . . the different stages of the birth: the first labor pains at two in the morning, a rapid progress toward the climax, half an hour of suffering, the last contraction. . . . His words reached me like news of a distant event, recollected only dimly by my senses" (62). But the woman's story, inseparable from her body, "my senses," is a memory fusing the past and the future, the now and the forever. It is a painful and humiliated recollection unrelated to and even at odds with the abstract chronology imposed onto the event by medical temporality: "I had become—was it for an instant or for an eternity?—a poor creature pleading for compassion" (63). The antagonism between women and linear time, and women's association instead with cyclical and monumental time, or repetition and eternity, has been discussed by Kristeva in "Women's Time"—a controversial text in which Kristeva provides a sophisticated elaboration of women's sexed embodiment, and consequently of the bonds between embodiment and conceptions of space and time. Analogously, Aleramo's text shows that bodies necessarily exist in a spatial and temporal context, yet we can only conceive of and represent space and time through the senses given to us by our bodies. And the senses, as is most obvious in the event of childbirth, are not univocal. Our perception of duration, our understanding of time, are relative to and dependent on multiple variables; for example, ideologies of narrative, a sense of production, sexed subjectivity.

The representation of childbirth in *A Woman* explicitly questions the validity of a teleological chronology of science, and of positivistic history, that is based on departure, progression, and arrival. The doctor's sequential temporality, whereby the woman's delivery is divided into "the phases of the delivery" that neatly move from the first to the last contractions (from "the first labor pains," that is, to "the last contraction"), contradicts the woman's own experience, in which the present and eternity, as also the self and the other, are intertwined and confused. Therefore, the protagonist does not recognize in *his* words *her* experience, in *his* language *her* body, in *his* univocity *her* paradoxical perspectives and ambivalent voice. In the lyrical reevocations of *Il passaggio* (The passage, 1919), an autobiographical text that revisits some of the events recounted in *A Woman*, Aleramo reiterates this bodily experience of temporality and its bond to the physiology of motherhood: "The fibers of a woman know the solitary slowness of time which swells up a womb, but to the innumerable moments stressed by a pleading heart there is a fixed end" (*Il passaggio*, 62). The thirteen intervening years have transformed Aleramo from mother to author, allowing her to recall the temporality of maternity as relatively fixed; antagonistic to the nine-month teleology of pregnancy is instead the uncertainty of written language: "Who on the other hand will be able to tell me if this work of mine will be finished in a year or in another ten years, this work which will then have to remain intangible, my work, star dust?" (*Il passaggio*, 62).

In *The Politics of Reproduction*, feminist political theorist Mary O'Brien claims that it is because of their different roles in the reproductive process that men and women have a different temporal consciousness, and that the link between birth and death, enfleshed in the mother's body, "is not antagonistic when it is perceived in terms of natural, cyclical [women's] time, but it becomes antagonistic when placed on the continuum of [men's] rectilinear time" (150). The clash of these two temporal perceptions—natural and cyclical versus cultural and rectilinear—is staged by Aleramo at the scene of her delivery. And like O'Brien, Aleramo relates this temporal irreconcilability with the impossible concurrence, within one body, of death and life. Childbirth is in this text the moment of oxymoron because it stages the very encounter of death and life, as Aleramo's narrator herself notes: "yes, at the point at which my son was entering the world I had thought I was about to die" (*A Woman,* 63). The poetic connection between birth and death as beginning and end was supported by the realities of maternal mortality in childbirth. Mantegazza pointed out in his *Fisiologia della donna* that one woman out of twenty-three died in her first childbirth, and one in forty-seven in later childbirths (2:63; Giorgio Cosmacini estimates women's mortality from childbirth in the mid-1800s to have been about one in fifty, "L'igiene e il medico di famiglia," 597). More recently, Luisa Accati has noted that "to examine childbirth means seeing in some way the relationship which a particular social group has with life and death" (44). And Poston evocatively writes: "We mothers are all physical keepers of graves; and at the moment when potential motherhood becomes actual—the moment of birth—we are surely seeing that in giving birth, one commits another human being, if not oneself, to death. It is material for the highest art; and that authentic voice, that of the birthing woman, needs now to be heard" (30). For in *A Woman,* childbirth, the culmination of the protagonist's life thus far, is also an ominous preview of her impending enslavement, a foreshadowing of the (self)destructiveness inherent in the maternal role: in *A Woman,* both the protagonist and her mother attempt suicide, and her mother dies in a sense when she is interned in an asylum for the rest of her days.

A mother in Aleramo's *A Woman* must die, lamentably, to give birth to another human being. Her subjectivity is lost, however temporarily, in the creation of another's. Aleramo polemically describes this social reality in the phrase that is most explicitly linked to the book's title: "But a good mother must not be simply a victim of self-sacrifice, as mine had been: she must be *a woman,* a human individual" (113). The joy of motherhood as experience is corrupted for Aleramo's protagonist and her mother by the institution of motherhood, to use Rich's well-known distinction, by its patriarchal trappings evident in the doctor's reformulation of the protagonist's temporality. And to break that "monstrous chain" handed down "from mother to daughter for so many centuries" (193), the author–protagonist has only the option of abandoning her husband and, with him, her beloved son—for the law would not have allowed her to take him along. This separation is poignantly described by Aleramo as a sort of therapeutic abortion or emergency cesarean section, thus underscoring the bodily connection, rooted in the economy of gestation, which she still entertained with her child: "How could I have done it? Why hadn't I been stronger? Yet I felt as if I had just had an operation to remove another person from my body—in order to save us both" (215). In the bond between mother and child, body and spirit, as well as life and death, are inextricably intertwined. As Claudia Pancino notes, "both experientially and symbolically, the knot of life being born touches death, and is entirely surrounded by fear;" and, until recently, because of its "elevated mortality, the event of birth must have been characterized by a strong drama, and this 'dramatic' dimension must be kept in mind when we speak of childbirth in past centuries" ("L'assistenza al parto," 66–67). Pizzini likewise points out that "*mortality* and *death* are words which appear immediately close to birth, both because the reconstruction of the passage from home to hospital is replete with threatening data on the mortality of both mother and child, and also because there is probably a connection in our unconscious between the two terminals of life, a connection which appears in the fears of death of the birthing woman and of those who assist her" ("Introduzione," 16). I return to a philosophical examination of this problematic connection between birth and death in the next section.

Parallel to this confrontation with death at the moment of delivery is the paradoxical moment of the encounter between speech and silence: Aleramo's self-exaltation precludes her debasement into a speechless animal (the birthing woman's fate in *L'innocente*), confirming Alice Adams's claim that women's narratives about giving birth "suggest that the birth process may be read not as regression but as an evolution in which a woman's understanding of herself becomes more complex and expansive" (26). If Aleramo's voice becomes a death-rattle and a scream—"[my] voice had changed into a hoarse death-rattle . . . [I] had screamed out rebellion" (63)—it nevertheless remains fully human, for it prepares to speak and tell its own story. In the immediate postpartum period, the author–narrator–protagonist–mother experiences "my first overwhelming impulse towards giving artistic expression to a torrent of new, distinctive emotions" (63). Silence is a prelude to literature; or, in Paolo Valesio's apt words, silence is seen and felt by the subject "not so much as the limit to verbal expression/communication, but rather as the reservoir or source of inspirations for a more profound use of language" (296). Postpartum silence can be regarded in many ways as equivalent to what Valesio describes as "The silence which precedes and follows explosions of creative energy, especially in artistic or scientific activity—a silence the duration of which can vary from a few minutes to many years;" "it is the silence of frustration, the silence of the artist (or thinker, or scientist) blocked on the other side of his/her creative project" (382–83). It is the "speaking" silence of bodily crisis and pain, a silence we must learn to read if we are to lift motherhood, metonymized in these texts as childbirth, out of the repression that characterizes it in Western discourse. Bodily crises such as childbirth impressively express, beyond and across their silence, an affirmative potential that demands to be deciphered and acknowledged. It is on this dimension of listening that the midwife care of old, at its best, was based, and it is this precious dimension that has been lost in the medicalized care of the pregnant and birthing woman. It is all the more significant then that in *A Woman* it should be a doctor rather than a midwife who attends the birth.

Let me jump forward a few decades and quote from Italian feminist thinker Alessandra Bocchetti, who writes in "The Indecent Difference" (1982):

> [W]omen's silence will keep coming up, and will be the phantasm that will continue to haunt our actions and thoughts, until we manage to make some sense of it, insert it into a historical perspective of thought, fill it with knowing; until we change the perspective in which to look at it; that is, at woman's implicit wretchedness. Our hypothesis is that we should take women's silence not as a sign of their poverty of language, but of the poverty of language. (151)

The notion and role of silence in the feminist movement at this turn of the millennium, as well as at the turn of the last century, is of central importance. How to explain, for example, the relative poverty of women's written production? Or women's apparent complicity in the institutions that silence them? But it is a complicated relationship that women entertain with language and with silence. Thus Bocchetti, instead of dismissing, denying, or covering over silence, invites us to listen to it, like Valesio, and fill it with a different, even an indecent meaning. It is this meaning of silence that Aleramo pursues throughout much of her writings. For example, the first chapter of Aleramo's *Il passaggio* is entitled "Il silenzio" (silence), and begins with the words "Silence waits. Silence, the most faithful thing fastened to me in life" (*Il passaggio*, 9).

The speechlessness of childbirth, expressed in a human and eloquent silence instead of a beastly, inarticulate cry, becomes for the narrator of *A Woman* the point of intersection between the bodily pain of the event (violent, negative) and the psychic and emotional exaltation of the experience (pleasurable, positive). The child being born incarnates such a silence and such an intersection, for as the narrator notes, in this new creature both her body and her spirit are enfleshed: "My body had created him, my spirit lived inside him" (*A Woman*, 63). In Aleramo's novel childbirth carries both a literal and a metaphorical value, as the birth and future upbringing of her son become fused in the narrator's mind with her project of writing an autobiographical book. In the postpartum week, as her son sleeps in his cradle, "two distinct plans came together in my mind: the first . . . concerned my son . . . the other . . . the plan of a book" (63–64). Against positivistic claims to the contrary, creation and procreation can be one, and Wood notes that for Aleramo "the experience of creativity, in motherhood or in writing, is—curiously—seen to have a single source" (77). (This is the opposite of the situation depicted just a few years later in Annie Vivanti's maternity novel *I divoratori* [The devourers, 1911] in which the protagonist's first feeling of fetal movement interrupts her from writing her book—a project she abandons as soon as she hears her newborn child's first cry of hunger, 144.) Nadia Fusini describes the parallel between giving birth and writing, noted by Aleramo, as analogous expulsive liberations that give birth to the self (as speaking subject) as well as to the other: "To separate oneself from one's book (or from one's child)—expelling it and/is freeing oneself—means the affirmation of birth, according to that etymological relationship that Lacan indicates: *se parere*, to generate oneself by oneself. *Parere* is 'first of all to obtain (a child for the husband)': to be born, then, is a double act of *giving* and *giving oneself* birth" (14). In Bocchetti's essay "The Indecent Difference," she quotes from an anonymous woman's metaphorical statement that women have to learn "to bring books into the world as we bring children into it," and interprets it to mean that "To bring a book into the world we have to lose it, accept its difference from us, be there at its birth, look at it living its own life, share it with others" (155). Even without the invocation of poststructuralist psychoanalysis, birthing and writing can be seen as analogous from a female perspective, not because both are productions (a patriarchal/capitalist view) but because both are ethical exercises in separation and division, splitting and difference. "This woman," notes Bocchetti, "theorized writing and creativity as an exercise in abandonment" (155). The ethical dimension of maternity surfaces once again, with maternity even posing as ethical emblem. As the body learns to let go of the child it gestates for nine months, so the writer learns to let go of a book, and a mother learns to let go of a growing, increasingly independent child.

But the ethical paradigm entails a constitutive linguistic dimension. Parturition demands an expulsion and a parting, which in generating the other also bring about the possibility of its entrance into language—through separation and the play between difference and communion that language involves. Throughout this process, communication springs from the maternal body and its semiotic dimension. Women's childbirth stories are multilayered, or, in Huff's words, "women's biographies of birth give us accounts which highlight the intricate relationships between the physical, cultural, and textual construction of delivery" (119–20). In its description of the narrator's son's birth, *A Woman* reflects on itself as both self and other, for the project of writing a book—a textual, linguistic, or symbolic construction—is inseparably connected with the author's experience of childbirth—a physical or semiotic construction. This blending, pointing to the inextricability of what is often referred to as gender and sex, leads back to *A Woman* itself as a complex cultural construction that, although clearly linguistic, repeatedly gestures toward a semiotic relation between mother and child in which the mother is always at once speaking subject and birthing body, or, alternately/simultaneously, birthing subject and speaking body, working on a process of differentiation and/as communion in which the ethical dimension is always-already present.

Mantegazza complacently proclaimed childbirth to be the capital event in a woman's life. With an analogous though much less romanticized definition, Pizzini notes, from a sociohistorical perspective, that "in every culture and period childbirth is a moment of synthesis of the condition of women in that society" ("Introduzione," 15)—its expression. Pizzini goes on to explain that "childbirth is the synthesis of woman's condition, because the key relationships in her life come together at childbirth: with her body first of all, but also with her man and her child, with her own mother and other women, all figures that are no longer real, today, on the scene of childbirth, but are nevertheless present in a phantasmatic way for every woman" (15). Likewise, we could say that the literary construction of childbirth may be read as emblematic of the cultural construction of woman. Thus for example D'Annunzio's poetics of birth in *L'innocente* revolves around a pathological animalization of the birthing woman—doubly passive because object of the narrator's gaze and because unable to speak—which tropes bodily production (childbirth) into bodily loss (amputation). Childbirth establishes woman's inactivity and even her destructiveness, for, as Rasy notes, the pathologization of childbirth is linked with woman's different body and antagonistic temporality, autonomous and irreducible to the reality principle that guides social progress (*La lingua della nutrice,* 119). Indeed, Aleramo's militant *roman à thèse* challenges constructions of childbirth as savage, barbaric, and loathsome through its association of childbirth with writing and its deconstruction of teleological chronology by means of a different temporal perception. This temporal perception is shaped, as O'Brien (from a Marxist perspective) and Rasy (from a psychoanalytic perspective) decades later theorized, by women's different relations to reproduction and, more specifically, to the event of childbirth. The woman's experience of pregnancy and childbirth cannot be reduced to the reality principle, Rasy argues, and, according to O'Brien, women experience the continuity of reproduction while men are alienated by the temporal gap between intercourse and the paternal appropriation of the child.

Parting and Parturition in Feminist Theory

The rending scream of childbirth provides the title, early images, and running metaphor to Anna Banti's autobiographical novel *Un grido lacerante, A Piercing Cry,* written in 1981 when Banti, a doyenne of twentieth-century Italian literature, was eighty-one years old. The literal translation of the participle in the title is *lacerating,* a recurring term in narratives of parturition, in novels such as Gabriele D'Annunzio's *L'innocente,* Sibilla Aleramo's *A Woman,* and Neera's *Duello d'anime.* The use of this word in the title of an important book that is not, after all, about childbirth, a book whose protagonist has no children and no apparent maternal instinct, is noteworthy. Yet it is birth and delivery that the protagonist dreams about, since early childhood; it is a nightmare, really, more than a dream, a nightmare from which she awakens trembling. It is the memory of her own birth, of that inception/conception to which she returns as she remembers her past—in the necessary retracing that the autobiographical task involves. The dream of her birth is her secret, the source of frequent and odd sensations ultimately amounting to a sense of placelessness, of foreignness to and alienation from the world that contains her, the world she inhabits. Her birth had been difficult, as her mother frequently recounted, and was followed by days of ceaseless cries and screams that figured the protagonist's exceptional relationship with language: At two months of age, she was already singing lullabies! The dream image of the gaping hole is both the child's mouth, figure of language, and the mother's sex, image of body. So laceration paradoxically characterizes both maternal flesh and daughterly speech, both the birth to and the death of language. It is a piercing cry that marks the protagonist's death at the end of the novel as her ultimate silence. Yet that same piercing cry points to her birth at the novel's beginning: her speech. Indeed, at the end of the book, one wonders whether what seems to be the memory of the experience of birth at its beginning is not in reality the audible divination of death.

Banti's novel is a difficult, plurivocal text that challenges the separation between women and literature. This rift is the newborn's piercing cry in the protagonist's recurring dream, as well the newborn protagonist's. She is clearly the author's alter ego, an exemplary yet highly specific figure for the woman writer. This scream is emblematic of her silent yet equally piercing cry before the exclusion of women from men's literary and artistic kingdom, and "of the depiction of a female life from the literary domain" (Lazzaro-Weis, 42), from the place where life and art can productively, prolifically merge.

Likewise, in "Travail, travaglio" (an untranslatable title underlining the connection between the labor of childbirth and labor as work), Battistina Costantino argues that childbirth and women's generative processes in general have traditionally been considered taboo not because of their relationship to sex, as is commonly believed, but rather because—as the term *labor* attests—pregnancy and delivery are work; and, in our society, work is what gives a human being the right to an income, to power, to status. Bearing a child and giving birth are productions for which the vocabulary of work and labor is the only possible one: in the hard labor of childbirth, as in heavy labor in fields or factories, the woman concentrates, breathes heavily, sweats, aches. There is even a by-product of her work, the placenta, an organ developed during pregnancy and finally expelled in the third phase of labor. As in hard work, in pregnancy and in childbirth the energy expended by the woman is much greater than the energy needed to just live.

This connection with work is reinforced by etymological observations. The word *gestation* comes from the Latin *gerere,* to carry as well as to act, to perform—an etymology shared by words such as *gesture, digestive, suggestion;* and the word *pregnancy* comes from *prehendere,* an active taking, getting hold of, seizing, grasping. Both etymologies point to pregnancy as an active undertaking on the mother's part. Indeed, with all pregnancy's do's and dont's—attention to the intake of and desire for food, to internal movements and lack thereof, to what can and cannot be looked at, or, in more contemporary terms, prenatal appointments and childbirth preparation classes, for example—it is certainly work, and not only unconscious work: decision making plays, or should play, a central role in both pregnancy and delivery. And yet, Rosalyn Diprose reminds us, "while women's labor is no longer explicitly excluded from the body politic, the labor of pregnancy and the maternal ethos remain foreign to the social contract," for "the maternal body is one kind of body not accommodated in the body politic" (26, 31).

The work of reproduction is especially apparent in practices such as surrogate motherhood today and, in the past, wet-nursing, practices for which women are/were financially compensated. In Italian, to look again at this matter from a linguistic point of view, *fare figli,* or "making children," is a common equivalent of "having children." As words such as *procreation, fruitfulness, reproductive,* and *prolific* confirm, the making of human beings is a kind of work, and the labor management of factories finds a linguistic equivalent in the obstetrician's management of labor. Yet, with the exception of breastfeeding, this work takes place inside the human body, inside the woman's body. And as I noted earlier, human reproduction is never really that because a human being is never the copy of another, but always an original. Perhaps this is why procreation is more often linked to intellectual work than to manual labor, as metaphors attest: a writer, a philosopher, a scholar is prolific, conceives ideas, gives birth to a book. As in maternity, intellectual work takes place inside the body, does not need external instruments, and is forever related to the person who brought it about; and our control over intellectual processes is limited, as it is in pregnancy and childbirth. (This metaphor of childbearing as work, of reproduction as production, however, can also be employed to women's disadvantage, leading for example to the commodification of children, as Emily Martin has shown in *The Woman in the Body,* 54–67.)

In Italian two terms refer to childbirth, and the choice between them is determined by whose experience is being recounted: while *parto,* an everyday Italian cognate of the more scientific *parturition* in English, is what the pregnant woman accomplishes at the end of nine months of gestation, her delivery, *nascita,* a cognate of *natal, natality, nascent,* refers to the child's birth. In English, on the other hand, *childbirth* usually refers to the experience of both mother and child, while the word *delivery,* unlike *parto,* does not only refer to what happens at the end of gestation (e.g., it can also refer to packages and speeches). So in her essay "Thinking Mothers/Conceiving Birth," Ruddick rather infelicitously (though, given the poverty of language in this area, understandably) chooses a cognate of *nascita,* with its implication of the child's perspective, to describe "natal thinking." Etymologically, *natal* refers to the birth of the child, not to the woman's delivery, though by "natal thinking" and "natal reflection" Ruddick means the birthgiver's acquisition of cognitive and emotional capacities, metaphysical attitudes, and values through her experience(s) of giving birth. (Ruddick sets forth multiple caveats concerning the concept of natal thinking, but not because of its shift of focus from mother to child; rather, she is afraid to perpetuate the essentialist identification of women with mothers, and of mothers with birthgivers.)

Nascita, literally birth, figures prominently in the work of Italian feminist theorist Adriana Cavarero, a member of the Diotima philosophical group in Verona, a specialist in ancient philosophy, and a major proponent of sexual difference. Among contemporary Italian feminists,

Cavarero is the thinker who has had the most works translated into English: two of her books, *In Spite of Plato* and *Relating Narratives*, and several essays in feminist anthologies. Cavarero insistently ties her discussion of birth with the mother's body and the mother's presence. The maternal is for this philosopher a major instance of sexual difference and a productive symbolic figure for its politics. Thus, Cavarero repeatedly argues against the elision of the mother from the discussion of the experience of the subject being born. For instance, Cavarero's *Relating Narratives* tackles the vast subject of autobiography from this perspective of birth, positing the uniqueness of the individual in the uniqueness of her/his birth of a unique mother: "The story of one's life always begins where that person's life begins. . . . The uniqueness of his identity, his *daimon*, has its origin in the event of this birth. . . . The link between personal identity and birth, according to Oedipus, is as materially founded as it is indubitable. His *daimon* is rooted in being born of a mother, *this* and not another" (11). Yet what for Cavarero is the philosophically fundamental fact that the subject is unique and unrepeatable—a fact, it is crucial to remember, that originates in one's birth of a mother—has traditionally and symptomatically attracted no interest on the part of Western philosophical discourse ("Il pensiero femminista," 160). Indeed, for Cavarero as for Irigaray and Muraro the symbolic dismissal of motherhood and of the mother's symbolic order constitutes one of the cornerstones of patriarchal power. Women's empowerment depends on, is structured around the redefinition, the reevaluation, the reappropriation of the maternal function and its impressiveness.

In her essay "Dire la nascita" (Telling birth), a discussion of the work of Hannah Arendt, as well as in her better-known volume *In Spite of Plato*—particularly in the chapter that discusses the mother–daughter myth of Demeter and Kore—Cavarero describes Arendt's category of natality as the rooting and center of individual existence. It is interesting, by the way, to note to what extent Italian feminists, and particularly the Diotima group, have rediscovered and reconsidered this philosopher, who did not consider herself a feminist and whom other philosophers such as Held and O'Brien have criticized, for example, for her conception of reproduction as mere repetition and as essentially natural rather than cultural (Held, 126, 132, 134). (Note that Cavarero in this essay and her other works uses the everyday word *nascita*, birth, not the philosophical term *natalità*.) For Cavarero as for Arendt, the subject being born is new, a production rather than a re-production, a factual and unpredictable subject, appearing in and belonging to the world. It is worth remembering at this point that, like Muraro and unlike French poststructuralist theorists such as Irigaray and Cixous, Cavarero does not reject the classic, unified subject of philosophy in favor of the postmodern shattered self. Rather, she elaborates a subject who is neither the substantive one of the metaphysical tradition nor the fragmented self of postmodernism. Her subject is sexed and embodied rather than universal; it is unrepeatable and intrinsically relational—all qualities that become especially evident if we think, as Cavarero convincingly impels us to do, of the subject's beginning in her/his birth of a mother. Just as in the scene of birth, this unique and unrepeatable subject is in constant need of an other who is equally unique and unrepeatable, an other whose identity is neither an effect of language, nor an agglomeration of fragments, nor a self-constituting substance. Instead, this feminist metaphysical identity is entirely external and exposed to the other; "it is to the gaze, gestures and words of this other that the subject entrusts her/his desire for meaning" ("Il pensiero femminista," 161). This identity can only be understood in philosophical discourse by asking the concrete question "who are you?" before asking the question "what are you?"—the question, that is, that sustains the binary economy of phallogocentrism. Before anything else, we need to ask the subject "who" she or he is, rather than insisting on defining "what" she or he is: Every subject is a unique and unrepeatable "someone" before being "something" to be boxed into a system of identities.

By emphasizing "who" the subject is rather than "what" the subject is, birth has in Cavarero's discussion a destabilizing effect on the patriarchal order as well as on the feminist arguments concerning essentialism and antiessentialism. In the patriarchal order, woman has no place, she is atopical because she is irreducibly other; but, with the reinscription of birth, this placelessness cannot be sustained, and it works instead to show that the patriarchal order does not correspond to reality as a whole and that, ultimately, there can be a symbolic order capable of representing both women and men—capable, that is, of representing the reality of sexual difference. And yet this reality is not "one" if we ask questions based on "who" rather than on "what"—questions that are not mutually exclusive, questions that do not form yet another binary. Indeed, the reality evoked in Cavarero's argument in turn dissolves, or should dissolve, the very system of binary thinking that characterizes metaphysics and patriarchy as well as much feminist thought (e.g., the ever popular sex/gender distinction) and that *pensiero della differenza* deconstructs. As Kamuf puts it, "whether one adopts the terms essentialism/anti-essentialism or others to qualify the nature of the opposition, the thinking that is called for must finally rethink, that is to say displace, opposition itself as the structuring agent of difference. This is the condition of marking a difference, making a difference that does not return, like a debt to be paid, to the concept of the same" (79–80).

In her study of Western philosophy and civilization, Cavarero encounters and interprets many sites where patriarchy and its essentialist constructs are destabilized by the signifier Woman. An important place for the inscription of sexual difference is the Greek mother–daughter myth of Demeter and Kore. This myth tells that when Hades, lord of the underworld, abducts and rapes Demeter's only daughter, Demeter causes the earth to become sterile and to no longer bear fruit; so Hades agrees to send Kore back to her mother every spring, in order that fertility may periodically return to the earth. The violation of the maternal order entails a violent, devastating response.

The myth of Demeter and Kore is read by Cavarero as "a disavowal of the maternal order of birth, an order that posits itself as a place from which human existence comes and takes signification . . . the myth evokes an original matricide" (*In Spite of Plato,* 63). But birth always implies coming from a mother, and is thus resistant to the logic of matricide. The philosophy of birth is identified by Cavarero, via Arendt (whom she reads against the grain and with her characteristic interdisciplinary style), as standing in opposition to that metaphysics of death on which Western thought is predicated and thus patriarchal power legitimated. It is this metaphysics of death that Cavarero's subversive work, through the theory and the practice of sexual difference, effectively and urgently deconstructs. Phallogocentric metaphysics is for Cavarero what makes the word *man* reductively signify both men and women, what has turned its gaze away from birth, and what has made of us all mortals instead of, as Arendt would put it, natals, defined by our death rather than by our birth. The condition of mortality is the countercurrent experience to Arendt's notion of human natality. This has important ethical as well as ontological ramifications: for while death is a solitary experience, birth, qua coming into the world, is necessarily communal; it always involves at least two, and it therefore points to an ethical situation (*In Spite of Plato,* 82).

Arendt understands natality from the standpoint of what she terms *amor mundi,* love for the world, love of the world. Human beginning, embodied in birth, is directed toward the world and for the sake of the world. Natality is a world-oriented phenomenon, which situates us qua natals (and thus not only, as the Greeks fatally defined us, mortals) in time and place, in a community. *Amor mundi* is the ultimate expression of natality, and, conversely, natality is the ultimate expression of *amor mundi.* This relationship is exemplified for Arendt by the birth of a child to the couple in love: "The child, this in-between to which the lovers are now related and which they hold in common, is representative of the world in that it also separates them; it is an indication that they will insert a new world into the existing world;" and, birth allows, impels love to become political because of its "world-creating faculty" (242).

Thanks to Arendt's elaboration, birth becomes speakable as a philosophical category; hence the title of Cavarero's essay, "speaking birth." In this process, birth deconstructs philosophy's privileging of death alone as speakable—the consequences of which, Cavarero argues, are the separation between thinking and bodiliness, the de-corporealization of thinking, and the contempt for a body whose signs are erased as insignificant ("Dire la nascita," 114). These consequences entail a devalorization of women, who lack a language of their own, who need to use the language of the other. There is no language of woman for Cavarero, the mother tongue is in effect the father tongue. Hence women's experience of the distance of language, an experience which in turn provokes ways of fleeing language: through silence, through unspoken residue, through the performance of a body divested of its connection to thought ("Towards a Theory of Sexual Difference," 197).

The speakability of birth, moreover, bestows on woman—the atopical in patriarchal discourse and therefore the one most irreducible to the matricidal order of death—the task of guarding the real. By "the real" Cavarero means not only the fact of sexual difference but also the possibility of a symbolic order that would represent the reality of the birth of both women and men, as opposed to a false, unreal patriarchal order from which women would be excluded. The myth of Demeter and Kore demands "a new philosophy of birth capable of winning some territory back from the metaphysics of death and from the social codes built upon it" (*In Spite of Plato*, 79). This territory, however, can be neither an unthinking celebration of motherhood nor the alternative prescription of a maternal ethics of care à la Carol Gilligan: rather, what is at stake in Cavarero's articulation of birth is the philosophical elaboration of a fluid personal identity and self-understanding based on a dynamic interplay of relations to the other—a feminist metaphysics that, through the ethical bond to the other exemplified by birth, aims to avoid the destructive alternative of either the full subject of metaphysics or the fragmented self of postmodernism (Cavarero, "Il pensiero femminista," 160).

Birth, then, becomes the unifying human experience insofar as it proclaims that women and men, who are born and live embodied in sexual difference, all and without exception originate in a woman's body. This common necessity should underline rather than erase the sexed identity of the subject. Indeed, at birth the first fact about the newborn to be announced to the mother and to the world is its sex: "it's a boy" or "it's a girl." This necessity, therefore, also underlines the unavailability of neutral universals, it invites the proclamation of difference, it acknowledges the impossibility both of separating mind from body and of eternal atemporality. It is no coincidence that sexual difference is much more prominent, according to Cavarero, at the time of birth than at the time of death, when we degenerate into nonhuman, inorganic matter (*In Spite of Plato*, 68). And "it is no coincidence," Cavarero continues in her essay on birth and natality, "that the category of birth, as an atopia that becomes speech/discourse, should have been given as a gift to philosophy by the thinking of a woman [Cavarero is referring to Arendt] and should have been gratefully accepted by the thinking of sexual difference (*pensiero della differenza*), namely by the thinking of some women [i.e., those in the Diotima group] who have turned their experience of atopia in the patriarchal 'scientific' and academic order, not into a discomfort that can be remedied through assimilation but rather into the place of a fertile rooting" ("Dire la nascita," 117).

It must be noted at this point that it is not so much the experience of giving birth that forms the basis for the elimination of birth and the elevation of death in philosophical thought; for not all women, Cavarero is quick to note, do or much less should give birth. The resemblance between mother and daughter evoked, for instance, by the myth of Demeter and Kore is not meant to impose biological reproduction on women. On the contrary, maternal power, maternal impressiveness, as the course of engendering, "demands a reciprocity in the gaze that the newborn female returns to the mother" (*In Spite of Plato*, 63).

In her book *Womanizing Nietzsche*, Kelly Oliver makes a similar statement when she discusses a new ethics based on the maternal body: Oliver's model, like Cavarero's, "is not developed on the basis of some supposition about how a mother feels or how it feels to be a mother. It is not a so-called ethics of care. Rather, the power of this theory comes from the fact that we all have mothers, dead or alive, known or unknown. So far, all human beings have been born of women's bodies" (186). As such, humans come into being through an intersubjective relationship, namely the relation to our mother and her body. According to Oliver, then, the autonomous individual, the unified subject, is impossible, because "all subjectivity is inherently and fundamentally intersubjectivity, constituted through communication and exchange" (187). (This is the model underscored by the theory of maternal impressions discussed in Chapter 1.)

Oliver's model is aimed at both men and women, as is the case for Cavarero's work, but Cavarero privileges in her discussion sexual difference, and thus the mother–daughter bond. For Cavarero, then, every woman, who is always a daughter even if not necessarily a mother, is rooted in the order of the female gaze, in the mutual recognition of a similarly female creature. Man is excluded from the scene of birth not so much because he is unable to give birth (since many women are also unable or unwilling to do so) but rather because of the sexual difference between him and his mother, which excludes him from the maternal continuum at the root of the order of birth (as noted earlier, Chodorow and Finzi also focus, from a psychoanalytic perspective, on the exclusion of men from the maternal continuum of birth). Hence man's own exclusion of this order from philosophical consideration. And yet in the order of birth, both men and women find the constitution of their subjectivity.

Cavarero has developed this theory in *Relating Narratives*, where she extends her notion of the formation of subjectivity through the process of mutual recognition to all newborns, female and male: "Besides being she from whom the existent comes, the mother is also the *other* to whom the existent first appears. . . . The primacy of appearance constitutes, through the other's gaze, the fundamental corporal aspect of identity. In other words, already on the corporeal level, in so far as a unique being is concerned, identity depends upon the presence of others" (*Relating Narratives*, 21). To deny this relationship to the mother as the first other is to risk stopping birth from ever taking place again, to invite barrenness, as the myth of Demeter and Kore attests: "maternal generation is just a root that welcomes the daughter within the horizon of similarity" (*In Spite of Plato*, 64). Without this welcome, recognition, acknowledgment, there is sterility and death.

Yet the power to generate is also, must also be the power *not* to generate: without that choice, there can be no power. Fruitlessness is in fact Demeter's reproductive choice when her daughter's gaze is removed from her own by the violent intervention of the patriarchal order, the masculine order of death, through Hades abduction of Kore into the underworld: "maternal power *per se* cannot be regulated" (*In Spite of Plato*, 80). Or, in Bocchetti's words, maternity is a place of indecency, a time when the sexually differentiated experience of women, of mothers, should lead to self-definition rather than the prohibitions and prescriptive exaltation engendered by external regulation:

> The old discourse of difference asserted maternity as its focal point: "Since the woman is mother she can't . . . she mustn't . . . ," and so became prescriptive and negative, grounded in what was evident. But what a mother is, only a mother can say.

> Maternity has been situated in, prescribed as one of the "good deeds," sacred even. But what is indecent in maternity, only a woman can say.
>
> "The ambiguous maternal," the only theme we put forward a couple of years ago, which hypothesized the maternal in the realm of passion, was an attempt to analyze the secret indecency of this experience. (159)

Indecently, perhaps, the fact that we are all "of woman born" forever roots man to the other sex, linking him to a genealogical female line, which at the same time inevitably, necessarily keeps him out: "every human born, male or female, is always born of a woman, who was born of a woman, who, in turn, was born of another woman, and so on, in an endless backward movement toward our origins. This maternal continuum delineates the feminine root of every human being" (*In Spite of Plato,* 60). Hence man's choice of death as philosophical criterion, one to which he has easier access. We are mortals rather than natals, inscribed in the patriarchal order of death perfectly symbolized by Hades kidnapping of Kore from her mother's generative earth, from the maternal order of birth, to his underworld of death. In this perspective, birth can be seen as just the beginning of man's race toward death. But even the scene of this beginning, birth, cannot be speakable by a sex that cannot be there except as an *infans,* one unable to speak: hence man's reluctance to acknowledge his debt to the mother, hence the reduction of motherhood to a social function, a demographic necessity, an unspoken and unspeaking non-subject. Maternal power is removed from the indecency of sovereign female subjectivity and reduced, depreciated into a reproductive function, the production of bodies, the transformation of woman into a receptacle for the unborn child—Bocchetti's "secret good deed."

Cavarero's discussion, for all its radicalism, can be usefully linked to other topics encountered thus far. Her approach assists us in legitimating women's epistemological claims by linking the birthing body with language and subjectivity, and ultimately with philosophical value. It establishes the category of birth as constitutive of an ethical self, defined through its fluid, changing relations to its other. And more generally, as Braidotti notes in her foreword to the English translation of *In Spite of Plato,* Cavarero's work affirms "the relevance and the range of social and political applications of philosophy itself" (ix). The speakability of birth, or natality, as philosophical category is intertwined with its speakability in literature—in turn related to the speakability of maternity in its diverse aspects, in multiple discourses. As Cavarero writes, "in silence the voice is quiet, but not the word" ("L'elaborazione filosofica," 177). By establishing birth as a discursive category, the maternal body, with its silence and its words, its impressions and its expressions, can become meaningful, and in this framework alone will meaning be restored as well to the reality of those who are born—a reality of sexual difference. Indeed, the philosophy of birth is meant to become a way of rethinking the world itself: the patriarchal order must be attacked, its matricidal culture defused, difference and the female symbolic order reestablished. For all this to happen, the reciprocal gaze exchanged between mother and daughter needs to be recognized and acknowledged.

The exclusion of the male sex from the scene of birth is predicated on the inclusion, in this same scene, of a female community: Cavarero refers in this context to the concept of female genealogies, discussed in Chapter 1 with the work of Muraro and Irigaray. Censored in traditional psychoanalytic theory, female genealogies link woman to mother, grandmother, daughter, and so on. This genealogical link expresses itself in both language and its other, silence—which takes us back to Kristeva's work. As Walker claims, "the way we can now talk about silence in philosophy is thoroughly altered because of [Kristeva's] work. In effect Kristeva moves us away from a silence/language opposition toward an understanding of the rather more complex relation between the logos and its other. We can use her work not to pit silence against this logos, but rather to think of silence as a metaphor for the otherness that inhabits the logos, an otherness that is anything but quiet" (99). This theoretical elaboration on silence, language, and the potential other of each emerges in the course of Kristeva's work on the mother and on the semiotic as the pre-Oedipal bond to the mother's body: if the semiotic, although preverbal and heterogeneous to verbal production, nevertheless inhabits language and impresses it with its marks, then any simple differentiation between silence and language is impossible. Their relationship is not an oppositional one, as the mystics knew—and we need only think of Angela of Foligno and Teresa of Avila (see my *Saint Hysteria*). Thus for example we might distinguish, with Valesio, between two fundamental types of silence: "silence as *interruption* (or fracture or breakage or cut . . .); and silence as *plenitude* (or fullness, or completeness)" (378). The plenitude of silence is in dangerous proximity with the fracturing interruption of silencing and, aware of this risk, I believe that it is important to listen to the words of maternity as well as to its pregnant silences. The two are inextricably intertwined: "there is an absolute unspeakable and there is a historically determined difficulty in speaking one's experience," argues Luisa Muraro in *L'ordine simbolico della madre,* complicating and complementing Valesio's bipartite division with a feminist perspective, "but the two unspeakables, which in theory can be distinguished, may result inseparable to the individual woman. Or she might not want to separate them, as if she had the premonition that her ordinary difficulty in speaking prefigures the absolutely unspeakable" (33).

The unspeakable is also unthinkable, and both are connected with the maternal dimension. In "Stabat Mater," Kristeva writes that "Man overcomes the unthinkable of death by postulating maternal love in its place—in the place and stead of death and thought" (252). Rather than repressing the maternal body, the body of birth and natality, in favor of that other, opposite existential experience to which his sex has access, namely death, the maternal body—love, life—becomes in Kristeva's discussion a means for man to avoid the painful, unbearable thought of death. A mother's love, expressed in semiotic traces and linked, in Kristeva's dual text, to the experience of birth, is a veil, a shield against the anguish of mortality. But it is also that which allows the unthinkable to be thought, the unspeakable to be said, through the substitution of the maternal experience of birthgiving, figured in mothering, for the masculine experience of death.

In returning to Muraro's *L'ordine simbolico della madre* with an emphasis on the symbolic order and its other, silence, let us remember that in Italian feminist thought the symbolic is regarded as a feminist practice—such as in *affidamento* and *disparità,* which I discussed in Chapter 1—rather than as an abstract philosophical speculation (see Cavarero, "Il pensiero femminista," 138–42). Its political, practical effectiveness is therefore considered central to its feminist value: What is the position of the mother, and of the maternal, with respect to language and silence? Is a mother the imaginary, pre-Oedipal fusion of female bodies, inaccessible to language? Does the maternal body simply replace the paternal law, is it a regressive utopia, or could it be instead the mediation through which language can be acquired, thus functioning as the authorization to freedom? And, perhaps most important, to what extent does the recognition of the symbolic order of the mother allow each woman to perform her feminist subjectivity?

According to Muraro, women are bound to remain silent unless they can reestablish the authority of that same mother from whom, after all and in spite of Lacanian psychoanalysis, they have historically learned how to talk: The mother signifies language more than body, as much as body, together with body. The mother's, and the daughter's, impressiveness is one with the mother's, the daughter's impressionability. She is the first, the primary figure of exchange in disparity, that *disparità* theorized by some Italian feminists as that without which women cannot attain authority. The mother is the one from whom we learn how to speak, and thus the one thanks to whom we become subjects through relationship—ethically, one might say. Individuation takes place not through separation but through mediation, through relationship with another woman—the mother. And language, in this framework, is inseparable from experience, as theory is inseparable from practice and the ethical self is inseparable from the recognition of the other.

Muraro's theory goes against poststructuralist psychoanalysis as embodied in the work of not only Lacan but also women theorists such as Kristeva. For the latter claims, in Muraro's critique, that the acquisition of language entails a "thetic cut" in the relationship with the mother; speaking is founded on the loss, however incomplete, of the semiotic in order to enter the symbolic. Muraro, on the other hand, asserts that such cut or severance from the mother is not necessary and that the symbolic order establishes itself in the relationship with the mother rather than in its destruction. Just as the body cannot be separated from the mind, the origin of life cannot be separated from the acquisition of language, from "the origin of the word" (*L'ordine simbolico*, 43). This relationship begins in utero, when the mother's voice is the most important one that the fetus hears. The desire to imitate such a voice, Muraro muses, is perhaps one of the incentives for birth. And birth, for Muraro, is defined as the introduction to language, its sine qua non: "The moment of birth must be seen as the decision made by the child about to be born to come out in the open, with a not inconsiderable renunciation of the advantages of uterine life, in order to have what it did not have there: air and breath, indispensable for the production of sound" (*L'ordine simbolico*, 43). Even before birth, then, language belongs to the connection between mother and child, with birth intervening to focus this connection on language even more. Our birth roots us and the maternal principle in history. It is the maternal authority—source of the mother tongue, of the first code, of the first mediation—that ultimately decides on speakability, according to Muraro (*L'ordine simbolico*, 102). "The issue of speakability is always also an issue of social order" (*L'ordine simbolico*, 98), and, as such, speakability is rooted in history just as language is historically determined. From this perspective, we might compare Muraro's position to Kristeva's if it is true, as Weir claims, that

> the symbolic order is not absolutely identical with the father's Law—that the mother, for instance, is not merely a victim of, but is also a participant in, the social symbolic order and is capable of representing aspects of symbolic ordering to the child. And, that through identification with her mother, *and*

> with the symbolic order, a female subject might take up a position as a participant in the given order, and in the creation of a different one. (89–90)

These are important statements in the context of speaking birth and of the potential ineffability of motherhood. For speakability is only possible if someone is there listening and assuring us that she understands what we mean, and who is better suited for this than the very source of our speaking ability, the one from whom we learned how to mean? Who best shares the same language with us? Muraro's theory, despite its initial shock value for the many of us weaned on the notion that language is learned through the Name of the Father and through separation from the mother, is actually in line with the maternal identification theory explained by Jessica Benjamin in a passage I quoted in Chapter 1. Individuality is not necessarily defined by a separateness brought about through paternal intervention, Benjamin notes, in turn at the basis of the girl's penis envy as her pitiful existential condition. Rather, individuality is a complex process of relationality and continuity, and sexual identity can be productively mediated for the girl by her identification with her mother. The mother, that is, becomes the mediator between her child and the world. Yet, as Muraro claims, the abandonment of the mother as the source of authority and/as language entails women's inability to speak, her unspeakability even, until the original relation with the mother, with language, is restored: "The mother's superiority and the necessity of its translation into symbolic authority . . . must be recognized as a principle" (*L'ordine simbolico*, 101). It is in the harmony of body and word—of semiotic and symbolic, of logic and experience—that the mother's authority provides the mediation necessary for speaking (of) both.

As we read about birth, language, and the maternal in the work of Cavarero, Kristeva, and Muraro, the analogies between turn-of-the-century literary texts and the elaborations of contemporary feminist thinkers are again striking and significant, as well as productive, prolific, fertile grounds for reconceiving our relationship to, our bearing and delivering the experiences of maternity. In self-consciously overusing these terms, I acknowledge the multiple connections between intellectual labor and the labor, my labor of human reproduction, those multiple and repeatedly intersecting lines that connect my reading, writing, birthing, mothering to which I referred in the Introduction. In all of these practices, language, and its other—silence—claim a role as central as the equally problematic relationship between theory and practice, self and other, separation and continuity. The difficulties of speaking about pregnancy, encountered throughout this book, become most visible in its culminating processes of labor and delivery, times of taboo and banishment for women in traditional societies, times that are today still imbued with fear and pleasure, creation and destruction, life and death. Unspeakable times, in many ways, yet times that many women cannot cease speaking about. The unspeakability of the forbidden, that which *should not* be spoken about, is however productively intertwined with the ineffability of the ecstatic moment, that which *cannot* be spoken about. And this complex cluster of relationships to the written word, and to the word as flesh, can in turn be rethought in light of feminist reconsiderations of the process through which we acquire language, through which we enter the symbolic order(s).

Conclusion

Impressive, Moving, Transforming, Paradoxical: Maternal Ethics

"According to traditional historiography, in order to enter 'History' we must get rid of our private dimension. Perhaps this is also why there is almost no trace left of how nineteenth-century women lived the experience of childbirth, maternity, breastfeeding, sexuality, the family" (*Libreria delle donne,* 52). With these words, the unnamed editors of a fascinating selection of photographs from the famed Alinari brothers Florentine photography studio, dated 1860–1910, begin the section entitled "Family Album." They note the striking absence from the Alinari archives of mothers with young children. Babies are portrayed either alone, in strange and elaborate nests and baskets reminiscent of those ubiquitous, oddly clad Anne Geddes babies we see today, or with their dolled-up wetnurses. As the editors point out, such an absence is all the more puzzling given that, at that time, the role of mother was practically the only one officially sanctioned for women to attain a personal identity. So why did the many women who went to get photographed in the Alinari studio not want to be represented as mothers? Even after all I have written, perhaps especially after all I have written, the answer is unclear. In some ways, for those mothers whom we will never be able to see in photographs, motherhood was impossible. It is all too significant, then, and noteworthy that the photographers were unable to capture and represent it.

The lifelong, multiple tasks of mothering, and of parenting, recapitulate the issues discussed in the preceding chapters in terms of the nine months of pregnancy and the hours or, at worst, days of labor and delivery. Indeed, the questions analyzed in Chapters 1 through 4 could be rephrased as follows to apply to parenting in general:

What *influence* do we have on the children we raise? (The question of maternal impressions).

How do we get to *know* our children and ourselves through our relationship with them? (The question of quickening).

What *effects* does mothering, parenting, have on us as subjects; how are we *changed* by it? (The question of maternal metamorphosis).

How can we talk about the experiences of mothering, of parenting, which cannot be adequately captured by *language*? (The question of paradoxical parturition).

These questions, involving relationality and dialogue, and traversed in turn by paradox and continuity, pervade the maternity matters I have been discussing throughout this book. In this process, I hope to have elicited in the reader a reflection not only on maternity, then, but also on how we come to be who we are in relation to others, to those whom we love and care for, and those who in turn love and care for us. These are the terms of ethics, and it is with a brief reflection on a possible ethics of maternity that I would like to end this book.

Ethics is a recurring theme in the discourse of feminism and of maternity. With the advent of poststructuralism and the fall of the strong Western subject, any reflection on ethical imperatives has become problematic in philosophical discourse. Yet the plurality in which the Western subject has dissolved is potentially fertile for women, as Italian feminist Alessandra Bocchetti has written: "Women have always carried within themselves this plural subject being: they have always experienced the impossibility of the split between affective life and social and cultural reason, between body and thought, an impossible one for them. Between passion and ethics, they have always lived this multiplicity, always embodied the crisis of a reason which was supposed to be singular and bodiless" (149). It is Bocchetti's association of ethics with passion that I find most compelling in this passage: through the mediation of sexual difference, ethics and passion demand that we recognize our engagement with and responsibility to the other, our reliance on reciprocal exchange and communication for our constitution as lovers and as subjects. For feminism cannot afford to do without the ethical. The very impetus for the feminist movement after all could be described as an ethical one: an impetus for social justice or equality, and for the cultural recognition of sexual difference. In the words of Margrit Shildrick, "The agenda for feminist ethics . . . revolves round issues of sameness and difference" (147). These are issues that the maternal body displays and performs. Thus in maternity a confrontation with the ethical, as we have seen in the texts encountered in the preceding chapters, is inevitable; at the same time, however, it is a confrontation that does not posit the necessity of maternal self-sacrifice, nor does it exclude the possibility of mothers who leave, mothers who hate, mothers who destroy.

The ethical relationship to the other is symbolized in the theory of maternal impressions and the concept of female genealogy (see Chapter 1). It is implicit in the epistemology of quickening and of female writing (see Chapter 2). It forms us and deforms us in ways that are at once corporeal, psychological, social, cultural (see Chapter 3). It impels us to speak beyond and across silence, and in speech and silence it asks us who we are and whom we make (see Chapter 4). The maternal imperative to ethics emerging in the most affirming of the texts we have encountered in this book encourages us to engage in reciprocal relationships without destroying the self or the other, with the implication that the hostile exclusion of otherness damages the self as well.

Thus, despite the obvious dangers of reducing women to maternity intrinsic in the choice of the maternal relation as a model for the ethical relation, I find it necessary, as a mother and as a scholar of maternity, to engage this model, reading it with a hermeneutics of suspicion, in the hope of deriving from what is my, and not only my, inevitable embodied reality the meaning necessary to experience maternity as a fully human, ethical activity. Maternal ethics is more than the reductive conflation of womanhood with motherhood, or of motherhood with lifelong selfless devotion. On the contrary, there is something subversive in the act of seeking and finding an ethical paradigm in the maternal model, a model that opposes self-transparency and isolation and that has traditionally been identified with the natural in opposition to the rational—and thus branded as unable to develop a mature personal morality.

But this ethical maternal model is not one, to paraphrase Luce Irigaray's seminal *This Sex Which Is Not One.* The child's first relation to the other is the relation to the mother, yet the possibility of modeling subsequent relations on this primary one is effectively excluded if the mother–child bond is viewed as dyadic and presocial, imaginary and unsymbolizable; rather than providing a model for interacting with others, this unethical bond threatens sociality itself. At the same time, one could look at the mother–child bond from the mother's perspective instead of the child's. Yes, the mother herself has had a primary bond to her own mother, a bond that, as the elaboration of female genealogy makes clear, must be acknowledged rather than repressed. But the mother's relation to her child, before, during, and after birth, is not her first relation. Rather, the mother's relation, like the mother's body, has a human history in which gender and sex, like nature and culture, are present, active, inseparable. To perceive the mother–child bond as preverbal, presymbolic, prelinguistic, premature, is to regard it from the child's perspective, as if the mother as body and subject came into being with the coming into being of her child. On the contrary, however, ethics is always-already present in a relationship in which at least one of the parties is an adult. In this perspective, Cynthia Willett writes that "the social eroticism of the nurturer-child relationship establishes the basis for an ethics that goes beyond the altruism-egoism dichotomy as well as the gender stereotypes that this dichotomy sustains in European cultures" (9). Indeed, Willett goes on to indict "one of the gravest injustices of the West: the effacement of maternal agency in the construction of sociality" (85).

Not all of the texts discussed in this book support a maternal imperative to ethics that encourages us to engage in reciprocal relationships without destroying the self or the other. Kristeva, for example, holds in her theory of abjection that instead we must construct our identity through the exclusion of the other. According to this theory, the exclusion operated by abjection is hostile, and its object remains a threat to our sense of self. The model of abjection is especially disturbing if we remember that the first object of abjection is the mother's body: the infant's first other would be constructed as its main obstacle to individuation, to its ability to become a social subject. But although abjection accurately describes the dynamics of oppression, as Kelly Oliver notes, we need not accept that abjection is necessary for the construction of self-identity (*Family Values,* 99). Other types of identity must be available. For if individuation and self-identity are predicated on the exclusion of the other, how can we have an ethical subject? Rather, for Oliver, our encounters with difference and otherness can help us form our identity: "Relationships bring us 'out of ourselves' in order to give us a sense of ourselves, to 'see' ourselves for the first time. It is only through our relationships that we become who we are" (*Family Values,* 102). Comparably, Rosalyn Diprose explores "the idea that sexed identity and difference is constituted through, rather than prior to, social exchange," noting that "if ethics is about taking a position in relation to others then it is also about the constitution of identity and difference" (x,

19). To read Kristeva differently—as she teaches us to read and thus, I believe, implicitly demands to be read—we become ourselves by being other to ourselves, which we achieve in our relationship with others who are different from us. Poetic language, psychoanalysis, and maternity are three privileged places where we encounter this ethical model of alterity. The maternal subject models ethics, or rather "herethics," as Kristeva calls it in "Stabat Mater," by embodying alterity within. For otherness, in the core of ourselves and in those with whom we entertain relationships, is fundamental to our identity and to our sense of who we are. The ethical relationship, for Kristeva, must originate in an ethics of difference.

This attention to maternal ethics as the relation to the other also emerges in a fascinating interview of Hélène Rouch conducted by Luce Irigaray and published in her book *Je, tu, nous.* Rouch, a biology teacher in a Paris lycée, has authored a text on the placenta as the third term between mother and fetus. In it, she describes the placenta as a mediator that is neither fetus nor mother, allowing interchange between the two terms that at the same time never touch; it is an organ produced by the fetus and anatomically dependent on it, but which later produces hormones for the mother, without ever becoming part of her body despite its imbrication in the uterine cavity. The placenta allows the fetus to grow without in this process destroying the mother, from whom the fetus's ability to grow nevertheless derives. From Rouch's theory, Irigaray extracts the notion of "the almost ethical character of the fetal relation" (*Je, tu, nous,* 46)—an ethical character symptomatically forgotten or misunderstood by discourses such as the scientific method, which can only imagine the relation between two bodies as either fusion or aggression (as in the rejection of a transplanted organ, for instance). The ethics of pregnancy, in Irigaray's understanding of Rouch's elaboration, is founded on order and the respect for the other, rather than on the unspeakable fusion imagined by much psychoanalysis and the patriarchal imagination in general.

This formulation can be productively reread in the context of maternal impression, the epistemology of quickening, the (de)forming of the mother's body, the paradoxical relations established by birth. The provocative model of the ethical in Rouch's placental economy, as in the bulk of my argument, is not so much the mother–child relation but rather the maternal body itself. Ethical mediation takes place through maternal impressions, in the course of which the mother's desire mediates between the child she carries and the outside world. In this model, ethics precedes ontology since the self comes into being, for better or for worse (as in Grazia Deledda's mouflon-like boy: deaf and mute), in relation to the other. Ethical mediation is central to the epistemology of quickening, a process of learning and knowing based on the continuity and difference between pregnant woman and moving fetus. Ethical mediation shapes the pregnant woman's transformation into mother, into other. And, finally, ethical mediation allows for communication in the midst of the paradoxes of parturition, its silences and screams, its pleasures and pains. And if medical discourse is one of the mechanisms through which the maternal body is produced, we ought to remember that "it is the fact that the body is the self expressed which gives medical practice its ethical dimension" (Diprose, 109).

The ethical mediation of maternity I am invoking is more complicated than the influential definition of the feminist ethics of care elaborated in Carol Gilligan's *In a Different Voice* (1983) because of its involvement with poststructuralist psychoanalysis and its deconstruction of binary opposition (which Gilligan, with her dichotomy between ethics of care and ethics of justice, instead reinforces). This ethical mediation of maternity belongs to the philosophical line along which maternal ethics is hinted at through the literary and theoretical texts by women I have been examining. The consciousness of an otherness, and of the subject's/the mother's responsibility toward this other, permeates the elaboration of maternal impressions, quickening, transformation, and paradox in turn-of-the-century and contemporary women's texts. The ethical questions raised by these elaborations are connected to topics that have long challenged moral theory—topics such as the complex relationship between reason and emotion, the development of a concept of the self, and the precarious distinction between private and public. An ethical understanding of maternity reconsiders and reframes the feminist slogan "the personal is political" by embedding the body with the development of the subject, and vice versa, by disrupting any easy separation between nature and culture, theory and practice, private morality and public life, and even self and other.

In this process, claiming an ethics of maternity dismantles as well the opposition between the distinctively human activity of political life and mothering as an activity that is not specifically human. To return to the claims made by Virginia Held in *Feminist Morality*, "Human mothering shapes language and culture, it forms human social personhood, it develops morality. . . . Human mothering is no more 'natural' or 'primarily biological' than is any human activity" (55). Even more directly, Sara Ruddick through her seminal book *Maternal Thinking* analyzes the implications of mothering as a practice paradigmatic of the conduct of peace politics. The maternal is the ethical, and as such it makes a difference. Thus Held argues, for example, that "From the point of view of those who give birth, the social, political, economic, legal, educational, cultural, and familial realms should be organized to be, *first of all,* hospitable to children" (172). Although I do not directly address politics in *Maternal Impressions,* Held's statement reminds us that a critique of politics is implicit in the ethical "remoralization" (Sarah Hoagland's term) of motherhood: The personal is not only ethical but also political; it interrogates public policy as well as psychology and epistemology.

Along these same lines, Silvia Vegetti Finzi argues that the ethical dimension of maternity has been unrecognized or denied in our culture because the mother–child relation has been naturalized, placed in a presocial and presymbolic realm. Yet according to the ethical paradigm of maternity, "the mother continually limits the impulse to completely possess her child," and "in so doing, she translates domination into responsibility;" thus, this paradigm can make a relevant contribution to the apparently unresolvable dilemmas of bioethics by helping us in "finding forms of rational control to counter the omnipotence of the scientific imaginary and the uncontrolled proliferation of its technical applications" (*Mothering,* 4–5; this paradigm again does not take into account mothers who leave, mothers who hurt, mothers, even, who kill—topics for another book, perhaps). More theoretically, Finzi argues that "No maternity exists, even potentially speaking, without some preliminary recognition of the other. Procreation is essentially a relationship, and gestation involves a silent dialogue in the shared space of the maternal body" (*Mothering,* 173). The period that precedes the mother–child relation interpreted by Finzi as an ethical paradigm, the period on which I concentrated throughout this book, is itself an ethical moment insofar as it is centered on the bond between self and other and the creation of the self through the other, the other through the self.

In birthgiving, the preponderant conjunction of pain, meaning, and silence is itself an ethical dimension: how to remain unmoved before a suffering other? I have already invoked Simone Weil's notion of attention, in Chapter 3, as the ability to be present to the pain of the other, to understand and articulate that affliction that "is by its nature inarticulate" (*The Simone Weil Reader,* 327). Closely related to attention and affliction is Weil's call for a politics willing and able to listen to the other's cry of pain, a politics characterized by "an attentive silence in which this faint and inept cry can make itself heard" (316). We can in turn relate this attentive silence to the concept of answer and responsibility, the root of which is the same as "response." The scope of personal responsibility, a central concern of traditional ethics, is an important question in Weil's social and philosophical analysis of affliction and attention as well as in Gilligan's ethics of care, and it is a guiding thread in the elaboration of maternal impressions, maternal epistemology, maternal transformations, maternal silence as (decentered) centers of moral choice. The formulations elaborated in the course of this book raise questions concerning the scope of our responsibility toward differences, especially as these differences are neither disembodied nor ahistorical, but rather invested in the other and in our own provisional self. By impersonating the leaky boundary between self and other, the pregnant, birthing body performs the ethical moment as the radical openness to the self's position among its others, as the self's risky recognition that it is embedded in the fate of others. In this perspective, knowledge can be pursued in order to connect with others, rather than as a verbal war or a philosophical contest. Because if knowledge can be sought only with reference to signification, and signification can arise only from difference, then our epistemic quest depends on our ethical relation to the other. Founded on attention to words, silence, and cries, the knowledge inscribed in maternal ethics pursues and is pursued in the recognition of the other in our self, of our self in the other, and in the permeable connections between what we are and who we are, who makes us and whom we make, in and through this impressive bond.

Bibliography

Accati, Luisa. "Il parto tra storia personale e storia sociale." Oakley et al., 43–46.

Adams, Alice E. *Reproducing the Womb: Images of Childbirth in Science, Feminist Theory, and Literature.* Ithaca: Cornell University Press, 1994.

Ainley, Alison. "The Ethics of Sexual Difference." In *Abjection, Melancholia, and Love: The Work of Julia Kristeva,* ed. John Fletcher and Andrew Benjamin, 53–62. London: Routledge, 1990.

Alcoff, Linda, and Elizabeth Potter, eds. *Feminist Epistemologies.* New York: Routledge, 1993.

Aleramo, Sibilla. *Una donna.* Milan: Feltrinelli, 1989.

——. *Il passaggio.* Milan: Serra e Riva, 1985.

——. *A Woman.* Trans. Rosalind Delmar. Berkeley: University of California Press, 1980.

Amerighi, Guglielmo, ed. *Proverbi delle donne.* Florence: Libreria Editrice Fiorentina, 1979.

Amoia, Alba. *No Mothers We! Italian Women Writers and Their Revolt Against Maternity.* Lanham, Md.: University Press of America, 2000.

——. *Women on the Italian Literary Scene: A Panorama.* Troy, N.Y.: Whitston, 1992.

Anderlini-D'Onofrio, Serena. "I Don't Know What You Mean by 'Italian Feminist Thought.' Is Anything Like That Possible?" Miceli Jeffries, 209–32.

Arendt, Hannah. *The Human Condition.* Chicago: University of Chicago Press, 1958.

Arslan, Antonia. "Ideologia e autorappresentazione: Donne intellettuali tra Ottocento e Novecento." Buttafuoco and Zancan, 164–77.

Arslan, Antonia, and Margherita Ganazzoli. "Neera e Paolo Mantegazza: Storia di una collaborazione (con 32 lettere inedite)." *Rassegna della letteratura italiana* 87.1–2 (1983): 102–24.

Atkinson, Clarissa. *The Oldest Vocation: Christian Motherhood in the Middle Ages.* Ithaca: Cornell University Press, 1991.

Azzolini, Paola, et al. *Mettere al mondo il mondo. Oggetto e oggettività alla luce della differenza sessuale.* Milan: La Tartaruga, 1990.

Babini, Valeria. "Il lato femminile della criminalità." Babini, Minuz, and Tagliavini, 25–77.

Babini, Valeria, Fernanda Minuz, and Annamaria Tagliavini. *La donna nelle scienze dell'uomo. Immagini del femminile nella cultura scientifica italiana di fine secolo.* Milan: Angeli, 1989.

——. "Introduzione." Babini, Minuz, and Tagliavini, 14–23.

Bakhtin, Mikhail. *Rabelais and His World.* Trans. Helene Iswolsky. Cambridge: MIT Press, 1968.

Banti, Anna. *A Piercing Cry.* Trans. Daria Valentini and Mark Lewis. New York: Peter Lang, 1996. (*Un grido lacerante.* Milan: Rizzoli, 1981.)

Bar On, Bat-Ami, and Ann Ferguson, eds. *Daring to Be Good: Essays in Feminist Ethico-Politics.* New York: Routledge, 1998.

Barthes, Roland. *A Lover's Discourse. Fragments.* Trans. Richard Howard. New York: Hill and Wang, 1978.

Bartky, Sandra Lee. "Foucault, Femininity and the Modernization of Patriarchal Power." Conboy, Medina, and Stanbury, 129–54.

Basile, Giambattista. "Petrosinella." In *The Pentamerone of Giambattista Basile.* Trans. N. M. Penzer. Westport, Conn.: Greenwood Press, 1979. 135–39.

Bassanese, Fiora. "*Una donna*: Autobiography as Exemplary Text." In Testaferri 131–52.

Beauvoir, Simone de. *The Second Sex.* Trans. H. M. Parshley. Intro. Deirdre Bair. New York: Vintage Books, 1989.

Belenky, Mary Field, Blythe McVicker Clinchy, Nancy Rule Goldberger, and Jill Mattuck Tarule. *Women's Ways of Knowing: The Development of Self, Voice, and Mind.* New York: Basic Books, 1997.

Benjamin, Jessica. "A Desire of One's Own: Psychoanalytic Feminism and Intersubjective Space." De Lauretis, *Feminist Studies/Critical Studies,* 78–101.

Berry, Philippa. "Woman and Space According to Kristeva and Irigaray." In *Shadows of Spirit: Postmodernism and Religion,* ed. Philippa Berry and Andrew Wernick, 250–64. London: Routledge, 1992.

Bianchi, Emanuela, ed. *Is Feminist Philosophy Philosophy?* Evanston: Northwestern University Press, 1999.

Blumenfeld-Kosinski, Renate. *Not of Woman Born: Representations of Caesarean Birth in Medieval and Renaissance Culture.* Ithaca: Cornell University Press, 1990.

Bocchetti, Alessandra. "The Indecent Difference." Bono and Kemp, *Italian Feminist Thought,* 148–61.

Bock, Gisela, and Susan James. *Beyond Equality and Difference: Citizenship, Feminist Politics and Female Subjectivity.* London: Routledge, 1992.

Bohjalian, Chris. *Midwives.* New York: Harmony Books, 1997.

Boito, Arrigo. "Lezione d'anatomia." In *Poesie e racconti,* ed. Rodolfo Quadrelli, 70–73. Milan: Mondadori, 1981.

Boito, Camillo. "Un corpo." *Narratori dell'Ottocento e del primo Novecento,* ed. Aldo Borlenghi, 585–617. Milan: Ricciardi, 1956.

Bono, Paola, and Sandra Kemp. "Introduction: Coming from the South." In *Italian Feminist Thought*, 1–29.

Bono, Paola, and Sandra Kemp, eds. *Italian Feminist Thought: A Reader.* Oxford: Blackwell, 1991.

——. *The Lonely Mirror: Italian Perspectives on Feminist Theory*. London: Routledge, 1993.

Bordo, Susan. *Unbearable Weight: Feminism, Western Culture, and the Body.* Berkeley: University of California Press, 1993.

Boston Children's Medical Center. *Pregnancy, Birth, and the Newborn Baby*. N.p.: Seymour Lawrence, 1972.

Braidotti, Rosi. "Foreword." Cavarero, *In Spite of Plato*, vii-xix.

——. "Of Bugs and Women: Irigaray and Deleuze on Becoming-Woman." Schor and Weed, 111–37.

——. *Nomadic Subjects: Embodiment and Sexual Difference in Contemporary Feminist Theory*. New York: Columbia University Press, 1994.

Brennan, Teresa, ed. *Between Feminism and Psychoanalysis.* London: Routledge, 1989.

Briziarelli, Susan. "Woman as Outlaw: Grazia Deledda and the Politics of Gender." *MLN* 110.1 (1995): 20–31.

Burke, Carolyn. "Irigaray Through the Looking Glass." Burke, Schor, and Whitford, 37–56.

——. "Translation Modified: Irigaray in English." Burke, Schor, and Whitford, 249–61.

Burke, Carolyn, and Jane Gallop. "Psychoanalysis and Feminism in France." Eisenstein and Jardine, 106–21.

Burke, Carolyn, Naomi Schor, and Margaret Whitford, eds. *Engaging with Irigaray: Feminist Philosophy and Modern European Thought.* New York: Columbia University Press, 1994.

Butler, Judith. *Bodies That Matter: On the Discursive Limits of "Sex."* New York: Routledge, 1993.

——. "The Body Politics of Julia Kristeva." Oliver, *Ethics, Politics, and Difference in Julia Kristeva's Writings*, 164–78.

——. *Gender Trouble: Feminism and the Subversion of Identity.* New York: Routledge, 1990.

Buttafuoco, Annarita, and Marina Zancan. *Svelamento. Sibilla Aleramo: Una biografia intellettuale.* Milan: Feltrinelli, 1988.

Buzzatti, Gabriella, and Anna Salvo, eds. *Corpo a corpo: Madre e figlia nella psicoanalisi.* Bari: Laterza, 1995.

Cavarero, Adriana. "Dire la nascita." Azzolini et al., 93–121.

——. "L'elaborazione filosofica della differenza sessuale." Marcuzzo and Rossi-Doria, 173–87.

——. "Il pensiero femminista. Un approccio teoretico." In *Le filosofie femministe*, Franco Restaino and Adriana Cavarero, 111–163. Turin: Paravia, 1999.

——. *In Spite of Plato: A Feminist Rewriting of Ancient Philosophy.* Trans. Serena Anderlini-D'Onofrio and Áine O'Healy. New York: Routledge, 1995.

——. *Relating Narratives: Storytelling and Selfhood.* Trans. Paul A. Koffman. London: Routledge, 2000.

——. "Towards a Theory of Sexual Difference." Bono and Kemp, *The Lonely Mirror,* 189–221.

Chanter, Tina. "Kristeva's Politics of Change: Tracking Essentialism with the Help of a Sex/Gender Map." Oliver, *Ethics, Politics, and Difference in Julia Kristeva's Writings,* 179–95.

Chianese, Gloria. *Storia sociale della donna in Italia (1800–1980).* Naples: Guida, 1980.

Chodorow, Nancy. "Gender Relation and Difference in Psychoanalytic Perspective." Eisenstein and Jardine, 3–19.

——. *The Reproduction of Mothering: Psychoanalysis and the Sociology of Gender.* Berkeley: University of California Press, 1978.

Cixous, Hélène. "Castration or Decapitation?" *Signs* 7.1 (1981): 41–55.

——. "Coming to Writing." *"Coming to Writing" and Other Essays,* 1–58.

——. *"Coming to Writing" and Other Essays.* Ed. Deborah Jenson. Trans. Sarah Cornell et al. Cambridge: Harvard University Press, 1991.

——. *The Hélène Cixous Reader.* Ed. Susan Sellers. London: Routledge, 1994.

——. "The Laugh of the Medusa." *Signs* 1.4 (1976): 875–93.

——. *Souffles. The Hélène Cixous Reader,* 49–55.

Cixous, Hélène, and Mireille Calle-Gruber. *Hélène Cixous, Rootprints: Memory and Life Writing.* Trans. Eric Prenowitz. London: Routledge, 1997.

Cixous, Hélène, and Catherine Clément. *The Newly Born Woman.* Trans. Betsy Wing. Minneapolis: University of Minnesota Press, 1986.

Code, Lorraine. "Taking Subjectivity into Account." Alcoff and Potter, 15–48.

Comba, Letizia. "Ciò che non è verificabile." Azzolini et al., 157–72.

Conboy, Katie, Nadia Medina, and Sarah Stanbury. *Writing on the Body: Female Embodiment and Feminist Theory.* New York: Columbia University Press, 1997.

Corona, Daniela, ed. *Donne e scrittura. Città di Palermo, Arcidonna: Atti del seminario internazionale (Palermo 9–11 giugno, 1990).* Palermo: La Luna, 1990.

Cosmacini, Giorgio. "L'igiene e il medico di famiglia." Melograni with Scaraffia, 589–627.

——. *Storia della medicina e della sanità in Italia: Dalla peste europea alla guerra mondiale (1348–1918).* Bari: Laterza, 1987.

Costantino, Battistina. "Travail, travaglio: Note intorno all'identità linguistica del lavoro e del travaglio di parto." In *Tematiche femminili. Seminario interdisciplinare Università di Torino 1987–1988,* ed. F. Balsamo and M. A. Sarti, 143–178. Turin: Il Segnalibro, 1988.

Cowley, Geoffrey. "The Biology of Beauty." *Newsweek* 127.23 (June 3, 1996): 61–66.

Curtis, Glade B. *Your Pregnancy Week-by-Week.* Tucson: Fisher Books, 1989.

Cutrufelli, Rosa. "Scritture, scrittrici. L'esperienza italiana." Corona, 237–45.

Dalmiya, Vrinda, and Linda Alcoff. "Are 'Old Wives' Tales' Justified?" Alcoff and Potter, 217–44.

Daniels, Cynthia R. "Fathers, Mothers, and Fetal Harm: Rethinking Gender Difference and Reproductive Responsibility." In *Fetal Subjects, Feminist Positions,* ed. Lynn M. Morgan and Meredith W. Michaels, 83–98. Philadelphia: University of Pennsylvania Press, 1999.

D'Annunzio, Gabriele. *L'innocente.* Milan: Mondadori, 1988.

Davis, Robert Con. "Woman as Oppositional Reader: Cixous on Discourse." *Papers on Language and Literature* 24.3 (1988): 265–82.

De Giorgio, Michela. *Le italiane dall'unità a oggi: modelli culturali e comportamenti sociali.* Bari: Laterza, 1992.

——. "Italiane fin de siècle." *Rivista di storia contemporanea* 2 (April 1987): 212–39.

De Grazia, Victoria. *How Fascism Ruled Women: Italy, 1922–1945.* Berkeley: University of California Press, 1992.

De Lauretis, Teresa. "The Essence of the Triangle, or Taking the Risk of Essentialism Seriously: Feminist Theory in Italy, the U.S., and Britain." Schor and Weed, 1–39.

——. "The Practice of Sexual Difference and Feminist Thought in Italy: An Introductory Essay." Milan Women's Bookstore Collective, 1–21.

De Lauretis, Teresa, ed. *Feminist Studies/Critical Studies.* Bloomington: Indiana University Press, 1986.

Deledda, Grazia. *Cosima.* Trans. Martha King. New York: Italica Press, 1988. (*Cosima.* In *Romanzi e novelle,* ed. Natalino Sapegno. Milan: Mondadori, 1971. 691–820.)

——. *Elias Portolu.* Trans. Martha King. Evanston: Northwestern University Press, 1995. (*Elias Portolu.* Turin: Roux e Viarengo, 1903.)

——. *The Mother.* Trans. Mary Steegmann. New York: Macmillan, 1927. (*La madre.* In *Romanzi e novelle,* ed. Natalino Sapegno. Milan: Mondadori, 1971. 387–511.)

Delphy, Christine. "The Invention of French Feminism: An Essential Move." Huffer, *Another Look, Another Woman,* 190–221.

Derrida, Jacques. "Opening Remarks." Bianchi, 10–16.

Dijkstra, Bram. *Idols of Perversity: Fantasies of Feminine Evil in Fin-de-Siècle Culture.* New York: Oxford University Press, 1986.

Diprose, Rosalyn. *The Bodies of Women: Ethics, Embodiment and Sexual Difference.* London: Routledge, 1994.

DiQuinzio, Patrice. *The Impossibility of Motherhood: Feminism, Individualism, and the Problem of Mothering.* New York: Routledge, 1999.

Dolfi, Anna. *Del romanzesco e del romanzo: Modelli di narrativa italiana tra Otto e Novecento.* Rome: Bulzoni, 1992.

Duden, Barbara. *Disembodying Women: Perspectives on Pregnancy and the Unborn.* Trans. Lee Hoinacki. Cambridge: Harvard University Press, 1993.

Dwyer, Susan. "Learning from Experience: Moral Phenomenology and Politics." Bar On and Ferguson, 28–44.

Eisenberg, Arlene, Heidi E. Murkoff, and Sandee E. Hathaway. *What to Expect When You're Expecting.* New York: Workman, 1991.

Eisenstein, Hester, and Alice Jardine. *The Future of Difference.* Boston: G. K. Hall, 1980.

Fallaci, Oriana. *Letter to a Child Never Born.* Trans. John Shepley. New York: Simon and Schuster, 1976. (*Lettera a un bambino mai nato.* Milan: Rizzoli, 1975.)

Feldman, George B., with Anne Felshman. *The Complete Handbook of Pregnancy: A Step-by-Step Guide from Preconception to the First Weeks Following Birth.* New York: Putnam, 1984.

Fenlon, Arlene, Ellen Oakes, and Lovell Dorchak. *Getting Ready for Childbirth: A Guide for Expectant Parents.* Boston: Little, Brown & Co., 1986.

Ferrucci, Carlo. "Grazia Cosima Deledda." *Nuovi argomenti* 53–54 (1977): 304–315.

Finke, Laurie. *Feminist Theory, Women's Writing.* Ithaca: Cornell University Press, 1992.

Finzi, Silvia Vegetti. "Alla ricerca di una soggettività femminile." Marcuzzo and Rossi-Doria, 228–48.

——. "L'altra scena del parto." Oakley et al., 185–93.

——. "The Female Animal." Bono and Kemp, *The Lonely Mirror,* 128–51.

——. "Female Identity Between Sexuality and Maternity." Bock and James, 126–45.

——. "Le isteriche o la parola corporea." In *Psicoanalisi al femminile,* ed. Silvia Vegetti Finzi, 2–50. Rome: Laterza, 1992.

——. *Mothering: Toward a New Psychoanalytic Construction.* Trans. Kathrine Jason. New York: Guilford, 1996.

Fiorenza, Elisabeth Schüssler. *Miriam's Child, Sophia's Prophet: Critical Issues in Feminist Christology.* New York: Continuum, 1994.

Folli, Anna. "Le arpe eolie. Lettura di Neera." *Rassegna della letteratura italiana* 91.1 (1987): 98–120.

——. "Lettura di Ada Negri." Buttafuoco and Zancan, 178–87.

Foucault, Michel. *The Birth of the Clinic: An Archaeology of Medical Perception.* Trans. A. M. Sheridan Smith. New York: Vintage Books, 1975.

Frabotta, Biancamaria. "Con la mano sinistra." In *Letteratura al femminile. Itinerari di lettura: a proposito di donne, storia, poesia, romanzo.* Bari: De Donato, 1980. 135–141.

Frati, Lodovico. *La donna italiana secondo i più recenti studi.* Turin: Bocca, 1899.

Freud, Sigmund. *Civilization and Its Discontents.* Trans. James Strachey. New York: W. W. Norton, 1962.

——. *Dora: An Analysis of a Case of Hysteria.* New York: Collier, 1963.

——. *The Interpretation of Dreams.* In *The Standard Edition of the Complete Psychological Works of Sigmund Freud.* Vols.4–5.

——. *Psychoanalytic Notes on an Autobiographical Account of a Case of Paranoia (Dementia Paranoides).* In *The Standard Edition of the Complete Psychological Works of Sigmund Freud.* Vol. 12: 1–82.

——. *The Standard Edition of the Complete Psychological Works of Sigmund Freud.* Trans. James Strachey. 24 vols. London: Hogarth Press, 1958.

——. "The Uncanny." In *Studies in Parapsychology.* New York: Collier, 1963. 17–60.

Fusini, Nadia. "Sulle donne e il loro poetare." *Nuova Donnawomanfemme* 5 (1977): 5–21.

Fuss, Diana. *Essentially Speaking.* New York: Routledge, 1989.

Gallop, Jane. *Reading Lacan.* Ithaca: Cornell University Press, 1985.

——. *Thinking Through the Body.* New York: Columbia Univerity Press, 1988.

Gélis, Jacques. *History of Childbirth: Fertility, Pregnancy and Birth in Early Modern Europe.* Trans. Rosemary Morris. Cambridge: Polity Press, 1991.

Giacanelli, Ferruccio. "Introduzione." In *La scienza infelice. Il museo di antropologia criminale di Cesare Lombroso,* by Giorgio Colombo. Turin: Boringhieri, 1975. 7–32.

Gilligan, Carol. *In a Different Voice: Psychological Theory and Women's Development.* Cambridge: Harvard University Press, 1983.

Ginzberg, Ruth. "The Personal is Philosophical, or Teaching a Life and Living the Truth: Philosophical Pedagogy at the Boundaries of the Self." Bianchi, 50–58.

Glenn, Evelyn Nakano, Grace Chang, and Linda Rennie Forcey, eds. *Mothering: Ideology, Experience, and Agency*. New York: Routledge, 1999.
Greenfield, Susan C., and Carol Barash. *Inventing Maternity: Politics, Science, and Literature, 1650–1865*. Lexington: University Press of Kentucky, 1999.
Grimm, Jakob and Wilhelm. "Rapunzel." In *About Wise Men and Simpletons: Twelve Tales from Grimm*. Trans. Elizabeth Shub. Etchings by Nonny Hogrogian. New York: Macmillan, 1971. 37–43.
——. "Rapunzel." In *Selected Tales*. Trans. David Luke. New York: Penguin Books, 1982. 66–69.
Grosz, Elizabeth. "Sexual Difference and the Problem of Essentialism." Schor and Weed, 82–97.
——. *Sexual Subversions: Three French Feminists*. Sydney: Allen and Unwin, 1989.
——. *Space, Time, and Perversion: Essays on the Politics of Bodies*. New York: Routledge, 1995.
——. *Volatile Bodies: Toward a Corporeal Feminism*. Bloomington: Indiana University Press, 1994.
Gubar, Susan. "The Birth of the Artist as Heroine: (Re)production, the Kunstlerroman Tradition, and the Fiction of Katherine Mansfield." In *The Representation of Women in Fiction*, ed. Carolyn Heilbrun and Margaret Higonnet, 19–59. Baltimore: Johns Hopkins University Press, 1983.
Gurrieri, Raffaele, and Ernesto Fornasari. *I sensi e le anomalie somatiche nella donna normale e nella prostituta*. Turin: Bocca, 1893.
Guttmacher, Alan. *Pregnancy, Birth, and Family Planning*. New York: Viking, 1973.
Haraway, Donna. *Simians, Cyborgs, and Women: The Reinvention of Nature*. New York: Routledge, 1991.
Harrowitz, Nancy A. *Antisemitism, Misogyny, and the Logic of Cultural Difference: Cesare Lombroso and Matilde Serao*. Lincoln: Univerity of Nebraska Press, 1994.
Hartouni, Valerie. *Cultural Conceptions: On Reproductive Technologies and the Remaking of Life*. Minneapolis: University of Minnesota Press, 1997.
Hartsock, Nancy. "The Feminist Standpoint: Developing the Ground for a Specifically Feminist Historical Materialism." Kemp and Squires, 152–60.
Heberle, Renee. "Remembering the Resistant Object: A Critique of Feminist Epistemologies." Bar On and Ferguson, 114–26.
Held, Virginia. *Feminist Morality: Transforming Culture, Society, and Politics*. Chicago: University of Chicago Press, 1993.
Henderson, Andrea. "Doll-Machines and Butcher-Shop Meat: Models of Childbirth in the Early Stages of Industrial Capitalism." *Genders* 12 (Winter 1991): 100–19.
Hendricks, Christina, and Kelly Oliver, eds. *Language and Liberation: Feminism, Philosophy, and Language*. Albany: State University of New York Press, 1999.
Hirsch, Marianne. "Mothers and Daughters." In *Ties That Bind: Essays on Mothering and Patriarchy*, ed. Jean F. O'Barr, Deborah Pope, and Mary Wyer, 177–99. Chicago: University of Chicago Press, 1990.
Hoagland, Sarah. *Lesbian Ethics*. Palo Alto, Calif.: Institute of Lesbian Ethics, 1988.
Holub, Renate. "Between the United States and Italy: Critical Reflections on Diotima's Feminist/Feminine Ethics." Miceli Jeffries, 233–60.

Horn, David G. *Social Bodies: Science, Reproduction, and Italian Modernity.* Princeton: Princeton University Press, 1994.

——. "This Norm Which Is Not One: Reading the Female Body in Lombroso's Anthropology." Terry and Urla, 109–28.

Hotchner, Tracie. *Pregnancy and Childbirth: The Complete Guide.* New York: Avon Books, 1990.

Hrdy, Sarah Blaffer. *Mother Nature: A History of Mothers, Infants, and Natural Selection.* New York: Pantheon Books, 1999.

Huff, Cynthia. "Delivery: The Cultural Re-presentation of Childbirth." In *Autobiography and Questions of Gender,* ed. Shirley Newman, 108–21. London: Cass, 1991.

Huffer, Lynne. *Maternal Pasts, Feminist Futures: Nostalgia, Ethics, and the Question of Difference.* Stanford: Stanford University Press, 1998.

——, ed. *Another Look, Another Woman: Retranslations of French Feminism. Yale French Studies* 87 (1995).

Invernizio, Carolina. "*Il bacio d'una morta.*" In *Romanzo storico sociale,* ed. Roberto Fedi. Milan: Mursia, 1989.

——. "La confessione d'una suicida." In *Il delitto di una madre,* 161–88.

——. *Cuore di madre.* Milan: Lucchi, 1977.

——. *Il delitto di una madre.* Milan: Lucchi, 1991.

——. *Odio di donna.* Milan: Lucchi, 1982.

——. "Il vero amore." In *Il delitto di una madre,* 61–102.

Iovine, Vicki. "Girlfriend to Girlfriend." *Child* (December/January 2000): 131–32.

Irigaray, Luce. "And the One Doesn't Stir Without the Other." *Signs* 7.1 (Autumn 1981): 60–67.

——. "Body Against Body: In Relation to the Mother." In *Sexes and Genealogies,* 7–21.

——. "Divine Women." In *Sexes and Genealogies,* 55–72.

——. "Each Sex Must Have Its Own Rights." In *Sexes and Genealogies,* 1–5.

——. *Elemental Passions.* Trans. Joanne Collie and Judith Still. New York: Routledge, 1992.

——. *An Ethics of Sexual Difference.* Trans. Carolyn Burke and Gillian Gill. Ithaca: Cornell University Press, 1993.

——. "Gesture in Psychoanalysis." In *Sexes and Genealogies,* 89–104.

——. *Je, tu, nous: pour une culture de la différence.* Paris: Grasset et Fasquelle, 1990.

——. *Sexes and Genealogies.* Trans. Gillian Gill. New York: Columbia University Press, 1993.

——. *Speculum of the Other Woman.* Trans. Gillian Gill. Ithaca: Cornell University Press, 1985.

——. *This Sex Which Is Not One.* Trans. Catherine Porter and Carolyn Burke. Ithaca: Cornell University Press, 1985.

Irigaray, Luce, and Sylvère Lotringer, eds. *Why Different? A Culture of Two Subjects. Interviews with Luce Irigaray.* Trans. Camille Collins. New York: Semiotext(e), 2000.

Jaberg, Karl. "The Birthmark in Folk Belief, Language, Literature, and Fashion." *Romance Philology* 12 (1956–1957): 307–42.

Jacobus, Mary. *Reading Woman: Essays in Feminist Criticism.* New York: Columbia University Press, 1986.

Jardine, Alice. "Prelude: The Future of Difference." Eisenstein and Jardine, xxv-xxvii.
Johnson, Elizabeth A. *She Who Is: The Mystery of God in Feminist Theological Discourse.* New York: Crossroad, 1992.
Jordanova, Ludmilla. *Sexual Visions: Images of Gender and Science in Medicine Between the Eighteenth and the Twentieth Centuries.* Madison: University of Wisconsin Press, 1989.
Kahane, Claire. "Questioning the Maternal Voice." *Genders* 3 (Fall 1988): 82–91.
Kahn, Robbie Pfeufer. *Bearing Meaning: The Language of Birth.* Urbana: University of Illinois Press, 1995.
Kamuf, Peggy. "To Give Place: Semi-Approaches to Hélène Cixous." Huffer, *Another Look, Another Woman,* 78–89.
Kaplan, E. Ann. "Look Who's Talking, Indeed: Fetal Images in Recent North American Visual Culture." Glenn, Chang, and Forcey, 121–37.
——. *Motherhood and Representation: The Mother in Popular Culture and Melodrama.* London: Routledge, 1992.
Keller, Evelyn Fox. "Making Gender Visible in the Pursuit of Nature's Secrets." De Lauretis, *Feminist Studies/Critical Studies,* 67–77.
——. *Secrets of Life, Secrets of Death: Essays on Language, Gender and Science.* New York: Routledge, 1992.
Kemp, Sandra, and Judith Squires. *Feminisms.* Oxford: Oxford University Press, 1997.
Knibiehler, Yvonne. "Bodies and Hearts." In *Emerging Feminisms from Revolution to World War I,* ed. Geneviève Fraisse and Michelle Perrot. Vol. 4 of *A History of Women in the West,* ed. Georges Duby and Michelle Perrot. 5 vols. Cambridge: Harvard University Press, Belknap Press, 1993. 325–68.
Knibiehler, Yvonne, and Catherine Fouquet. *Histoire des mères du Moyen Âge à nos jours.* Paris: Montalba, 1977.
Kofman, Sarah. *The Enigma of Woman: Woman in Freud's Writings.* Trans. Catherine Porter. Ithaca: Cornell University Press, 1985.
Korte, Barbara. "In Sorrow Thou Shalt Bring Forth Children—On Childbirth in Literature." *Orbis Litterarum* 45.1 (1990): 30–48.
Kristeva, Julia. "Discrezione." Rasy, *La lingua della nutrice,* 7–10.
——. *The Kristeva Reader.* Ed. Toril Moi. New York: Columbia University Press, 1986.
——. "Motherhood According to Giovanni Bellini." In *Desire in Language: A Semiotic Approach to Literature and Art,* ed. Leon S. Roudiez. Trans. Thomas Gora, Alice Jardine, and Leon S. Roudiez. New York: Columbia University Press, 1980. 237–70.
——. "A New Type of Intellectual: The Dissident." In *The Kristeva Reader,* 292–300.
——. *Powers of Horror: An Essay on Abjection.* Trans. Leon S. Roudiez. New York: Columbia University Press, 1982.
——. *La Révolution du langage poétique.* Paris: Seuil, 1974.
——. "Stabat Mater." In *Tales of Love.* Trans. Leon S. Roudiez. New York: Columbia University Press, 1987. 234–63.
——. "Women's Time." In *The Kristeva Reader,* 187–213.

Kroha, Lucienne. *The Woman Writer in Late-Nineteenth-Century Italy: Gender and the Formation of Literary Identity.* Lewiston, N.Y.: Edwin Mellen, 1992.

Kurella, Hans. *Cesare Lombroso: A Modern Man of Science.* Trans. M. Eden Paul. London: Rebman, 1911.

Lacan, Jacques. *The Psychoses 1955–1956.* Book III of *The Seminar of Jacques Lacan.* Ed. Jacques-Alain Miller. Trans. with notes by Russell Grigg. New York: W. W. Norton, 1993.

Landucci, Giovanni. *Darwinismo a Firenze: Tra scienza a ideologia.* Florence: Olschki, 1977.

——. "I positivisti e la 'servitù' della donna." In *L'educazione delle donne: Scuole e modelli di vita nell'Italia dell'Ottocento,* ed. Simonetta Soldani, 463–95. Milan: Angeli, 1991.

Lazzaro-Weis, Carol. "Stranger Than Life? Autobiography and Historical Fiction." In *Gendering Italian Fiction: Feminist Revisions of Italian History,* ed. Maria Ornella Marotti and Gabriella Brooke, 31–48. Cranbury, N.J.: Associated University Presses, 1999.

Leavitt, Judith Walzer. *Brought to Bed: Childbearing in America, 1750 to 1950.* New York: Oxford University Press, 1986.

Leder, Drew. *The Absent Body.* Chicago: University of Chicago Press, 1990.

Libreria delle donne, ed. *Oltre la posa. Immagini di donne negli Archivi Alinari.* Firenze: Alinari, 1984.

Lombroso, Cesare, and Guglielmo Ferrero. *La donna delinquente, la prostituta e la donna normale.* Turin: Roux, 1893.

——. *La donna delinquente, la prostituta e la donna normale.* Milan: Bocca, 1915.

Lonzi, Carla. "Let's Spit on Hegel." Bono and Kemp, *Italian Feminist Thought,* 40–59.

Loux, Françoise. *Le jeune enfant et son corps dans la médecine traditionnelle.* Paris: Flammarion, 1978.

Macalpine, Ida, and A. Richard Hunter. "Observations on the Psychoanalytic Theory of Psychosis: Freud's 'A Neurosis of Demoniacal Possession in the Seventeenth Century.' " *The British Journal of Medical Psychology* 27 (1954): 175–95.

——. "The Schreber Case: A Contribution to Schizophrenia, Hypochondria, and Psycho-Somatic Symptom-Formation." *The Psychoanalytic Quarterly* 22 (1953): 328–71.

Maitland, Sara. *Virgin Territory.* New York: Beaufort Books, 1984.

Mantegazza, Paolo. *Gli amori degli uomini.* Milan: P. Mantegazza, 1886.

——. *L'arte di prender moglie.* Milan: Treves, 1892.

——. *Fisiologia della donna.* 2 vols. Milan: Treves, 1893.

——. *Fisiologia dell'amore.* Florence: Bemporad, n.d.

——. *Fisiologia del piacere.* Pordenone: Studio Tesi, 1982.

——. *The Physiology of Love.* New York: Cleveland, 1894.

——. *The Sexual Relations of Mankind.* Largs, Scotland: Banton Press, 1990.

Maraini, Dacia. *Il treno per Helsinki.* Turin: Einaudi, 1984.

Marcuzzo, Maria Cristina, and Anna Rossi-Doria, eds. *La ricerca delle donne: Studi femministi in Italia.* Turin: Rosenberg & Sellier, 1987.

Martin, Emily. "Medical Metaphors of Women's Bodies: Menstruation and Menopause." Conboy, Medina, and Stanbury, 15–41.

——. *The Woman in the Body: A Cultural Analysis of Reproduction.* Boston: Beacon Press, 1987.

Mathews, Joan J., and Kathleen Zadak. "The Alternative Birth Movement in the United States: History and Current Status." In *Mothers and Motherhood: Readings in American History,* ed. Rima D. Apple and Janet Golden, 278–92. Columbus: Ohio State University Press, 1997.

Mathieu, Deborah. *Preventing Prenatal Harm: Should the State Intervene?* Washington: Georgetown University Press, 1996.

Matus, Jill. *Unstable Bodies: Victorian Representations of Sexuality and Maternity.* Manchester: Manchester University Press, 1995.

Mayer, Marianna. "Rapunzel." In *Little Golden Book Storyland. 40 of the Best Little Goden Books Ever Published.* New York: Golden Books, 1992. 235–40.

Mazzoni, Cristina. "Is Beauty Only Skin Deep? Constructing the Female Corpse in Scapigliatura." *Italian Culture* 12 (1994): 175–87.

——. *Saint Hysteria: Neurosis, Mysticism, and Gender in European Culture.* Ithaca: Cornell University Press, 1996.

Melograni, Piero, with Lucetta Scaraffia, eds. *La famiglia italiana dall'Ottocento a oggi.* Bari: Laterza, 1988.

Merry, Bruce. "Neera (Anna Radius Zuccari)." Russell, 286–94.

Messina, Maria. *Alla deriva.* Milan: Treves, 1920.

——. *L'amore negato.* Palermo: Sellerio, 1993.

——. *A House in the Shadows.* Trans. John Shepley. Marlboro, Vt.: The Marlboro Press, 1989. (*La casa nel vicolo.* Palermo: Sellerio, 1992.)

Miceli Jeffries, Giovanna, ed. *Feminine Feminists: Cultural Practices in Italy.* Minneapolis: University of Minnesota Press, 1994.

Michie, Helena, and Naomi R. Cahn. *Confinements: Fertility and Infertility in Contemporary Culture.* New Brunswick: Rutgers University Press, 1997.

Milan Women's Bookstore Collective. *Sexual Difference: A Theory of Social-Symbolic Practice.* Trans. Patricia Cicogna and Teresa De Lauretis. Bloomington: Indiana University Press, 1990.

Miller-McLemore, Bonnie J. *Also a Mother: Work and Family as Theological Dilemma.* Nashville: Abingdon Press, 1994.

Minicuci, Maria. "Nascere e partorire tra passato e presente." Oakley et al., 55–61.

Minuz, Fernanda. "Femmina o donna." Babini, Minuz, and Tagliavini, 114–60.

Moi, Toril. "Introduction." In *French Feminist Thought: A Reader.* Oxford: Blackwell, 1987. 1–13.

——. "Patriarchal Thought and the Drive for Knowledge." Brennan, 189–205.

——. *Sextual/Textual Politics.* London: Methen, 1985.

Morandini, Giuliana. "Introduzione." In *La voce che è in lei: Antologia della narrativa femminile italiana tra '800 e '900.* Milan: Bompiani, 1980. 5–41.

Mortensen, Ellen. *The Feminine and Nihilism: Luce Irigaray with Nietzsche and Heidegger.* Oslo: Scandinavian University Press, 1994.

Mossman, Carol A. *Politics and Narratives of Birth: Gynocolonization from Rousseau to Zola.* Cambridge: Cambridge University Press, 1993.

Mosso, Angelo. *L'educazione fisica della donna. L'educazione fisica della gioventù—della donna.* Milan: Treves, 1911.

Muraro, Luisa. "Female Genealogies." Burke, Schor, and Whitford, 317–33.

——. *Maglia o uncinetto: Racconto linguistico-politico sulla inimicizia tra metafora e metonimia.* Milan: Feltrinelli, 1981.

——. *L'ordine simbolico della madre.* Milan: Editori Riuniti, 1991.

Neera (Anna Radius Zuccari). "Angelica." In *Monastero e altri racconti,* ed. Antonia Arslan and Anna Folli, 85–91. Milan: Scheiwiller, 1987.

——. *Crevalcore.* Milan: Lombardi, 1991.

——. *Duello d'anime.* Milan: Treves, 1911.

——. *Una giovinezza del secolo XIX.* Milan: Feltrinelli, 1980.

——. *Le idee di una donna.* Florence: Vallecchi, 1977.

——. *L'indomani.* Milan: Galli, 1889.

——. *Il romanzo della fortuna.* Milan: Antongini, 1906.

——. *Teresa.* Trans. Martha King. Evanston: Northwestern University Press, 1999. (*Teresa.* Lecco: Periplo, 1995.)

——. *La vecchia casa.* Milan: Baldini, Castoldi & C., 1900.

Negri, Ada. *Poesie.* Ed. Bianca Scalfi and Egidio Bianchetti. Milan: Mondadori, 1956.

——. *Prose.* Ed. Bianca Scalfi and Egidio Bianchetti. Milan: Mondadori, 1954.

The New American Bible. Nashville: Catholic Bible Press, Thomas Nelson Publishers, 1987.

Noddings, Nel. *Caring: A Feminine Approach to Ethics.* Berkeley: University of California Press, 1984.

Nozzoli, Anna. *Tabù e coscienza. La condizione femminile nella letteratura italiana del Novecento.* Florence: La Nuova Italia, 1978.

Oakley, Ann. *The Captured Womb: A History of the Medical Care of Pregnant Women.* Oxford: Blackwell, 1984.

——. "A Case of Maternity: Paradigms of Women as Maternity Cases." *Signs* 4.4 (1979): 607–31.

——. "Feminism, Motherhood and Medicine—Who Cares?" In *What Is Feminism? A Re-examination,* ed. Juliet Mitchell and Ann Oakley, 127–50. New York: Pantheon Books, 1986.

——. "Il parto: un evento biosociale." Oakley et al., 3–11.

Oakley, Ann, et al. *Le culture del parto.* Milan: Feltrinelli, 1985.

O'Brien, Mary. *The Politics of Reproduction.* Boston: Routledge & Kegan Paul, 1981.

Oliver, Kelly. *Family Values: Subjects Between Nature and Culture.* New York: Routledge, 1997.

——. *Reading Kristeva: Unraveling the Double-Bind.* Bloomington: Indiana University Press, 1993.

——. *Subjectivity without Subjects: From Abject Fathers to Desiring Mothers.* Lanham, Md.: Rowman and Littlefield, 1998.

——. *Womanizing Nietzsche: Philosophy's Relation to the 'Feminine.'* New York: Routledge, 1995.

——, ed. *Ethics, Politics, and Difference in Julia Kristeva's Writings.* New York: Routledge, 1993.

Pancino, Claudia. "L'assistenza al parto dalla pratica femminile all'intervento medico." Pizzini, *Sulla scena del parto,* 62–80.

——. *Il bambino e l'acqua sporca: Storia dell'assistenza al parto dalle mammane alle ostetriche (secoli XVI-XIX).* Milan: Franco Angeli, 1984.

——. *Voglie materne. Storia di una credenza.* Bologna: CLUEB, 1996.

Pansa, Raimondo Collino. "Una femminista d'altri tempi: Neera." *Martinella* 31 (1977): 71–72.

Parto e maternità: Momenti della autobiografia femminile. Bologna: Il Mulino, 1980.

Pateman, Carole. *The Sexual Contract.* Stanford: Stanford University Press, 1988.

Petcheski, Rosalind Pollack. "Fetal Images: The Power of Visual Culture in the Politics of Reproduction." *Feminist Studies* 13.2 (Summer 1987): 263–92.

Piazza, Carlotta. "Un nuovo stile di vita." *Io e il mio bambino* 13.147 (July 1996): 94–97.

Pickering-Iazzi, Robin. "Unseduced Mothers: Configurations of a Different Female Subject Transgressing Fascistized Femininity." Miceli Jeffries, 16–42.

——, ed. *Mothers of Invention: Women, Italian Fascism, and Culture.* Minneapolis: University of Minnesota Press, 1995.

Pierobon, Ermenegilda. "La diversità del femminile: Neera femminista ed antifemminista." *Studi d'italianistica nell'Africa Australe* 9.2 (1996): 30–44.

Pitt, Susan J. "Technology and the Mediation of Gender Relations in Childbirth in Post-war Britain." In *Gender and Material Culture in Historical Perspective,* ed. Moira Donald and Linda Hurcombe, 192–208. New York: St. Martin's Press, 2000.

Pizzini, Franca. "Introduzione: Parole del parto." Pizzini, *Sulla scena del parto,* 9–34.

——. *Maternità in laboratorio: Etica e società nella riproduzione artificiale.* Turin: Rosenberg & Sellier, 1992.

Pizzini, Franca, ed. *Sulla scena del parto: Luoghi, figure, pratiche.* Milan: Angeli, 1981.

Poovey, Mary. " 'Scenes of an Indelicate Character': The Medical 'Treatment' of Victorian Women." *Representations* 14 (Spring 1986): 137–68.

Porter, Elisabeth. *Feminist Perspectives on Ethics.* London: Longman, 1999.

Poston, Carol H. "Childbirth in Literature." *Feminist Studies* 4.2 (June 1978): 18–31.

Prelinger, Elizabeth. *Käthe Kollwitz.* Washington, D.C.: National Gallery of Art, 1992.

Probyn, Elspeth. *Sexing the Self: Gendered Positions in Cultural Studies.* London: Routledge, 1993.

Rasy, Elisabetta. *Le donne e la letteratura.* Rome: Editori Riuniti, 1984.

——. *La lingua della nutrice: Percorsi e tracce dell'espressione femminile con una introduzione di Julia Kristeva.* Rome: Edizioni delle donne, 1978.

Re, Lucia. "Fascist Theories of 'Women' and the Construction of Gender." Pickering-Iazzi, *Mothers of Invention,* 76–99.

——. "Mythic Revisionism: Women Poets and Philosophers in Italy Today." In *Italian Women Writers from the Renaissance to the Present: Revising the Canon,* ed. Maria

Ornella Marotti, 187–233. University Park: Pennsylvania State University Press, 1996.

Reddy, Maureen T., Martha Roth, and Amy Sheldon. *Mother Journeys: Feminists Write About Mothering.* Minneapolis: Spinsters Ink, 1994.

Rich, Adrienne. *Of Woman Born: Motherhood as Experience and Institution.* New York: W. W. Norton, 1976.

Rothman, Barbara Katz. "Beyond Mothers and Fathers: Ideology in a Patriarchal Society." Glenn, Chang, and Forcey, 139–57.

——. *Recreating Motherhood: Ideology and Technology in a Patriarchal Society.* New York: W. W. Norton, 1989.

Ruddick, Sara. "Maternal Thinking." *Feminist Studies* 6.2 (Summer 1980): 342–67.

——. *Maternal Thinking: Toward a Politics of Peace.* Boston: Beacon Press, 1989.

——. "Thinking Mothers/Conceiving Birth." In *Representations of Motherhood,* eds. Donna Bassin, Margaret Honey, and Meryle Mahrer Kaplan, 29–45. New Haven: Yale University Press, 1994.

Russell, Rinaldina, ed. *Italian Women Writers: A Bio-Bibliographical Sourcebook.* Westport, Conn.: Greenwood Press, 1994.

Russo, Mary. "Female Grotesques: Carnival and Theory." De Lauretis, *Feminist Studies/Critical Studies,* 213–29.

Santoro, Anna. "Introduzione." In *Narratrici italiane dell'Ottocento.* Napoli: Federico & Ardia, 1987. 5–20.

Scaraffia, Lucetta. "Essere uomo, essere donna." Melograni, 193–258.

Scarry, Elaine. *The Body in Pain: The Making and the Unmaking of the World.* New York: Oxford University Press, 1985.

Schiebinger, Londa. *Natures' Body: Gender in the Making of Modern Science.* Boston: Beacon Press, 1993.

Schor, Naomi. "Previous Engagements: The Reception of Irigaray." Burke, Schor, and Whitford, 3–13.

Schor, Naomi, and Elizabeth Weed, eds. *The Essential Difference.* Bloomington: Indiana University Press, 1994.

Schreber, Daniel Paul. *Memoirs of My Nervous Illness.* Trans., Edited, with Introduction, Notes, and Discussion by Ida Macalpine and Richard A. Hunter. London: Dawson, 1955.

Serao, Matilde. *Cuore infermo.* Florence: Salani, 1914.

Serono, Cesare. *Femminismo e maternità.* Rome: n.p., 1913.

Shiach, Morag. "Their 'Symbolic' Exists, It Holds Power—We, the Sowers of Disorder, Know It Only Too Well." Brennan, 153–67.

Shildrick, Margrit. *Leaky Bodies and Boundaries: Feminism, Postmodernism and (Bio)Ethics.* London: Routledge, 1997.

Sighele, Scipio. *La donna e l'amore.* Milan: Treves, 1913.

Simkin, Penny, Janet Whalley, and Ann Keppler. *Pregnancy, Childbirth, and the Newborn: The Complete Guide.* Deephaven, Minnesota: Meadowbrook Press, 1991.

Spackman, Barbara. "Fascist Women and the Rhetoric of Virility." Pickering-Iazzi, *Mothers of Invention,* 100–20.

Spivak, Gayatri Chakravorti. "French Feminism Revisited: Ethics and Politics." In

Feminists Theorize the Political, ed. Judith Butler and Joan W. Scott, 54–85. New York: Routledge, 1992.

——, with Ellen Rooney. "In a Word: *Interview.*" Schor and Weed, 151–84.

Stanton, Domna C. "Difference on Trial: A Critique of the Maternal Metaphor in Cixous, Irigaray and Kristeva." In *The Poetics of Gender,* ed. Nancy K. Miller, 157–82. New York: Columbia University Press, 1986.

——. "Language and Revolution: The Franco-American Dis-Connection." Eisenstein and Jardine, 73–87.

Stanworth, Michelle. *Reproductive Technologies: Gender, Motherhood and Medicine.* Minneapolis: University of Minnesota Press, 1987.

Suleiman, Susan Rubin. Introduction. In *The Female Body in Western Culture: Contemporary Perspectives,* ed. Susan Rubin Suleiman, 1–4. Cambridge: Harvard University Press, 1986.

Synnott, Anthony. *The Body Social: Symbolism, Self, and Society.* London: Routledge, 1983.

Tagliavini, Annamaria. "Il fondo oscuro dell'anima femminile." Babini, Minuz, and Tagliavini, 78–113.

Tatar, Maria. *The Hard Facts of the Grimms' Fairy Tales.* Princeton: Princeton UP, 1987.

Terry, Jennifer, and Jacqueline Urla, eds. *Deviant Bodies: Critical Perspectives on Difference in Science and Popular Culture.* Bloomington: Indiana University Press, 1995.

——. "Introduction: Mapping Embodied Deviance." Terry and Urla, 1–18.

Testaferri, Ada, ed. *Donna: Women in Italian Culture.* Toronto: Dovehouse, 1989.

Tew, Marjorie. *Safer Childbirth? A Critical History of Maternity Care.* London: Free Association Books, 1998.

Valesio, Paolo. *Ascoltare il silenzio: La retorica come teoria.* Bologna: Il Mulino, 1986.

Verga, Giovanni. *Tutte le novelle.* Milan: Mondadori, 1988. 2 vols.

Vivanti, Annie. *I divoratori.* Florence: Bemporad, 1925.

——. *Vae Victis!* Milan: Quintieri, 1924.

Walker, Michelle Boulous. *Philosophy and the Maternal Body: Reading Silence.* London: Routledge, 1998.

Walsh, Lisa. "Writing (into) the Symbolic: The Maternal Metaphor in Hélène Cixous." Hendricks and Oliver, 347–65.

Washbourn, Penelope. *Becoming Woman: The Quest for Wholeness in Female Experience.* New York: Harper & Row, 1977.

Weil, Simone. *The Simone Weil Reader.* Ed. George A. Panichas. New York: McKay, 1977.

Weinbaum, Alys Eve. "Marx, Irigaray, and the Politics of Reproduction." Bianchi, 132–63.

Weir, Alison. "Identification with the Divided Mother: Kristeva's Ambivalence." Oliver, *Ethics, Politics, and Difference in Julia Kristeva's Writings,* 79–91.

Whitford, Margaret. *Luce Irigaray: Philosophy in the Feminine.* London: Routledge, 1991.

Willett, Cynthia. *Maternal Ethics and Other Slave Moralities.* New York: Routledge, 1995.

Wood, Sharon. *Italian Women's Writing, 1860–1994.* London: Athlone, 1995.

Yaeger, Patricia. "The Poetics of Birth." In *Discourses of Sexuality: From Aristotle to AIDS,* ed. Domna Stanton, 262–96. Ann Arbor: University of Michigan Press, 1992.

Young, Iris Marion. "Pregnant Embodiment: Subjectivity and Alienation." *Journal of Medicine and Philosophy* 9 (1984): 45–62.

Zambon, Patrizia. "Leggere per scrivere. La formazione autodidattica delle scrittrici tra Otto e Novecento: Neera, Ada Negri, Grazia Deledda, Sibilla Aleramo." *Studi novecenteschi* 16.38 (1989): 287–324.

Zelinsky, Paul O. *Rapunzel.* New York: Dutton Children's Books, 1997.

Zerilli, Linda. "A Process without a Subject: Simone de Beauvoir and Julia Kristeva on Maternity." *Signs* 18.1 (1992): 111–35.

Ziarek, Ewa. "At the Limits of Discourse: Heterogeneity, Alterity, and the Maternal Body in Kristeva's Thought." Hendricks and Oliver, 323–46.

Zingarelli, Nicola. *Vocabolario della lingua italiana.* 10th ed. Bologna: Zanichelli, 1970.

Zipes, Jack. *When Dreams Came True: Classical Fairy Tales and Their Tradition.* New York: Routledge, 1999.

Zolli, Paolo. "La maternità nelle tradizioni popolari." In *Maternità trasgressiva e letteratura,* ed. Ada Neiger, 15–26. Naples: Liguori, 1993.

Index